BEST BOOK OF TRUE SEA STORIES

BEST BOOK OF TRUE SEA STORIES

Edited by

ROBERT A. ROSENBAUM

Illustrated by

KIYOAKI KOMODA

Doubleday & Company, Inc., Garden City, New York

Library of Congress Catalog Card Number AC 66-10738

Printed in the United States of America

The Best Book Series

BEST BOOK OF ADVENTURE STORIES
BEST BOOK OF ANIMAL STORIES
BEST BOOK OF BEDTIME STORIES
BEST BOOK OF DOG STORIES
BEST BOOK OF FAIRY TALES
BEST BOOK OF FUN AND NONSENSE
BEST BOOK OF HEROES AND HEROINES
BEST BOOK OF HORSE STORIES
BEST BOOK OF MYSTERY STORIES
BEST BOOK OF NATURE STORIES
BEST BOOK OF READ ALOUD STORIES
BEST BOOK OF SPORTS STORIES
BEST BOOK OF STORIES OF BOYS AND GIRLS
BEST BOOK OF TRUE SEA STORIES

For Hope and Emily
—a good crew

Introduction

In human history, the sea has played many roles. It has been source of food, road of discovery, highway of commerce, bridge of migration, arena of conflict, life line of empire, pleasure ground for sportsmen and tourists. But it has been something more. It has been a stage where men, solitary or in small companies, cut off from all the rest of their kind, have tested themselves—their purpose, their endurance, their skill, their science, their humanity—and come to view life in a special way.

Sailors are not usually articulate. They have always found it difficult to communicate their experience of the sea to landsmen, although they have been quick to detect the false notes in the writings of others. This does not mean that seafaring men have not written about the sea. There is, in fact, a large literature about the sea written by sailors. Some of these works possess great literary distinction. All, however modest their literary pretensions, possess one quality that landsmen who write about the sea can only envy—authenticity. In an age of much mechanically produced literature and entertainment of all kinds, this is a quality greatly to be prized.

The true stories gathered in this volume are told by the men who lived them. They all share that quality of authenticity which the works of other writers can only simulate. "I was there," each of these authors can say, "and this is how it was." No one who was not there could tell these stories.

R.A.R.

Acknowledgments

Grateful acknowledgment is made for the use of the following copyrighted material:

"Cape Horn," from *Ships and Women,* by Bill Adams. Reprinted by permission of Jacques Chambrun, Inc.

"Commander of the *Triton,*" from *Around the World Submerged,* by Edward L. Beach, U.S.N. Copyright 1962 by Edward L. Beach. Reprinted by permission of Holt, Rinehart & Winston, Inc.

"The Sinking of the *Titanic,*" from *Tramps and Ladies,* by Sir James Bisset. Copyright 1959 by S. G. Phillips, Inc. Reprinted by permission of S. G. Phillips, Inc., and Angus & Robertson, Ltd.

Selection from *The Mirror of the Sea,* by Joseph Conrad. Reprinted by permission of J. M. Dent & Sons, Ltd., and the Trustees of the Joseph Conrad Estate.

"Down to the *S-4,*" from *Men under the Sea,* by Edward Ellsberg. Copyright 1939 by Edward Ellsberg. Reprinted by permission of Dodd, Mead & Company, Inc.

"Battle Station," from *Pacific War Diary,* by James Fahey. Copyright 1963 by James J. Fahey. Reprinted by permission of Houghton Mifflin Company.

"Reconnaissance at Wewak" (original title, "Mush the Magnificent"), from *War Fish,* by George Grider as told to Lydel Sims. Copyright 1958 by George Grider and Lydel Sims. Reprinted by permission of Little, Brown and Company and the Sterling Lord Agency.

"Decision at Leyte Gulf," from *Admiral Halsey's Story,* by Fleet Admiral William F. Halsey, U.S.N., and J. Bryan III. Published by Whittlesey House, McGraw-Hill Book Company, Inc. Copyright 1947 by William F. Halsey; copyright 1947 by the Curtis Publishing Company. Reprinted by permission of Brandt & Brandt.

"The Reef," from *Kon-Tiki: Across the Pacific by Raft,* by Thor Heyerdahl. Copyright 1950 by Thor Heyerdahl. Reprinted by permission of Rand McNally & Company and George Allen & Unwin Ltd.

"Tramp Steamer," from *In the First Watch,* by William McFee. Copyright 1946 by William McFee. Reprinted by permission of Random House, Inc., and the author.

"Trans-Atlantic Race," from *Passage East,* by Carleton Mitchell, published by W. W. Norton & Company, Inc. Copyright 1953 by Carleton Mitchell. Reprinted by permission of the author.

Selection from *Seven Came Through,* by Captain Edward V. Rickenbacker. Copyright 1943 by Doubleday & Company, Inc. Reprinted by permission of the publisher.

"The Boat Journey," from *South,* by Ernest Shackleton. Reprinted by permission of William Heinemann, Ltd.

"Escape from the *Inquisition,*" from *Blow the Man Down!,* by James H. Williams, arranged and edited by Warren F. Kuehl. Copyright 1959 by Warren F. Kuehl. Reprinted by permission of E. P. Dutton & Co., Inc.

Contents

FROM

The Mirror of the Sea

JOSEPH CONRAD

Twenty years at sea provided the Polish-born British novelist Joseph Conrad with the materials for his memorable novels and stories. Conrad also wrote two volumes of autobiography and reminiscence. In one of them, The Mirror of the Sea (1906), *he recalled the incident that had stripped him of his youthful, romantic notions about the sea and made him "a seaman at last."*

Initiation

THE love that is given to ships is profoundly different from the love men feel for every other work of their hands—the love they bear to their houses, for instance—because it is untainted by the pride of possession. The pride of skill, the pride of responsibility, the pride of endurance there may be, but otherwise it is a disinterested sentiment. No seaman ever cherished a ship, even if she belonged to him, merely because of the profit she put in his pocket. No one, I think, ever did, for a shipowner, even of the best, has always been outside the pale of that sentiment embracing in a feeling of intimate, equal fellowship the ship and the man, backing each other against the implacable, if sometimes dissembled, hostility of their world of waters. The sea—this truth must be confessed—has no generosity. No display of manly qualities—courage, hardihood, endurance, faithfulness—has ever been known to touch its irresponsible consciousness of power. The ocean has the conscienceless temper of a savage autocrat spoiled by much adulation. He cannot brook the slightest appearance of defiance, and has remained the irreconcilable enemy of ships and men ever since ships and men had the unheard-of audacity to go afloat together in the face of his frown. From that day he has gone on swallowing up fleets and men without his resentment being glutted by the number of victims—by so many wrecked ships and wrecked lives. Today, as ever, he is ready to beguile and betray, to smash and to drown the incorrigible optimism of men who, backed by the fidelity of ships, are trying to wrest from him the fortune of their house, the dominion of their world, or only a dole of food for their hunger. If not always in the hot mood to smash, he is always stealthily ready for a drowning. The most amazing wonder of the deep is its unfathomable cruelty.

I felt its dread for the first time in mid-Atlantic one day, many years ago, when we took off the crew of a Danish brig homeward bound from the West Indies. A thin, silvery mist softened the calm and majestic splendour of light without shadows—seemed to render the sky less remote and the ocean less immense. It was one of the days, when the might of the sea appears indeed lovable, like the nature of a strong man in moments of quiet intimacy. At sunrise we had made out a black speck to the westward, apparently suspended high up in the void behind a stirring, shimmering veil of silvery blue gauze that seemed at times to stir and float in the breeze which fanned us slowly along. The peace of that enchanting forenoon was so profound, so untroubled, that it seemed that every word pronounced loudly on our deck would penetrate to the very heart of that infinite mystery born from the conjunction of water and sky. We did not raise our voices. "A water-logged derelict, I think, sir," said the second officer, quietly, coming down from aloft with the binoculars in their case slung across his shoulders; and our captain, without a word, signed to the helmsman to steer for the black speck. Presently we made out a low, jagged stump sticking up forward—all that remained of her departed masts.

The captain was expatiating in a low conversational tone to the chief mate upon the danger of these derelicts, and upon his dread of coming upon them at night, when suddenly a man forward screamed out, "There's people on board of her, sir! I see them!" in a most extraordinary voice—a voice never heard before in our ship; the amazing voice of a stranger. It gave the signal for a sudden tumult of shouts. The watch below ran up the forecastle head in a body, the cook dashed out of the galley. Everybody saw the poor fellows now. They were there! And all at once our ship, which had the well-earned name of being without a rival for speed in light winds, seemed to us to have lost the power of motion, as if the sea, becoming viscous, had clung to her sides. And yet she moved. Immensity, the inseparable companion of a ship's life, chose that day to breathe upon her as gently as a sleeping child. The clamor of our excitement had died out, and our living ship, famous for never losing steerage way as long as there was air enough to float a feather, stole, without a ripple, silent and white as a ghost, towards her mutilated and wounded sister, come upon at the point of death in the sunlit haze of a calm day at sea.

With the binoculars glued to his eyes, the captain said in a quavering tone: "They are waving to us with something aft there." He put down the glasses on the skylight brusquely, and began to walk about the poop. "A shirt or a flag," he ejaculated, irritably. "Can't make it out. . . . Some damn rag or other!" He took a few more turns on the poop, glancing down over the rail now and then to see how fast we were moving. His nervous footsteps rang sharply in the quiet of the ship, where the other men, all looking the same way, had forgotten themselves in a staring immobility. "This will never do!" he cried out, suddenly. "Lower the boats at once! Down with them!"

Before I jumped into mine he took me aside, as being an inexperienced junior, for a word of warning:

"You look out as you come alongside that she doesn't take you down with her. You understand?"

He murmured this confidentially, so that none of the men at the falls should overhear, and I was shocked. "Heavens! as if in such an emergency one stopped to think of danger!" I exclaimed to myself mentally, in scorn of such cold-blooded caution.

It takes many lessons to make a real seaman, and I got my rebuke at once. My experienced commander seemed in one searching glance to read my thoughts on my ingenuous face.

"What you're going for is to save life, not to drown your boat's crew for nothing," he growled, severely, in my ear. But

as we shoved off he leaned over and cried out: "It all rests on the power of your arms, men. Give way for life!"

We made a race of it, and I would never have believed that a common boat's crew of a merchantman could keep up so much determined fierceness in the regular swing of their stroke. What our captain had clearly perceived before we left had become plain to all of us since. The issue of our enterprise hung on a hair above that abyss of waters which will not give up its dead till the Day of Judgment. It was a race of two ships' boats matched against Death for a prize of nine men's lives, and Death had a long start. We saw the crew of the brig from afar working at the pumps—still pumping on that wreck, which already had settled so far down that the gentle, low swell, over which our boats rose and fell easily without a check to their speed, welling up almost level with her head-rails, plucked at the ends of broken gear swinging desolately under her naked bowsprit.

We could not, in all conscience, have picked out a better day for our regatta had we had the free choice of all the days that ever dawned upon the lonely struggles and solitary agonies of ships since the Norse rovers first steered to the westward against the run of Atlantic waves. It was a very good race. At the finish there was not an oar's length between the first and second boat, with Death coming in a good third on the top of the very next smooth swell, for all one knew to the contrary. The scuppers of the brig gurgled softly all together when the water rising against her sides subsided sleepily with a low wash, as if playing about an immovable rock. Her bulwarks were gone fore and aft, and one saw her bare deck low-lying like a raft and swept clean of boats, spars, houses—of everything except the ringbolts and the heads of the pumps. I had one dismal glimpse of it as I braced myself up to receive upon my breast the last man to leave her, the captain, who literally let himself fall into my arms.

It had been a weirdly silent rescue—a rescue without a hail, without a single uttered word, without a gesture or a sign, without a conscious exchange of glances. Up to the very last moment those on board stuck to their pumps, which spouted two clear streams of water upon their bare feet. Their brown skin showed through the rents of their shirts; and the two small bunches of half-naked, tattered men went on bowing from the waist to each other in their back-breaking labour, up and down, absorbed, with no time for a glance over the shoulder at the help that was coming to them. As we dashed, unregarded, alongside a voice let out one, only one hoarse howl of command, and then, just as they stood, without caps, with the salt drying gray in the wrinkles and folds of their hairy, haggard faces, blinking stupidly at us their red eyelids, they made a bolt away from the handles, tottering and jostling against each other, and positively flung themselves over upon our very heads. The clatter they made tumbling into the boats had an extraordinarily destructive effect upon the illusion of tragic dignity our self-esteem had thrown over the contests of mankind with the sea. On that exquisite day of gentle breathing peace and veiled sunshine perished my romantic love to what men's imagination had proclaimed the most august aspect of Nature. The cynical indifference of the sea to the merits of human suffering and courage, laid bare in this ridiculous, panic-tainted performance extorted from the dire extremity of nine good and honorable seamen, revolted me. I saw the duplicity of the sea's most tender mood. It was so because it could not help itself, but the awed respect of the early days was gone. I felt ready to smile bitterly at its enchanting charm and glare viciously at its furies. In a moment, before we shoved off, I had looked coolly at the life of my choice. Its illusions were gone, but its fascination remained. I had become a seaman at last.

We pulled hard for a quarter of an hour, then laid on our oars waiting for our ship. She was coming down on us with swelling sails, looking delicately tall and exquisitely noble through the mist. The captain of the brig, who sat in the stern sheets by my side with his face in his hands, raised his head and began to speak with a sort of sombre volubility. They had lost their masts and sprung a leak in a hurricane; drifted for weeks, always at the pumps, met more bad weather; the ships they sighted failed to make them out, the leak gained upon them slowly, and the seas had left them nothing to make a raft of. It was very hard to see ship after ship pass by at a distance, "as if everybody had agreed that we must be left to drown," he added. But they went on trying to keep the brig afloat as long as possible, and working the pumps constantly on insufficient food, mostly raw, till "yesterday evening," he continued, monotonously, "just as the sun went down, the men's hearts broke."

He made an almost imperceptible pause here, and went on again with exactly the same intonation:

"They told me the brig could not be saved, and they thought they had done enough for themselves. I said nothing to that. It was true. It was no mutiny. I had nothing to say to them. They lay about aft all night, as still as so many dead men. I did not lie down. I kept a lookout. When the first light came I saw your ship at once. I waited for more light; the breeze began to fail on my face. Then I shouted out as loud as I was able, 'Look at that ship!' but only two men got up very slowly and came to me. At first only we three stood alone, for a long time, watching you coming down to us, and feeling the breeze drop to a calm almost; but afterwards others, too, rose, one after another, and by and by I had all my crew behind me. I turned round and said to them that they could see the ship was coming our way, but in this small breeze she might come too late after all, unless we turned to and tried to keep the brig afloat long enough to give you time to save us all. I spoke like that to them, and then I gave the command to man the pumps."

He gave the command, and gave the example, too, by going himself to the handles, but it seems that these men did actually hang back for a moment, looking at each other dubiously before they followed him. "He! he! he!" He broke out into a most unexpected, imbecile, pathetic, nervous little giggle. "Their hearts were broken so! They had been played with too long," he explained, apologetically, lowering his eyes, and became silent.

Twenty-five years is a long time—a quarter of a century is a dim and distant past; but to this day I remember the dark-brown feet, hands, and faces of two of these men whose hearts had been broken by the sea. They were lying very still on their sides on the bottom boards between the thwarts, curled up like dogs. My boat's crew, leaning over the looms of their oars, stared and listened as if at the play. The master of the brig looked up suddenly to ask me what day it was.

They had lost the date. When I told him it was Sunday, the twenty-second, he frowned, making some mental calculation, then nodded twice sadly to himself, staring at nothing.

His aspect was miserably unkempt and wildly sorrowful. Had it not been for the unquenchable candor of his blue eyes, whose unhappy, tired glance every moment sought his abandoned, sinking brig, as if it could find rest nowhere else, he would have appeared mad. But he was too simple to go mad, too simple with that manly simplicity which alone can bear men unscathed in mind and body through an encounter with the deadly playfulness of the sea or with its less abominable fury.

Neither angry, nor playful, nor smiling, it enveloped our distant ship growing bigger as she neared us, our boats with the rescued men and the dismantled hull of the brig we were leaving behind, in the large and placid embrace of its quietness, half lost in the fair haze, as if in a dream of infinite and tender clemency. There was no frown, no wrinkle on its face, not a ripple. And the run of the slight swell was so smooth that it resembled the graceful undulation of a piece of shimmering gray silk shot with gleams of green. We pulled an easy stroke; but when the master of the brig, after a glance over his shoulder, stood up with a low exclamation, my men feathered their oars instinctively, without an order, and the boat lost her way.

He was steadying himself on my shoulder with a strong grip, while his other arm, flung up rigidly, pointed a denunciatory finger at the immense tranquillity of the ocean. After his first exclamation, which stopped the swing of our oars, he made no sound, but his whole attitude seemed to cry out an indignant "Behold!" . . . I could not imagine what vision of evil had come to him. I was startled, and the amazing energy of his immobilized gesture made my heart beat faster with the anticipation of something monstrous and unsuspected. The stillness around us became crushing.

For a moment the succession of silky undulations ran on innocently. I saw each of them swell up the misty line of the horizon, far, far away beyond the derelict brig, and the next moment, with a slight friendly toss of our boat, it had passed under us and was gone. The lulling cadence of the rise and fall, the invariable gentleness of this irresistible force, the great charm of the deep waters, warmed my breast deliciously, like the subtle poison of a love potion. But all this lasted only a few soothing seconds before I jumped up, too, making the boat roll like the veriest landlubber.

Something startling, mysterious, hastily confused was taking place. I watched it with incredulous and fascinated awe, as one watches the confused, swift movements of some deed of violence done in the dark. As if at a given signal, the run of the smooth undulations seemed checked suddenly around the brig. By a strange optical delusion the whole sea appeared to rise upon her in one overwhelming heave of its silky surface where in one spot a smother of foam broke out ferociously. And then the effort subsided. It was all over, and the smooth swell ran on as before from the horizon in uninterrupted cadence of motion, passing under us with a slight friendly toss of our boat. Far away, where the brig had been, an angry white stain undulating on the surface of steely gray waters, shot with gleams of green, diminished swiftly without a hiss, like a patch of pure snow melting in the sun. And the great stillness after this initiation into the sea's implacable hate seemed full of dread thoughts and shadows of disaster.

"Gone!" ejaculated from the depths of his chest my bowman in a final tone. He spat in his hands, and took a better grip on his oar. The captain of the brig lowered his rigid arm slowly, and looked at our faces in a solemnly conscious silence, which called upon us to share in his simple-minded, marveling awe. All at once he sat down by my side, and leaned forward earnestly at my boat's crew, who, swinging together in a long, easy stroke, kept their eyes fixed upon him faithfully.

"No ship could have done so well," he addressed them, firmly, after a moment of strained silence, during which he seemed with trembling lips to seek for words fit to bear such high testimony. "She was small, but she was good. I had no anxiety. She was strong. Last voyage I had my wife and two children in her. No other ship could have stood so long the weather she had to live through for days and days before we got dismasted a fortnight ago. She was fairly worn out, and that's all. You may believe me. She lasted under us for days and days, but she could not last for ever. It was long enough. I am glad it is over. No better ship was ever left to sink at sea on such a day as this."

He was competent to pronounce the funereal oration of a ship, this son of ancient sea folk, whose national existence, so little stained by the excesses of manly virtues, had demanded nothing but the merest foothold from the earth. By the merits of his sea-wise forefathers and by the artlessness of his heart, he was made fit to deliver this excellent discourse. There was nothing wanting in its orderly arrangement—neither piety nor faith, nor the tribute of praise due to the worthy dead, with the edifying recital of their achievement. She had lived, he had loved her; she had suffered, and he was glad she was at rest. It was an excellent discourse. And it was orthodox, too, in its fidelity to the cardinal article of a seaman's faith, of which it was a single-minded confession. "Ships are all right." They are. They who live with the sea have got to hold by that creed first and last; and it came to me, as I glanced at him sideways, that some men were not altogether unworthy in honor and conscience to pronounce the funereal eulogium of a ship's constancy in life and death.

After this, sitting by my side with his loosely clasped hands hanging between his knees, he uttered no word, made no movement till the shadow of our ship's sails fell on the boat, when, at the loud cheer greeting the return of the victors with their prize, he lifted up his troubled face with a faint smile of pathetic indulgence. This smile of the worthy descendant of the most ancient sea folk whose audacity and hardihood had left no trace of greatness and glory upon the waters, completed the cycle of my initiation. There was an infinite depth of hereditary wisdom in its pitying sadness. It made the hearty bursts of cheering sound like a childish noise of triumph. Our crew shouted with immense confidence—honest souls! As if anybody could ever make sure of having prevailed against the sea, which has betrayed so many ships of great "name," so many proud men, so many towering ambitions of fame, power, wealth, greatness!

As I brought the boat under the falls my captain, in high good-humor, leaned over, spreading his red and freckled elbows on the rail, and called down to me sarcastically out of the depths of his cynic philosopher's beard:

"So you have brought the boat back after all, have you?"

Sarcasm was "his way," and the most that can be said for it is that it was natural. This did not make it lovable. But it is decorous and expedient to fall in with one's commander's way. "Yes. I brought the boat back all right, sir," I answered. And the good man believed me. It was not for him to discern upon me the marks of my recent initiation. And yet I was not exactly the same youngster who had taken the boat away—all impatience for a race against Death, with the prize of nine men's lives at the end.

Already I looked with other eyes upon the sea. I knew it capable of betraying the generous ardor of youth as implacably as, indifferent to evil and good, it would have betrayed the basest greed or the noblest heroism. My conception of its magnanimous greatness was gone. And I looked upon the true sea—the sea that plays with men till their hearts are broken, and wears stout ships to death. Nothing can touch the brooding bitterness of its soul. Open to all and faithful to none, it exercises its fascination for the undoing of the best. To love it is not well. It knows no bond of plighted troth, no fidelity to misfortune, to long companionship, to long devotion. The promise it holds out perpetually is very great, but the only secret of its possession is strength, strength—the jealous, sleepless strength of a man guarding a coveted treasure within his gates.

FROM

In the First Watch

WILLIAM McFEE

"It was a beautiful life," the Anglo-American author William McFee recalled of his years as an engineer on British tramp steamers before World War I. He had not forgotten "our poor pay, salt meat, canned vegetables, verminous bunks, oil lamps, no heat in winter or fans in summer, no radio and no vacations except those we took when we were paid off." But the seafarers of those distant days were happier than modern merchant sailors, he believed. The sea was a way of life then, with respected traditions and loyalties, not just another way to earn money.

No idyl, however, is this description of his encounter with an Atlantic storm in 1912, when he was chief engineer of the little tramp steamer Fernfield.

Tramp Steamer

We went ashore and had dinner at the Grosvenor in Glasgow to celebrate our captain's return in such fine fettle. We loaded for Leghorn and went to sea. The great Seamen's Strike was over, the shipowners had given in, and the men were now getting nine pounds a month instead of four pounds ten. We got a good crew from the union and the union was under an obligation to keep them good. It had been a miserable business for us while it lasted. We had to take the owners' side while our sympathies were with the men. The owners declared they would be ruined if they paid the new wages; but somehow they survived, and, if the truth be told, began to make more money. Trade revived because more people had something to spend. The owners talked about socialism, red ruin, and the breaking up of laws, the dictatorship of the proletariat, and the end of merry England. But they managed to stay in business. They even restored our wages to what they had been before the cuts.

The season was spring and the Mediterranean had been in a bad mood the whole voyage. We went light ship to the Greek Islands to load iron ore for Rotterdam, and we had a duster going around Cape Matapan. We had to run out of our island harbor twice to avoid being smashed on the rocks. Aegean storms are not to be sneezed at. I have always been impressed by the stories of Greek seamanship in the classic tales.

No sooner had we passed Gibraltar than we ran into the tail end of an Atlantic storm. The wind wasn't much, but the seas! They came in from the westward, mountains high. If the Aegean squalls explained much in classical mythology, those great seas, their height and immensity, gave me a fresh respect for the early navigators like Columbus, Da Gama, Magellan, and the Zeni brothers, who got as far as Greenland in the thirteenth century. Their ships were not much larger than our lifeboats, and how they did it is beyond my understanding.

We had six thousand tons of ore in the holds, and although the ship was laboring heavily and taking a lot of water on the foredeck, we were not worrying. The captain was in Mr. Ede's cabin when I went around after eight o'clock in my pajamas to have a smoke and a yarn. They were talking about the chief's trip to Canada to see his niece. He had a lot of snapshots of the place where she was living with her husband, somewhere in Alberta. Mr. Ede pointed out the magnificent scenery. He had been at sea so long he had a great longing for mountains, and he had an idea, too, he would like to fish. He said it was the sort of job he thought he would like in his old age. Just sit and hold a rod, and when he got a bite, haul in his dinner.

"We all want to have a farm when we get old," the captain said, "but I was on a farm when I was a kid, and I say I'd as soon be in jail. Nothing but work from four o'clock in the mornin' till late at night. Now *I'd* like to have a country pub."

I was just saying that I wouldn't mind a pub myself, when the carpenter, a Norwegian who had been in the ship for years, came to the door.

"What's the matter, Chips?" the captain said.

"Plenty watter in the wells, sir," Chips said, "in number-one 'old. Can't keep de chalk dry."

The *Fernfield* had transverse wells between the double-bottom tanks, into which the water from the wings was supposed to drain. I used to argue that it made her really a single-bottom ship if anything happened. Mr. Ede wouldn't discuss it.

"How much?" Mr. Ede asked.

"T'ree feet." Chips held out his sounding rod and put his thumb on the three-foot mark.

Captain Williams eased himself out of the wicker chair. Mr. Ede searched around for his sea boots.

"I'll put the pump on that well," I said. I went down in my pajamas and told the donkeyman. Hassan Izzet, a Turk, had been so long in the ship we used to say he was geared to the engines. He was better than many junior watchkeepers.

I was feeling fine in part of my mind, but there was an underlying feeling of anxiety. I was in my twenty-ninth year. Very few men had chiefs' jobs before they were thirty. I was definitely lucky. I had been at sea only five years. Most men had ten years' service before a job at the top loomed.

I was feeling fine because my novel had been getting along well during this voyage in spite of the bad weather. While we were in Leghorn I had taken a weekend trip to Florence, and that had done something to me. I suppose nobody with any interest in the arts can ever get over Florence. It had had its effect on my writing, given me an impetus, so to speak.

But there was underneath a feeling of worry whether I would succeed as chief. This weather in the Atlantic made it worse.

As I turned in, the ship began to take heavier seas. I could hear and feel them thundering overhead. But I slept like a baby. We had had plenty of bad weather in my years at sea.

At one bell (3:45 A.M.) Mr. Ede called me. He was in a boiler suit with a hood. He carried a flashlight. He looked like a gigantic gnome. His beard was wet with spray, his eyes grave.

He said number-one well had a lot of water in it. They could not be sure because the seas came over onto the forward deck so constantly it was a job to keep the sounding rod dry. In fact it was impossible. Chips, however, by long experience, was sure the rod went into water as into a full tank. He could tell by the feel of it as he lowered.

I sat on the edge of my bunk and looked at the chief, who fumbled a bit and brought out his cigarette holder.

"Leak somewhere," he said, and struck a match.

The ship wasn't behaving any better, either. There were long deceptive pauses, and then a sound like an express train coming at us through a tunnel. There would follow a great deal of water—about as much as you would get at Niagara, and some of it would wash around Mr. Ede's sea boots. I had rolled up my carpet and stowed everything high above the desk. Sea water can be mopped up.

I got down to the settee without touching the floor and put on my socks and engine-room slippers. I asked about the well. Mr. Ede said it was full. Couldn't get any fuller. It was coming in from somewhere. The suction was choked. Wouldn't draw. The main engine bilge pumps were on it. No good. Ship was down by the head too. She was getting it, all right.

He broke off to let one of the express trains go by. Then he got up and went out, bracing himself in the dark alleyway.

When I went on watch I relieved the third, a young Scotsman who was having his first real taste of bad weather. Mr. Ede came down and we tried to clear the line. Hold bilges often jammed with mud, dead rats, pieces of waste, coal, iron-ore dust, and all the detritus of general cargo. We took out the valve from the manifold, put the cover back and opened the sea injection fast. We left it open for a few seconds, closed it, replaced the valve, primed the pump, and set it away at a fast clip. The idea was, the sea rushing back into the hold would wash the muck out of the suction box and give us a chance to pump. It did, but the strum soon choked again. The remedy was as bad as the disease, and we still had the disease.

Down below it seemed as if the weather had moderated. The ship was steadier. The reason was, she had her forehold full of water. Some twelve hundred tons of iron ore were under water in that hold. It held her head to the gale and the seas were smashing on the foredeck like rocks. The men who were supposed to relieve mine at eight o'clock could not get along until the mate rigged double lifelines. Once along, they could not get back. They had breakfast in the fiddle grating above the boilers and later they turned in to sleep in the 'tween deck bunker.

The weather, however, had not moderated. We were laboring out into a waste of tumbling waters. There would have been nothing to worry about if she could only have risen to them. Captain Williams was afraid that one of those waves, landing on top of the hatches, would stove them in. Mr. Ede couldn't see what difference it would make.

"She's full to sea level already. Number one is," he pointed out.

The captain said Mr. Ede 'ud soon find out the difference if those hatches gave way.

We had to pump out the regular bilges, of course, and in the meanwhile we concentrated on the leak. Where was it? Mr. Ede went down into the forepeak, the triangular tank in the bow of the ship below the chain locker. He showed the mate the patent oil sprayer in the bows. This was a mechanical oil bag. It was a cylinder full of thick fish-oil under pressure of a piston with a spring. Two small copper pipes led to holes in the bow plates. When working, the oil slick covered the plates and the seas glanced off. This was the invention of an old shipmate of my father, a retired skipper named Cooves, a fine old codger who gave me my first Bible when he was staying with us.

The change was remarkable. The mate had never heard of it. All he knew was the old-fashioned canvas oil bags slung over the bows, which were always carried away and lost after an hour or two.

Mr. Ede found the forepeak dry. The suction was clear, so we decided that if we could cut through the bulkhead the water in the hold would run into the dry forepeak and we could pump it out. This meant the third and I had to get down into the very forefoot of the ship, under the chain locker. The frames were narrow and covered with yellow slime like excrement. There was no ventilation. We had two candles and a slush lamp. We rigged a ratchet brace and started to drill holes. Just over our heads, in that narrow submarine dungeon, echoing with the boom and crash of great seas and the low, menacing sound of chain links grinding over each other, crouched Mr. Ede, his beard in a blue calico bag and the pointed hood of his boiler suit making an enormous shadow on the plates, watching us.

We toiled all day drilling holes and nothing came out but a few dribbles of wet iron ore. We were as far as ever from finding where the water was coming in. We had tried all we could think of.

Mr. Ede looked at his bunkers and told the Old Man he would have to put in somewhere for coal. The trash we had received in Oran was burning like paper. So we earned a few hours quiet by going in behind Cape Finisterre and taking fifty tons in Corcubión. Perhaps the weather would ease now, but with the Bay of Biscay ahead the chances were poor.

I remember that voyage because I was preoccupied with the coming job as chief. It seemed Fate was determined to give Mr. Ede the time of his life before letting him go to see his niece in Canada. Here we were, leaking, short of coal, a dirty ship, and the bay like nothing we had seen so far.

We had one comfort, those good old main engines of Blair's and his massive boilers were all right. It was a treat to get into that warm, dry, engine room. My cabin had a couple of inches of water in it all the time. Poor Jack had to sleep on the chief's settee and he couldn't get any exercise at all.

I would find Mr. Ede contemplating the blueprint of the ship's pumping arrangement. He would shake his head mournfully.

"The connections aren't like this now," he would say.

All old ships are like that. The blueprints are what she was at first, often only what they were supposed to be. Our pipes ran differently. Well, we knew that; but where was the water coming from? It was now twenty-one feet, which meant level with the sea outside. Something we didn't know about, Mr. Ede said. What worried him was whether the office would be satisfied with that sort of answer.

I might have been more cheerful if I hadn't begun to wonder whether we would ever get home. No use being promised a chief's job on a ship we couldn't bring in except in a sinking condition.

These dark thoughts were inspired by the fact that the ship now had a list in addition to being far down by the bows. She was in the position a vessel takes when about to make a dive to the bottom. When she rolled she barely came upright. She was over to port. Now we had trouble keeping our other bilges drained.

The cook could keep nothing on his range without a complicated series of wedges and lashings. The sea flew in and doused his fire. It is quite a job to relight a galley range after sea water has put it out. He was finally barricaded in the galley, both doors cleated tight with spun yarn caulked in, and the grub passed up through his skylight. Our meals were passed down our skylight, over the mess table.

We lived lonely lives. Captain Williams was cut off from us. We could not read, and I had no time for writing. We spoke only when necessary. There was a feeling of insecurity among us younger and less experienced men. If only she wouldn't lie down in such a disconsolate position! The ship had no heart. Nor had we.

Off Ushant the weather moderated. The waves grew longer, the wind was on our quarter, and we had the after well deck clear of water. Mr. Ede and I, in the shelter of the overhang under the ladder to the bridge deck, looked out over immense gray slopes. It was on this occasion that Mr. Ede quoted a phrase, one of the loveliest metaphors in the language of an island race. He said, "Look at them! The fenceless meadows of the sea! Don't you wish you were a farmer?"

Captain Williams, when he raised Ushant Light, made a decision. We had no wireless in those days. We could only communicate by flags. It so happened neither of our mates could use the Morse Code or the semaphore.

The captain decided he could not risk going up Channel. The ship was not steering smartly. She fell away. As Mr. Ede put it, "She'd never get through the Straits of Dover unless they held up the traffic." The only thing to do was make Falmouth and signal for orders.

We thought we were out of our troubles. They were just beginning. The weather, when we were clear of the land and heading due north, grew worse. It became a dark, furious, westerly gale, with rain. In the course of my life at sea in steamers, I have rarely been in storms with rain. Rain, to me, was something that always came on sailing day and made us miserable. This gale came out of the northwest. The ship took a heavier list. She was lying down in the water on her left ear. The seas went over her green. The captain had to slow down or we would have been swept. His fear for the hatches was understandable. If number-two hatch covers carried away we'd be in trouble.

The worst came off the Scillies. There was no thought now of Falmouth. She was sinking slowly. We were heading for the Bristol Channel where we could refit.

"Always supposing," Mr. Ede said in a faint voice, "that we get there."

We got better weather in the Bristol Channel. In fact it began to get much better. The sea went down. Instead we had a swell which started us rolling. Mr. Ede told me the Old Man was going to Milford Haven. He had been studying the charts. There was a fine sloping beach there.

"She wouldn't get over Swansea Bar in this condition," Mr. Ede said. "They couldn't unload her."

I couldn't bear to look at my engine room. Here I was, going chief, bringing her into a home port so dirty I dreaded anyone from ashore looking into the engine room. We'd done nothing but pump, pump, pump, with hours of bilge diving, clearing suctions, opening valve boxes and manifolds.

She was beginning to make water in the main hold.

We were off Lundy Island by breakfast, the wind and tide

taking us eastward out of our course. It was not so bad now. In fact the weather was clearing. We saw tramps following each other out of Barry Dock and Swansea, tramps who must have given us some curious glances. A Blue Funnel boat passed close by. She had been loading tin plates in Swansea for China. She signaled, "Do you need assistance?" Captain Williams said to us, as the mate ran up a reply, "Yes, I do, but not from Alfred Holt!" The Blue Funnel mates did some wigwagging, but our mates had not learned it, so it was ignored.

We had a long, slow-moving second mate, who had spent a good many years in large steel grain carriers, full-rigged sailing ships. He was a sailor, but he was a bad-tempered shipmate. He was the only officer we ever carried who ignored Jack. Jack would lie in his box glaring at this chap when he came down with the noonday chit.

When he paid no attention to the Blue Funnel ship's signal, Captain Williams said, "Can't you read that?"

The second mate walked to the other end of the bridge and said, very loud:

"Not for seven pound a month, Cap'n!"

Soon we had St. Anne's Head on our beam and we entered that noble haven. There was a light-gray cruiser coming out of Pembroke Dockyard and some fishing boats coming in. Captain Williams headed for the south side, and somewhere opposite the town of Milford Haven the ship ran her bows up a gently sloping mud beach and came to rest.

The captain went ashore in a boat and sent a wire to London.

The ship, as the tide dropped, went down by the stern. For the hundredth time the third and I had the valves out and primed the line to number-one well. We did it to ease our consciences. We still did not know where the water was coming in. The superintendent, Mr. Huggins, would bark, "You ought to know!" He was right, I thought drearily as I climbed up to the deck, not to look at the lovely Pembrokeshire scenery, but to look over the side and see if anything came out. He was right, we ought to know.

I saw Mr. Ede looking at the discharges. I joined him. I was amazed. A solid curved torrent of rust-red water was pouring out. Up on the bridge Chips with his sounding rod was gazing at the same phenomenon. Up came the third. He was a small, wiry, black-haired lad from the north of Scotland, with sharp rabbits' front teeth and an unintelligible accent. He was, in my private opinion, not a Scot at all, but a Pict. He was at this moment excited, which made him almost unintelligible.

"She's poompin' the noo!" he observed. Seeing the gush of water, he added, "Aye, the noo!" He talked as if his mouth was full of plums.

Mr. Ede said the trim of the ship was doing it.

"Never mind what's doing it!" I cried, and hurried along with Chips to take a sounding. "Eighteen feet already," I sang out to Mr. Ede and the captain, up on the bridge deck.

We had it dry by noon. The office wired that Mr. Huggins had been caught by a telegram from them at Newport on his way to Cardiff, and was coming straight on to Pembroke.

He came out in a boat. It was too far for us to see what was going on, but Captain Williams, who had gone ashore to meet him, told us about it when we got to sea. The boat was a few yards from the beach. Mr. Huggins came out of a fly he had chartered at Pembroke. He was a small, sharp man who knew everything about every ship and officer in the company. Or thought he did. I had never forgiven him for telling me, before I went to sea in one of the hardest ships he had, that "It was an ideal life for a lazy man; eight hours watch, eight hours sleep, and eight hours play." He would have made a good recruiting sergeant, a good advertising copywriter.

When he saw the boat, he said, "I won't get my feet wet! You'll have to carry me." So Captain Williams, who had sea boots on, took him on his back and carried him through the water to the boat. I would have liked to have witnessed that scene. When I spotted him he was hunched up in an ulster on the thwarts, holding his bowler hat on in the breeze. The word went round at once: "Super's coming aboard."

We regarded Mr. Huggins with admiration, respect, and fear. There is often a conviction among seamen, when one of them is hoisted into a position of prominence on shore, that it is due largely to luck or cunning, or to a combination. We had no such feeling about Mr. Huggins. We knew him for a man of resource, energy, and intelligence. He was just, too, like my uncle, his colleague. He had no sentiment in him, but even if he had, it was not likely to show on this occasion.

He climbed the rope ladder and was officiously helped over the bulwarks by the mate. I saw Mr. Ede come out of his alleyway and I at once effaced myself.

A man of sixty, suddenly deflected from a routine professional visit to Cardiff, forced to make a tedious journey in a local train, to be carried pickaback through the sea to a rowboat, to have to climb a dirty rope ladder, is not in an angelic mood. Mr. Huggins was too artful to ask why the teak accommodation ladder wasn't rigged and lowered for him. He knew the captain would ask, who was to do it with the crew we carried? Accommodation ladders are for ships carrying quartermasters, apprentices, and a full crowd of AB's. We had six men on deck and three of them were off watch. The carpenter had been on duty for nearly two days and nights.

"You must have left something open."

"No, sir."

Mr. Huggins knew Mr. Ede hadn't left anything open, but he had to blame us, on principle. He came down into the engine room, grotesquely attired in one of Mr. Ede's boiler suits. He was a smallish man, sharp as a terrier. He ordered us to cut holes into the forepeak. We had done that, so we all went down to let him poke a stick through and see the dribble of mud. It was a close fit for three of us with a slush lamp, far down in that stifling tank. I thought, How nice it would be to have electric light.

Mr. Huggins gave us a time. He had all the floor plates up in the engine room. Where did this go to? What was that pipe? Must be a leak in the suction. He made us prime the lines and hold lamps here and there. No leaks. Then we'd left something open. Mr. Ede said the valves were non-return, and got his head snapped off. Bit of waste or a chip of wood under it, of course!

The tide was coming in. When it was at the full we put the engines astern and slid off into deep water to anchor. Mr. Huggins, secluded in the chief's cabin, was nonetheless remarkably among those present on board. There was a peculiar atmosphere. We spoke low, as though he could hear us through several decks and a couple of steel bulkheads, as though someone was dying in one of the cabins. The mate, in a daze, unshipped the accommodation ladder and lowered it. He set a sailor washing the gratings. The steward could be seen hurriedly setting the cabin in a harbor condition at high speed. Even the sea kept out of the ship. Number-one well remained dry. We felt foolish after all the misery we had been through. Instead of being commended, it seemed that we were responsible for that water getting into the ship.

Mr. Huggins never said an unnecessary word. He made no further charges in Mr. Ede's cabin. He had known the chief for twenty years. I learned later he became human. He spoke of his son.

Mr. Huggins' son was his trouble. He had sent him to a fine grammar school and apprenticed him to one of the big yards in the North. Mr. Huggins' son, however, was a black sheep. He was always in trouble during his apprenticeship. When he finished there, Mr. Huggins got him into a famous line running passengers and mails to Australia, with frozen mutton homeward. After a couple of voyages, during which Mr. Huggins had poor reports, his son ran away in Melbourne and went up country. It was a shocking thing for Mr. Huggins, a man whose philosophy was built on discipline, duty, integrity, loyalty. He expected and got all these from us. He gave them to us in return. Mr. Ede told me later that he spoke of his son. He said Mr. Ede was "Damn lucky to have no children, only a married niece —in Canada!"

Now he was on board he seemed reluctant to leave us. At last he went down the clean accommodation ladder to the boat waiting. Captain Williams went with him. They went ashore to Milford Haven town. A rumor went around that we were not going to Rotterdam. We argued in the engine room. Hassan Izzet, the Turkish donkeyman, who spoke a sort of sibilant basic English consisting of a dozen words, reported what he had heard from his roommate, Chips, a Norwegian with his own twanging basic English (two dozen words). The gist of this was "Da mate say no Rotterdam dis time." I wanted to know how the hell the mate, who did not know enough to get out of his own road, could know where we were going? Had we not seen him start to hoist the accommodation ladder, and then lower it again hastily, when he remembered the Old Man was still ashore?

I sat on the hatch that afternoon, smoking happily and admiring the lovely views of Pembrokeshire. I had time now to meditate on the coming chief's job, seventeen pounds a month and no watch to keep. Hassan was far better than any junior. I wondered what sort of second I would get, and where we would go. I wanted a few days' leave, too, before we sailed.

Captain Williams came back while we were having tea. We were to go to Glasgow. Mr. Huggins had done some long-distance telephoning. He had not been as sure as he pretended that we were a lot of lazy, incompetent piano tuners. He thought a home dry dock would be a good thing for us. So up came the accommodation ladder, up came the anchor and down went I to the starting platform. We got out of Milford Haven as a dusky red sun set over the Bristol Channel.

When I came off watch at eight o'clock, the carpenter, Nillsson, had his head in the chief's room. I went in and looked over his shoulder.

"How's the well, Chips?"

"Nodding yet," Chips sang out, looking over at me. "She ain't 'ad no wedder." He meant "no weather."

I turned in.

The "wedder" came in the Irish Sea. What a spring that was! Gales all along the coast. Fishing smacks lost with all hands. Coasters driven ashore. No stars. Rain driving horizontally against the weather cloth on the bridge.

At one bell next morning I was waked by the third tumbling into my cabin and crashing the door open. The ship gave a sudden roll. I heard the dreary, everlasting swash of the sea overhead, the clank, clank of gear swinging in the storeroom below, the stagger and the sudden, hurrying hiss of the engines as the stern went up.

I looked at the lamp on its gimbals, and then at the third's dirty, tired face.

"Is she makin' water again?" I said.

He wiped his nose with the back of his hand and sniffed. Nobody looks his best at 4 A.M. after a lot of bilge diving. Young Linklatter wasn't much to look at even when going ashore. Now he was a mess.

I turned out. Seagoing is occasionally a boring business. Anyone can be a hero in wartime. The stimulation of the nervous system by explosions and the excitement of words like "guns," "torpedoes," "mines," "the enemy" and so on generally keep a man going in wartime. We had nothing of that. Our stimulation lay in the stark fact that a job had to be done. The dock was lined with men who could and would do the job if we didn't. Economic necessity is an even more austere mistress than patriotism.

I put on my clothes. Since I had heard from Mr. Ede that I was to get his job, I had not written a line. I tried to blame the weather, but I succeeded only to a limited extent. I remembered bad weather during which I had gone on writing. I even blamed the ship making water. The plain fact was, I was allowing other interests to delay my novel. I felt depressed. I went down below filled with a determination to get the ship out of her troubles, so that I could return to *Casuals of the Sea.*

We were off Holyhead that morning. Mr. Ede said the Kingstown mail packet crossed our bows, "doing everything except turn over." He came down while I was having my morning tea at the vise bench under the clock. Number-one well was full up and rising.

"Why didn't it fill when the Super was on board?" I demanded.

"He had his thumb on the leak," Mr. Ede said sourly.

He looked like an Old Testament prophet in his nightgown and sea boots, a prophet who had not had much luck in his prophesyings lately.

"You'll get a lot of luck like this, if you stick to the sea."

"I'll stick to it until you come back," I said.

"I'm not gone yet," he pointed out. "We're in for a picnic in the Clyde if she gets full again."

He suddenly looked hard at his clenched fist.

He made a further remark which I didn't catch. Owing to the ship being slowed down, on account of the weather, the safety valves suddenly roared. They made a thuttering noise like heavy machine guns.

"What did you say, sir?" I bawled.

"I said, 'Oh, Gawd damn and blast it!' "

He gave me a comical look.

He climbed the ladder while I went to the main damper and closed it some more. There was such a wind coming down the stokehold ventilators you would have thought we had forced draft.

Now and again, when a wave lifted the bows high, we got the pump going, but the trim made it impossible most of the time. All day we labored—no other word describes the motion of a water-logged ship in a quartering sea—toward the North Channel, between Scotland and Ireland. I went to bed that night resigned to arriving in Glasgow with a dirty engine room. It was raining and some of it was coming in, blown by the wind, under the skylight lifts. The cylinder covers were not a pretty sight. The handrails were rusty, the gratings foul. Mr. Ede had taken no indicator cards. The ship's motion had made it impossible.

Next morning we were in the Firth. When I went out on deck at quarter to four it was terribly cold, but I could see the lights of Ayr and, ahead, Ardrossan. Burns's country, they called it. We were going full speed past it. The sea was smooth by comparison. We were out of the wind. There was less chance of the old ship taking a dive.

Mr. Ede was up and dressed and had coffee ready. He had some old-fashioned ways that made you love him and his beard. I saw his log all laid out on his table. Next trip, I thought, by Jove, I'll be doing that!

Mr. Huggins was on the dock when we got in. So was my respected relative, the "ship's husband," as he was technically known. They stood watching us being warped in, in their black suits, black boots, black umbrellas, black hats, black mustaches and mutton-chop whiskers, like two black birds of misfortune. There was a glass porthole in our top-store in the 'tween-deck, a porthole which was really illegal, for it was under water when we were deep-loaded. As we came alongside it was level with the dock. I was in there, looking through the smudged little circle of three-quarter-inch plate glass, and I had a close-up of our lords and masters as they stood waiting for the gangway to be unshipped. Two of the best! I thought, but they were not at all sure about themselves. They knew no more than we where the water was coming in.

Number-one hatch, when it was opened, left no doubt in anybody's mind that we were leaking. Instead of a mountain of bright-red iron ore, the stuff was dark-red and full of puddles. It was leveled off almost flat. The cargo men who were to dig it out looked at it askance. This was not going to be the usual dry dusty job, but it would be work. I was not worrying about them and their work. We had plenty to do. As soon as the ore was out, six thousand tons, we were to go into dry dock for a survey.

Mr. Ede and I sat in the Grosvenor Bar that evening, among the students from the university, some of whom did most of their studying there, and tried to concentrate on life ashore. We had had curried prawns and rice with mango chutney, followed by cheese and celery. At the Grosvenor we had a double Scotch with Apollinaris, followed by a chaser of large Bass Ale. The place closed at ten, owing to the peculiar sumptuary laws of the land, so we left the students drinking up their parents' savings and went to the second house at the Empire, where Little Tich made us laugh because he was so like our third, Linklatter, whom we called Little Tich. Mr. Ede and I kept thinking of Little Tich down in the bilges, or getting his face all blacked on the boiler tops. Then Harry Tate with his motorcar and his imbecile college-boy son put us in stitches, in fact, gave Mr. Ede the hiccups, which lasted all the way down Renfield Street and as far as the Queen's Dock.

We had forgotten that damned number-one hold for a while, anyway.

"You've pulled some rivets," Mr. Huggins said to Mr. Ede. "That's the only thing. We've called a survey."

He made the statement *ex cathedra* and we accepted it, as it were, *in statu pupillari*. It was a perfectly logical, reasonable assumption, though sixteen-year-old ships built by Furness Withy did not customarily pull rivets out of their limber strakes. Who were we to contradict authority? We waited until the order came to move into the graving dock.

Mr. Ede said to me, in a voice that seemed to be ambushed in his beard (we were in the fire room and Mr. Huggins was ashore), "Funny sort of rivets! They go in and out like concertinas. Why doesn't she make water now? There's a couple of feet in the well, mud mostly. Chips says the rod sticks in it."

Mr. Huggins wasn't the sort of man to have two tugs when he had us to work the engines. We juggled the old lady into the dock and finally received the order F. W. E. (Finished With Engines). Mr. Ede went over the things we had to do, a class of work known as "underwater connections." They can be done only in dry dock, but that is not their peculiar impact upon the ship's personnel. What gives them their slightly awesome significance is that they have to be examined again and again, not only while opened up but when completed. If the water is let into the dock and there is anything wrong with them . . .

This is a subject almost too serious for discussion outside of the confessional.

The old ship had such solidly built connections that we had nothing to worry about. It was the leak which obsessed us. So stealthily does time erode impressions, convictions, and suspicions it was hard to believe we had gone through all that misery at sea. Was it possible that, when the Old Man had put the ship around, stern to the gale, we had congregated on the wet, blowy foredeck, had watched the carpenter chalk his line as well as his rod, had seen him lower it slowly, carefully, until it stuck in ore mud at the bottom and finally had seen him haul it up showing twenty-one feet of water? We had difficulty in holding onto the fact that we had indeed seen all this.

I was working furiously on the stern gland (which had been leaking) when I saw Mr. Ede, lamp in hand, coming along the shaft-tunnel. His boots rang on the loose floor planks. He might have been Diogenes with his lamp searching for an honest man. His expression was gay, as though, when he saw me, he had at last found what he was looking for.

He watched me drive a final turn of inch and a half packing into the stuffing box and start the gland into place.

"All new?" he inquired.

"All new," I said. I was going to have no stern-gland trouble when I was chief.

"They've found it," he said.

"The leak?" I left the fireman to screw all the nuts up snug and turned to Mr. Ede.

"In the well. Two-inch drain plug fell out at sea!"

"Two inch . . . ? A two-inch hole in the bottom of the ship? Why didn't she fill up when we were anchored in Milford Haven?"

"Clay. When we beached her she drove a clay plug into it. Took a day to wash it out."

"What did the Super say?"

Mr. Ede made a sound which in anybody else might be called a snigger. In him it was too ventriloquial. It seemed to come down the ventilator.

"He said he knew it was a plug gone. Said he told us at the time. It was just as he expected. Not surprised."

"Good God!"

Relief at finding what had plagued us, the knowledge that we were in no way responsible for what had occurred, prevented us from brooding over Mr. Huggins' assumption of omniscience. After all, he had to say something. He couldn't admit he didn't know it all. It was like papal infallibility. Nobody really believes in it, but everybody wants to. If the boss knows everything, he has to carry the responsibility.

"Come up when you've finished the job," Mr. Ede said, in a tone I understood.

I went up and found him with Captain Williams. There was a bottle open and a siphon. The divine aroma of Crabbie's Export Scotch filled the room I was to occupy for a few voyages.

"After all, she's due for a cleanin'," the captain said.

The ship in an empty dock had a dead feel about her, quite different from being tied up in a wet dock. Stentorian shouts echoed as in a cavern from the vast cistern of the dock and mingled with the clink-clink-clink-clack-clack, of riveters and the heavy thwack of the swinging maul tightening the propeller nut. Fires glowed on deck where smiths straightened rails and hatch coamings. Cranes lifted out boat davits and carried them, swinging in wide arcs, down to the forges in the yard. Sailors were making a distant tack-tack with chipping hammers. Everybody, from time to time, hurried ashore to the lavatories. Everything on board was locked up until we were once more water-borne. There was a constant passage of men and boys to and fro up the two long gangways. The boys were very black, very greasy, in clothing and in face, and they had an air of importance beyond anything we seniors could achieve.

"It's always a great day, Mac, when you take charge," the captain said. We drank to success in general.

I suppose it is, but the fact was plain enough to me in later years that, in our way of life, a man, like Brown or myself, had such a long, arduous preparation for chief that when he finally took charge he had only himself to worry about.

That was my trouble. It is the imaginative man who suffers the agonies when he is in the driver's seat. The tortures I went through, during my first voyage as chief, all over nothing! Mere chimeras, dire anticipations, and almost voluptuous dreads! I was a victim, at times, of accidental terrors. Mr. Ede's room had a window hinged at the top and fastened at the bottom with a catch, looking down into the engine room. It had a tight rubber strip around it to keep out the noise. I had turned in about midnight, having seen the third safely on watch. I put out the lamp and went off to sleep. All was well.

About two o'clock the ship gave a gentle roll. The window catch came loose, the window opened and let in the thunderous clangor of the engine room.

I was out of my bunk and halfway down the engine room ladder in my bare feet before I realized what had happened.

I went back and made the window secure. It sounds silly, but it was a shock. The captain, when I told him, said,

"You get used to it after a while, Mac."

FROM

Kon-Tiki

THOR HEYERDAHL

To support his theory that the mysterious original settlers of the South Pacific islands had migrated from South America, Thor Heyerdahl, a thirty-four-year-old Norwegian anthropologist, and five companions sailed from Callao, Peru, on April 28, 1948, aboard a balsa-wood raft much like those built by the pre-Inca inhabitants of the country. One hundred and one days and 4300 miles later, the raft crashed on the reef surrounding Raroia Island in the Tuamotu Archipelago. Here is Heyerdahl's account of the perilous climax of that voyage.

The Reef

WE were drifting straight toward the ominous Takume and Raroia reefs, which together blocked up forty to fifty miles of the sea ahead of us. We made desperate efforts to steer clear, to the north of these dangerous reefs, and things seemed to be going well till one night the watch came hurrying in and called us all out.

The wind had changed. We were heading straight for the Takume reef. It had begun to rain, and there was no visibility at all. The reef could not be far off.

In the middle of night we held a council of war. It was a question of saving our lives now. To get past on the north side was now hopeless; we must try to get through on the south side instead. We trimmed the sail, laid the oar over, and began a dangerous piece of sailing with the uncertain north wind behind us. If the east wind came back before we had passed the whole façade of the fifty-mile-long reefs, we should be hurled in among the breakers, at their mercy.

We agreed on all that should be done if shipwreck was imminent. We would stay on board the *Kon-Tiki* at all costs. We would not climb up the mast, from which we should be shaken down like rotten fruit, but would cling tight to the stays of the mast when the seas poured over us. We laid the rubber raft loose on the deck and made fast to it a small watertight radio transmitter, a small quantity of provisions, water bottles, and medical stores. This would be washed ashore independently of us if we ourselves should get over the reef safe but empty-handed. In the stern of the *Kon-Tiki* we made fast a long rope with a float which also would be washed ashore, so that we could try to pull in the raft if she were stranded out on the reef. And so we crept into bed and left the watch to the helmsman out in the rain.

As long as the north wind held, we glided slowly but surely down along the façade of the coral reefs which lay in ambush below the horizon. But then one afternoon the wind died away, and when it returned it had gone round into the east. According to Erik's position we were already so far down that we now had some hope of steering clear of the southernmost point of the Raroia reef. We would try to get round it and into shelter before going on to other reefs beyond it.

When night came, we had been a hundred days at sea.

Late in the night I woke, feeling restless and uneasy. There was something unusual in the movement of the waves. The *Kon-Tiki's* motion was a little different from what it usually was in such conditions. We had become sensitive to changes in the rhythm of the logs. I thought at once of suction from a coast, which was drawing near, and was continually out on deck and up the mast. Nothing but sea was visible. But I could get no quiet sleep. Time passed.

At dawn, just before six, Torstein came hurrying down from the masthead. He could see a whole line of small palm-clad islands far ahead. Before doing anything else we laid the oar over to southward as far as we could. What Torstein had seen must be the small coral islands which lay strewn like pearls on a string behind the Raroia reef. A northward current must have caught us.

At half-past seven palm-clad islets had appeared in a row all along the horizon to westward. The southernmost lay roughly ahead of our bow, and thence there were islands and clumps of palms all along the horizon on our starboard side till they disappeared as dots away to northward. The nearest were four or five sea miles away.

A survey from the masthead showed that, even if our bow pointed toward the bottom island in the chain, our drift sideways was so great that we were not advancing in the direction in which our bow pointed. We were drifting diagonally right in toward the reef. With fixed centerboards we should still have had some hope of steering clear. But sharks were following close astern, so that it was impossible to dive under the raft and tighten up the loose centerboards with fresh guy ropes.

We saw that we had now only a few hours more on board the *Kon-Tiki*. They must be used in preparation for our inevitable wreck on the coral reef. Every man learned what he had to do when the moment came; each one of us knew where his own limited sphere of responsibility lay, so that we should not fly around treading on one another's toes when the time came and seconds counted. The *Kon-Tiki* pitched up and down, up and down, as the wind forced us in. There was no doubt that here was the turmoil of the waves created by the reef—some waves advancing while others were hurled back after beating vainly against the surrounding wall.

We were still under full sail in the hope of even now being able to steer clear. As we gradually drifted nearer, half sideways, we saw from the mast how the whole string of palm-clad isles was connected with a coral reef, part above and part under water, which lay like a mole where the sea was white with foam and leaped high into the air. The Raroia atoll is oval in shape and has a diameter of twenty-five miles, not counting the adjoining reefs of Takume. The whole of its longer side faces the sea to eastward, where we came pitching in. The reef itself, which runs in one line from horizon to horizon, is only a few hundred yards clear, and behind it idyllic islets lie in a string around the still lagoon inside.

It was with mixed feelings that we saw the blue Pacific being ruthlessly torn up and hurled into the air all along the horizon ahead of us. I knew what awaited us; I had visited the Tuamotu group before and had stood safe on land looking out over the immense spectacle in the east, where the surf from the open Pacific broke in over the reef. New reefs and islands kept on gradually appearing to southward. We must be lying off the middle of the façade of the coral wall.

On board the *Kon-Tiki* all preparations for the end of the voyage were being made. Everything of value was carried into the cabin and lashed fast. Documents and papers were packed into watertight bags, along with films and other things which would not stand a dip in the sea. The whole bamboo cabin was covered with canvas, and especially strong ropes were lashed across it. When we saw that all hope was gone, we opened up the bamboo deck and cut off with machete knives all the ropes which held the centerboards down. It was a hard job to get the centerboards drawn up, because they were all thickly covered with stout barnacles. With the centerboards up the draught of our vessel was no deeper than to the bottom of the timber logs, and we would therefore be more easily washed in over the reef. With no centerboards and with the sail down, the raft lay completely sideways on and was entirely at the mercy of wind and sea.

We tied the longest rope we had to the homemade anchor and made it fast to the step of the port mast, so that the *Kon-Tiki* would go into the surf stern first when the anchor was thrown overboard. The anchor itself consisted of empty water cans filled with used radio batteries and heavy scrap, and solid mangrove-wood sticks projected from it, set crosswise.

Order number one, which came first and last, was: Hold on to the raft! Whatever happened, we must hang on tight on board and let the nine great logs take the pressure from the reef. We ourselves had more than enough to do to withstand the weight of the water. If we jumped overboard, we should become helpless victims of the suction which would fling us in and out over the sharp corals. The rubber raft would capsize in the steep seas or, heavily loaded with us in it, it would be torn to ribbons against the reef. But the wooden logs would sooner or later be cast ashore, and we with them, if we only managed to hold fast.

Next, all hands were told to put on their shoes for the first time in a hundred days and to have their life belts ready. The last precaution, however, was not of much value, for if a man fell overboard he would be battered to death, not drowned. We had time, too, to put our passports and such few dollars as we had left into our pockets. But it was not lack of time that was troubling us.

Those were anxious hours in which we lay drifting helplessly sideways, step after step, in toward the reef. It was noticeably quiet on board; we all crept in and out from cabin to bamboo deck, silent or laconic, and carried on with our jobs. Our serious faces showed that no one was in doubt as to what awaited us, and the absence of nervousness showed that we had all gradually acquired an unshakable confidence in the raft. If it had brought us across the sea, it would also manage to bring us ashore alive.

Inside the cabin there was a complete chaos of provision cartons and cargo, lashed fast. Torstein had barely found room for himself in the radio corner, where he had got the shortwave transmitter working. We were now over four thousand sea miles from our old base at Callao, where the Peruvian Naval War School had maintained regular contact with us, and still farther from Hal and Frank and the other radio amateurs in the United States. But, as chance willed, we had on the previous day got in touch with a capable radio "ham" who had a set on Rarotonga in the Cook Islands, and the operators, quite contrary to all our usual practice, had arranged for an extra contact with him early in the morning. All the time we were drifting closer and closer in to the reef, Torstein was sitting tapping his key and calling Rarotonga.

Entries in the *Kon-Tiki's* log ran:

—8:15: *We are slowly approaching land. We can now make out with the naked eye the separate palm trees inside on the starboard side.*

—8:45: *The wind has veered into a still more unfavorable quarter for us, so we have no hope of getting clear. No nervousness on board, but hectic preparations on deck. There is something lying on the reef ahead of us which looks like the wreck of a sailing vessel, but it may be only a heap of driftwood.*

—9:45: *The wind is taking us straight toward the last island but one we see behind the reef. We can now see the whole coral reef clearly; here it is built up like a white and red speckled wall which barely sticks up out of the water as a belt in front of all the islands. All along the reef white foaming surf is flung up toward the sky. Bengt is just serving up a good hot meal, the last before the great action!*

It is a wreck lying in there on the reef. We are so close now that we can see right across the shining lagoon behind the reef and see the outlines of other islands on the other side of the lagoon.

As this was written, the dull drone of the surf came near again; it came from the whole reef and filled the air like thrilling rolls of the drum, heralding the exciting last act of the *Kon-Tiki.*

—*9:50: Very close now. Drifting along the reef. Only a hundred yards or so away. Torstein is talking to the man on Rarotonga. All clear. Must pack up log now. All in good spirits; it looks bad,* but we shall make it!

A few minutes later the anchor rushed overboard and caught hold of the bottom, so that the *Kon-Tiki* swung around and turned her stern inward toward the breakers. It held us for a few valuable minutes, while Torstein sat hammering like mad on the key. He had got Rarotonga now. The breakers thundered in the air and the sea rose and fell furiously. All hands were at work on deck, and now Torstein got his message through. He said we were drifting toward the Raroia reef. He asked Rarotonga to listen in on the same wave length every hour. If we were silent for more than thirty-six hours, Rarotonga must let the Norwegian Embassy in Washington know. Torstein's last words were:

"O.K. Fifty yards left. Here we go. Good-by."

Then he closed down the station, Knut sealed up the papers, and both crawled out on deck as fast as they could to join the rest of us, for it was clear now that the anchor was giving way.

The swell grew heavier and heavier, with deep troughs between the waves, and we felt the raft being swung up and down, up and down, higher and higher.

Again the order was shouted: "Hold on, never mind about the cargo, hold on!"

We were now so near the waterfall inside that we no longer heard the steady continuous roar from all along the reef. We now heard only a separate boom each time the nearest breaker crashed down on the rocks.

All hands stood in readiness, each clinging fast to the rope he thought the most secure. Only Erik crept into the cabin at the last moment; there was one part of the program he had not yet carried out—he had not found his shoes!

No one stood aft, for it was there the shock from the reef would come. Nor were the two firm stays which ran from the masthead down to the stern safe. For if the mast fell they would be left hanging overboard, over the reef. Herman, Bengt, and Torstein had climbed up on some boxes which were lashed fast forward of the cabin wall, and, while Herman clung onto the guy ropes from the ridge of the roof, the other two held onto the ropes from the masthead by which the sail at other times was hauled up. Knut and I chose the stay running from the bow up to the masthead, for, if mast and cabin and everything else went overboard, we thought the rope from the bow would nevertheless remain lying inboard, as we were now head on to the seas.

When we realized that the seas had got hold of us, the anchor rope was cut and we were off. A sea rose straight up under us, and we felt the *Kon-Tiki* being lifted up in the air. The great moment had come; we were riding on the wave back at breathless speed, our ramshackle craft creaking and groaning as she quivered under us. The excitement made one's blood boil. I remember that, having no other inspiration, I waved my arm and bellowed "Hurrah!" at the top of my lungs; it afforded a certain relief and could do no harm anyway. The others certainly thought I had gone mad, but they all beamed and grinned enthusiastically. On we ran with the seas rushing in behind us; this was the *Kon-Tiki's* baptism of fire. All must and would go well.

But our elation was soon dampened. A new sea rose high up astern of us like a glittering, green glass wall. As we sank down it came rolling after us, and, in the same second in which I saw it high above me, I felt a violent blow and was submerged under floods of water. I felt the suction through my whole body, with such great power that I had to strain every single muscle in my frame and think of one thing only—hold on, hold on! I think that in such a desperate situation the arms will be torn off be-

fore the brain consents to let go, evident as the outcome is. Then I felt that the mountain of water was passing on and relaxing its devilish grip of my body. When the whole mountain had rushed on, with an earsplitting roaring and crashing, I saw Knut again hanging on beside me, doubled up into a ball. Seen from behind, the great sea was almost flat and gray. As it rushed on, it swept over the ridge of the cabin roof which projected from the water, and there hung the three others, pressed against the cabin roof as the water passed over them.

We were still afloat.

In an instant I renewed my hold, with arms and legs bent round the strong rope. Knut let himself down and with a tiger's leap joined the others on the boxes, where the cabin took the strain. I heard reassuring exclamations from them, but at the same time I saw a new green wall rise up and come towering toward us. I shouted a warning and made myself as small and hard as I could where I hung. In an instant hell was over us again, and the *Kon-Tiki* disappeared completely under the masses of water. The sea tugged and pulled with all the force it could bring to bear at the poor little bundles of human bodies. The second sea rushed over us, to be followed by a third like it.

Then I heard a triumphant shout from Knut, who was now hanging onto the rope ladder:

"Look at the raft—she's holding!"

After three seas only the double mast and the cabin had been knocked a bit crooked. Again we had a feeling of triumph over the elements, and the elation of victory gave us new strength.

Then I saw the next sea come towering up, higher than all the rest, and again I bellowed a warning aft to the others as I climbed up the stay, as high as I could get in a hurry, and hung on fast. Then I myself disappeared sideways into the midst of the green wall which towered high over us. The others, who were farther aft and saw me disappear first, estimated the height of the wall of water at twenty-five feet, while the foaming crest passed by fifteen feet above the part of the glassy wall into which I had vanished. Then the great wave reached them, and we had all one single thought—hold on, hold on, hold, hold, hold!

We must have hit the reef that time. I myself felt only the

strain on the stay, which seemed to bend and slacken jerkily. But whether the bumps came from above or below I could not tell, hanging there. The whole submersion lasted only seconds, but it demanded more endurance than we usually have in our bodies. There is greater strength in the human mechanism than that of the muscles alone. I determined that, if I were to die, I would die in this position, like a knot on the stay. The sea thundered on, over and past, and as it roared by it revealed a hideous sight. The *Kon-Tiki* was wholly changed, as by the stroke of a magic wand. The vessel we knew from weeks and months at sea was no more; in a few seconds our pleasant world had become a shattered wreck.

I saw only one man on board besides myself. He lay pressed flat across the ridge of the cabin roof, face downward with his arms stretched out on both sides, while the cabin itself was crushed in, like a house of cards, toward the stern and toward the starboard side. The motionless figure was Herman. There was no other sign of life, while the hill of water thundered by, in across the reef. The hardwood mast on the starboard side was broken like a match, and the upper stump, in its fall, had smashed right through the cabin roof, so that the mast and all its gear slanted at a low angle over the reef on the starboard side. Astern, the steering block was twisted round lengthways and the crossbeam broken, while the steering oar was smashed to splinters. The splashboards at the bow were broken like cigar boxes, and the whole deck was torn up and pasted like wet paper against the forward wall of the cabin, along with boxes, cans, canvas, and other cargo. Bamboo sticks and rope ends stuck up everywhere, and the general effect was of complete chaos.

I felt cold fear run through my whole body. What was the good of my holding on? If I lost one single man here, in the run in, the whole thing would be ruined, and for the moment there was only one human figure to be seen after the last buffet. In that second Torstein's hunched-up form appeared outside the raft. He was hanging like a monkey in the ropes from the masthead and managed to get onto the logs again, where he crawled up onto the debris forward of the cabin. Herman, too, now turned his head and gave me a forced grin of encouragement, but did not move. I bellowed in the faint hope of locating the others and heard Bengt's calm voice call out that all hands were aboard. They were lying holding onto the ropes behind the tangled barricade which the tough plaiting from the bamboo deck had built up.

All this happened in the course of a few seconds, while the *Kon-Tiki* was being drawn out of the witches' caldron by the backwash, and a fresh sea came rolling over her. For the last time I bellowed "Hang on!" at the top of my lungs amid the uproar, and that was all I myself did; I hung on and disappeared in the masses of water which rushed over and past in those endless two or three seconds. That was enough for me. I saw the ends of the logs knocking and bumping against a sharp step in the coral reef without going over it. Then we were sucked out again. I also saw the two men who lay stretched out across the ridge of the cabin roof, but none of us smiled any longer. Behind the chaos of bamboo I heard a calm voice call out:

"This won't do."

I myself felt equally discouraged. As the masthead sank farther and farther out over the starboard side, I found myself hanging onto a slack line outside the raft. The next sea came. When it had gone by I was dead tired, and my only thought was to get up onto the logs and lie behind the barricade. When the backwash retreated, I saw for the first time the rugged red reef naked beneath us and perceived Torstein standing, bent double, on gleaming red corals, holding onto a bunch of rope ends from the mast. Knut, standing aft, was about to jump. I shouted that we must all keep on the logs, and Torstein, who had been washed overboard by the pressure of water, sprang up again like a cat.

Two or three more seas rolled over us with diminishing force, and what happened then I do not remember, except that water foamed in and out and I myself sank lower and lower toward the red reef over which we were being lifted in. Then only crests of foam full of salt spray came whirling in, and I was able to work my way in onto the raft, where we all made for the after end of the logs which was highest up on the reef.

At the same moment Knut crouched down and sprang up onto the reef with the line which lay clear astern. While the backwash was running out, he waded through the whirling water some thirty yards in and stood safely at the end of the line when the next sea foamed in toward him, died down, and ran back from the flat reef like a broad stream.

Then Erik came crawling out of the collapsed cabin, with his shoes on. If we had all done as he did, we should have got off cheaply. As the cabin had not been washed overboard but had been pressed down pretty flat under the canvas, Erik lay quietly stretched out among the cargo and heard the peals of thunder crashing above him while the collapsed bamboo walls curved downward. Bengt had had a slight concussion when the mast fell but had managed to crawl under the wrecked cabin alongside Erik. We should all of us have been lying there if we had realized in advance how firmly the countless lashings and plaited bamboo sheets would hang onto the main logs under the pressure of the water.

Erik was now standing ready on the logs aft, and when the sea retired he, too, jumped up onto the reef. It was Herman's turn next, and then Bengt's. Each time the raft was pushed a bit farther in, and, when Torstein's turn and my own came, the raft already lay so far in on the reef that there was no longer any ground for abandoning her. All hands began the work of salvage.

We were now twenty yards away from that devilish step up on the reef, and it was there and beyond it that the breakers came rolling after one another in long lines. The coral polyps had taken care to build the atoll so high that only the very tops of the breakers were able to send a fresh stream of sea water past us and into the lagoon, which abounded in fish. Here inside was the corals' own world, and they disported themselves in the strangest shapes and colors.

A long way in on the reef the others found the rubber raft, lying drifting and quite waterlogged. They emptied it and dragged it back to the wreck, and we loaded it to the full with the most important equipment, like the radio set, provisions, and water bottles. We dragged all this in across the reef and piled it up on the top of a huge block of coral which lay alone on the inside of the reef like a large meteorite. Then we went back to the wreck for fresh loads. We could never know what the sea would be up to when the tidal currents got to work around us.

In the shallow water inside the reef we saw something bright shining in the sun. When we waded over to pick it up, to our astonishment we saw two empty tins. This was not exactly what we had expected to find there, and we were still more surprised when we saw that the little boxes were quite bright and newly opened and stamped "Pineapple," with the same inscription as that on the new field rations we ourselves were testing for the quartermaster. They were indeed two of our own pineapple tins which we had thrown overboard after our last meal on board the *Kon-Tiki.* We had followed close behind them up on the reef.

We were standing on sharp, rugged coral blocks, and on the uneven bottom we waded now ankle-deep, now chest-deep, according to the channels and stream beds in the reef. Anemones and corals gave the whole reef the appearance of a rock garden covered with mosses and cactus and fossilized plants, red and green and yellow and white. There was no color that was not represented, either in corals or algae or in shells and sea slugs and fantastic fish, which were wriggling about everywhere. In the deeper channels small sharks about four feet long came sneaking up to us in the crystal-clear water. But we had only to smack the water with the palms of our hands for them to turn about and keep at a distance.

Where we had stranded, we had only pools of water and wet patches of coral about us; farther in lay the calm blue lagoon. The tide was going out, and we continually saw more corals sticking up out of the water round us, while the surf which thundered without interruption along the reef sank down, as it were, a floor lower. What would happen there on the narrow reef when the tide began to flow again was uncertain. We must get away.

The reef stretched like a half-submerged fortress wall up to the north and down to the south. In the extreme south was a long island densely covered with tall palm forest. And just above us to the north, only six hundred or seven hundred yards away, lay another but considerably smaller palm island. It lay inside the reef, with palm tops rising into the sky and snow-white sandy beaches running out into the still lagoon. The whole island looked like a bulging green basket of flowers, or a little bit of concentrated paradise.

This island we chose.

Herman stood beside me beaming all over his bearded face. He did not say a word, only stretched out his hand and laughed quietly. The *Kon-Tiki* still lay far out on the reef with the spray flying over her. She was a wreck, but an honorable wreck. Everything above deck was smashed up, but the nine balsa logs from the Quevedo forest in Ecuador were as intact as ever. They had saved our lives. The sea had claimed but little of the cargo, and none of what we had stowed inside the cabin. We ourselves had stripped the raft of everything of real value, which now lay in safety on the top of the great sun-smitten rock inside the reef.

Since I had jumped off the raft, I had genuinely missed the sight of all the pilot fish wriggling in front of our bow. Now the great balsa logs lay up on the reef in six inches of water, and brown sea slugs lay writhing under the bows. The pilot fish were gone. The dolphins were gone. Only unknown flat fish with peacock patterns and blunt tails wriggled inquisitively in and out among the logs. We had arrived in a new world. Johannes had left his hole. He had doubtless found another lurking place here.

I took a last look around on board the wreck and caught sight of a little baby palm in a flattened basket. It projected from an eye in a coconut to a length of eighteen inches, and two roots stuck out below. I waded in toward the island with the nut in my hand. A little way ahead I saw Knut wading happily landward with a model of the raft, which he had made with much labor on the voyage, under his arm. We soon passed Bengt. He was a splendid steward. With a lump on his forehead and sea water dripping from his beard, he was walking bent double pushing a box, which danced along before him every time the breakers outside sent a stream over into the lagoon. He lifted the lid proudly. It was the kitchen box, and in it were the Primus and cooking utensils in good order.

I shall never forget that wade across the reef toward the heavenly palm island that grew larger as it came to meet us.

When I reached the sunny sand beach, I slipped off my shoes and thrust my bare toes down into the warm, bone-dry sand. It was as though I enjoyed the sight of every footprint which dug itself into the virgin sand beach that led up to the palm trunks. Soon the palm tops closed over my head, and I went on, right in toward the center of the tiny island. Green coconuts hung under the palm tufts, and some luxuriant bushes were thickly covered with snow-white blossoms, which smelled so sweet and seductive that I felt quite faint. In the interior of the island two quite tame terns flew about my shoulders. They were as white and light as wisps of cloud. Small lizards shot away from my feet, and the most important inhabitants of the island were large blood-red hermit crabs which lumbered along in every direction with stolen snail shells as large as eggs adhering to their soft hinder parts.

I was completely overwhelmed. I sank down on my knees and thrust my fingers deep down into the dry warm sand.

The voyage was over. We were all alive. We had run ashore on a small uninhabited South Sea island. And what an island! Torstein came in, flung away a sack, threw himself flat on his back and looked up at the palm tops and the white birds, light as down, which circled noiselessly just above us. Soon we were all six lying there. Herman, always energetic, climbed up a small palm and pulled down a cluster of large green coconuts. We cut off their soft tops with our machete knives, as if they were eggs, and poured down our throats the most delicious refreshing drink in the world—sweet, cold milk from young and seedless palm fruit. On the reef outside resounded the monotonous drumbeats from the guard at the gates of paradise.

"Purgatory was a bit damp," said Bengt, "but heaven is more or less as I'd imagined it."

We stretched ourselves luxuriously on the ground and smiled up at the white trade-wind clouds drifting by westward up above the palm tops. Now we were no longer following them helplessly; now we lay on a fixed, motionless island, in Polynesia.

And as we lay and stretched ourselves, the breakers outside us rumbled like a train, to and fro, to and fro, all along the horizon.

Bengt was right; this was heaven.

FROM

Ships and Women

BILL ADAMS

In sailing-ship days, no man was truly a deep-water sailor who had not experienced a passage around Cape Horn. Violent, changeable winds, towering seas, ice-coated decks and rigging, and always the danger of being dashed against the gloomy, savage rocks of Tierra del Fuego—there was no greater test of seamanship.

Some seventy years ago, young Bill Adams, an apprentice aboard the clipper Silberhorn, *made that passage from the Atlantic to the Pacific, from boyhood to manhood. Here is his description of how it was.*

Cape Horn

THE vertigo was always with me when I had to go aloft. Height was my utter horror. I dreaded taking sail in, dreaded setting it. On deck I loved my ship, but up aloft I feared her with a ghastly fear. And God knows how I hid it. Sailors don't notice things perhaps. At any rate none ever knew of it. I lived with horror ever at my elbow. And so did Wood. He suffered just as I, but he let others know. Daytime was worst, but night was bad enough. I mind the first time I went to a royal, the highest sail of all, above the big topgallant. I went up on the mainmast. The ship was racing through a windy sea, sprays flying high. Hickley went first, ahead of me. Two lads to a royal. I somehow made my way to the high spar, a hundred and seventy feet from the hard deck and farther from the sea that waited me. I set my foot upon the swaying footrope, no thicker than my thumb; and I walked out along it. I could not see a thing with any clearness. All was a dim and sickening blur. The tall mast swayed through a terrific arc. I don't know how I did it, but I gathered up the flapping sail, lashed it, and came down. And, God, how good it was to feel the solid planks beneath my feet again! *I was not fit to be a sailor!* I did not wonder could I ever live it down. I lived just day by day, and night by night. And when at work on deck I put it out of my mind, or did so mostly. I could have told the mate, of course, and he would have been easy on me. But I kept my fear a secret hidden thing, because of pride; deeming myself a coward. Wood told MacDonald of his dread. MacDonald said, "Why, Jesus Christ, forget it! Hop up aloft and overhaul that mizzen royal buntline!" And up went Wood, shaking like any leaf, a hundred and seventy feet or so, and all alone. Death at his elbow.

Pleasant it was upon the tropic sea. We sat upon the hatch at evening, singing. Sometimes we danced, for Alexander had a queer old fiddle made of coal-oil cans. We boxed, we wrestled, had tugs of war, played leapfrog. Billings and Thornton often sat apart, talking of women.

"Remember Katie Jacobs on the Boca, Buenos Ayres?"

"Aye, an' Liverpool Liz? Is she in Portland yet, d'ye s'pose?"

They spoke of "Number nine" in Yokohama. They said, "Them coolie gals is swell out in Calcutta."

I liked the names of ports, not women.

And then one sunny afternoon I sat out on the boom's far end with Douglas, fishing for bonito. They sported in their thousands under our bare feet, leaping, playing. And now and then a school of flying fish flashed from the sea to dart away downwind. Seated out there, we could watch the tall ship coming, her cutwater lifting, up, up, and up; then pitching deep, deep down. Dancing she came, and swaying lightly with a gentle roll. Oh, lovely thing! And I forgot my vertigo in her great loveliness. Oh, yes, I loved her well.

Then Douglas spoke. "A few more weeks and we'll be off the Horn."

The Horn! There was a sort of something in that name. A dread. Or, call it challenge. And could I meet that challenge? I said no word. I wondered. Cape Horn. Vertigo.

"You'll find it a hard life, my son." Funny! I'd never thought of that, not even when I'd trembled up aloft with vertigo.

Well, I forgot Cape Horn. For when I went on duty the mate said, "Get down the forepeak, you boys. Get up a barrel of pork, and one of junk, and fill the harness casks."

The harness casks were two fine teakwood casks that stood on top of our half-deck. Bound with wide bands of brightly shining brass they were. The varnished teakwood glistened in the sun. And when we opened up the barrel of pork, a reek spread all along the lovely ship. A stink of rotten pork. We took it from its barrel piece by piece, and piece by piece we put it in the harness cask. And then, for many days, we ate it. Putrid pork. And back in Liverpool the owner ate roast beef, and maybe Yorkshire pudding. We didn't think of *him.* We damned our grim Old Man, blaming it on him; as we blamed all things hard, never realizing in our hot youth that he as much as any of us was the sea's slave, serving a shipowner.

We ran from the tropics, and came soon to the roaring forties. Rain beat down. Wind blew cold. Sailors and boys knelt in a long row on the rain-wet planks, each with a bucket of salt water and a large flat sandstone. To and fro, to and fro, we pushed the holystones, scouring her long decks white. Monotony, day after day. A housemaid could have done it. "Who wouldn't sell a farm and go to sea?" One does not love his ship on days like those days were. But the mate says, "Come on, now! Keep those holystones moving!"

And soon we were preparing for Cape Horn. Lashing the weatherboards to the taffrail, to make a solid bulwark lest the seas burst on the high poop. Long ago the most skilled of the sailors had got all her rigging ready for the hurricanes.

Darker the dark sea grew while each day passed. Colder the air. June. Midwinter off the Horn. The Old Man's eyes were solemn. The mate was mute. MacDonald cursed more mightily than ever. And flocks of little black and white sea pigeons circled all about the ship, and now and then came larger birds. Cape hens and mollyhawks. At dusk one day a pod of sperm whales passed within a hundred yards. They rose to spout, and dived, and rose again. Playing as trout play in a mountain pool, they sported. One monster bull leapt from the sea, his whole bulk leaving it; and falling back to his cold element brought down his tail with a great crash, flat on the sullen water. A bull sperm whale, ninety feet long or more, with bulk of four or five big elephants. They passed, sporting toward Cape Horn.

That night MacDonald looked in at an open port. "Aye, sing, by God! Sing now ye've the chance!" he said. For Glynn Williams was singing:

Merry are we, merry are we,
There's no one on earth like a sailor at sea.

Wood's eyes were as the eyes of a poor rabbit that the snake approaches. And as for me, I wondered.

Another evening came. The wind was fallen quite. The sea was level. The clouds hung high and dark, without a break; a canopy of omen. The horizon a sharp line around a solemn sea. The ship lay motionless, her sails all hanging flat. Sea pigeons in hundreds sat on the dark water. A few Cape hens and mollyhawks and one lone snowy albatross. All utter still, to fly an effort on the windless air. And from the distant west there rose a slow-upcreeping glow; a fan-shaped lurid light that slowly spread from the sharp-cut horizon toward the higher sky.

The center of that glow, where the cold winter sun was setting, was a ruby light. The outer glow was as slain bullocks' blood. The ruby faded, and all the western sky was one great bloody light. Old blood, and dull; not from a fresh-made wound. It was as though the gods had slaughtered bullock herds for sacrifice, and their hot blood had dripped and soaked into the canopy of cloud, empurpling it. Old Man, mates, apprentices, sailors, gazed at that bloody west. Sheer silence. No voice. No footfall. No rope creaking. And then the lights went out, as though a curtain had been dropped. The sun was gone. The cook came from his door and flung a hunk of pork rind to the sullen water. An instant flurry rose, of hungry birds all winging toward the rind. They screamed and fought above it. The albatross winged thither, and lesser birds made way for his white majesty. The silence fell again. The Old Man turned and murmured to the mate. The mate came down to the main deck.

"Clew up the royals!"

The royal yards slid down, to rest upon the heads of the topgallant masts. We waited word to go aloft and furl them. Instead came, "Clew up the topgallant sails!" Their heavier halyards groaning, they slid down. Again we waited word. Instead came, "Clew up the cross-jack!" We hauled that great sail up, a hundred feet across its head, by forty-five or fifty deep. And after it we hauled up the yet larger mainsail. The foresail next. And then we lowered the upper topsails, and slid the staysails down. Then the sole sail left set was one small narrow strip upon each towering mast. Three narrow strips of board-hard canvas. The lower topsails. It was pitch dark by now. Nigh to five o'clock. And then the order came to go aloft and furl the lot of them, and up we went and gathered in her wings, the canvas rustling in the sheer sea silence. Blocks creaked, and sailors cried, *"Ho, roll and bunt her!"* And *"Yo—ho—ho—roll her, bullies!"* And Alexander sang, *"That's the way we'll pay Paddy Doyle for his——"*—rolling the mainsail up he sang that, and all hands, giving the sail a last roll, roared together, *"Boots."* And of a sudden I remembered my felt-lined sea boots and wondered how I'd fare off the Horn. We stripped the ship of almost all her dress, left her a scant-clothed lady on the hidden sea. And all night long there was not any sound or any motion. Only her clanging bells, to tell the hours away. Only at each hour's passing the lookout man's clear high cry, "All's well, sir." Then the mate's quiet answer, "All right." Her sidelights gleamed, throwing a red and a green glimmer on the forward water. We saw some sea birds floating, red and green. There was an eeriness about the night. And just ere I went below to roll into my bunk at four of the freezing morning, there came a sort of moaning from the far dark west. The sound of a great gale yet far away. And when they wakened me for breakfast, there was a thundering outside our half-deck. A rage. A roar. The ship was labouring. And I heard water crashing to and fro upon the deck. It was my day to fetch the breakfast coffee from the cook's galley. I stepped from the half-deck door into barbarous fury. The sky was inky, close on the reeling mastheads. The lower topsails strained, tighter than war drums. I could not see a hundred yards away on either side, for mountain seas black as the lowering sky. I ran for the cook's door, and passed the carpenter's. He stood in his door. He looked at me and shouted. Wind swept his words away. But I just caught them. "*This is the Horn!*"

All day it blew, and all the next, and all the next, and all the next; and then blew on, and on, and on, and ever on. Ofttimes the snow whirled by. Darkness till nine, and dark again soon after four. Salt pork, salt junk, pea soup, bean soup, and Harriet Lane on Sunday. And margarine in place of marmalade now when Monday came. And vinegar, of course, and daily lime juice. And no man had a dry rag on the second day. Though all wore rope yarns tied about wrists and ankles, about the oilskin trousers and the jacket sleeves, to keep the water out, water got in. We call those rope yarns "Soul and body lashings," because they keep our souls and bodies in one piece. We stuffed towels within our oilskin collars to keep the water out. They didn't, for you can't have great seas sweep over you and water not get in. And everybody's sea boots as they stepped went "squelch." Felt linings didn't matter very much.

Day upon bitter day, we hauled the braces tight to hold her rolling spars from having too much play. Sails worked loose from lashings. We went aloft to lash them. One yelling day the galley stove was swamped because the cook, for just a moment's space, left his door a half inch too wide open. We ate hard-tack at every meal that day. The thick skin on our palms split open at every finger-joint, in the barbaric cold. Beneath the splits we saw the raw red flesh. The sails, with ice upon them, knocked our knuckles raw; bare to the cold white bone. Our oilskins, chafing at wrists and neck, caused salt water boils. Poor sons of Job were we, and kin to Lazarus. But they had sun, ashore! And yet we laughed at one another, too, mocking a comrade's miseries. Seeing a comrade knocked down by a boarding sea, and soaked afresh, we'd yell, "Why didn't you stay on the farm, you clumsy lubber?" I had that yelled at me many times. But Wood yet many more. His face was a ghost's face. When in the evenings we were all together in the half-deck, the ports closed, our pipes puffing comforting smoke, he'd sit and stare straight before him and never speak a word. If spoken to he'd often never change that stare or say a word.

At last there came a morning when the wind was low, out of the frozen south. We put some sail on the ship. I went aloft to loose an upper topsail, and had that vertigo. And on the rigging there was ice, and on the sails. I almost slipped and fell from the ice-sheathed rigging. And then I all but fell from the frozen footrope of the frozen sail. It would have been quite bad enough without the vertigo. God knows how I got up, or how came down again. I did, and that is all I know. We hoisted that topsail in a lightly falling snow, and Alexander sang:

Boney was a warrior,
To me waye, aye, yoh!
A warrior and a tarrier,
A long time ago.

Then, as the mate called, "Good! Make fast that rope!" the snow ceased. And, about to walk off, old One Eye turned and gazed across the northern water. And all hands stopped, and gazed where he gazed. And there I saw a hard black triangle of land, a dark hill snow-capped.

"Cape Stiff!" said One Eye. And looking around at us he grinned and rubbed his horny hands together, saying, "I 'opes she makes a long voyage. I'm goin' to save me pay-day. More days, more dollars, b'ys!"

Then snow came back and hid Cape Stiff. Before the day was gone, the wind was savage as ever. On, on, and ever on we fought the hurricane. And I lost count of days, of weeks. So, too, did everyone, save One Eye maybe. Sometimes, in lulls, we set a little sail and all hands sang. You cannot hoist a sail without a song for sailormen to pull by:

Oh, blow today, and blow tomorrow,
Blow, boys, blow!
Oh, blow for all poor tars in sorrow,
Blow, my bully boys, blow!

There came a murderous day when we were taking in an upper topsail. All hands were at the gear. Great flakes whirled by. The bitter sprays beat on us. "Aloft and make it fast!" MacDonald shouted when it was ready for furling. The crowd climbed into the reeling ice-sheathed rigging till only Glynn and Wood and I were left on deck.

"Get up there, you!" MacDonald bawled to Wood.

But Wood was beaten. He could not face the Horn's mad music any more. He ran, and vanished through the half-deck door. I felt like following, God knows. But Glynn, catching my eye, laughed merrily and cried, "Who wouldn't sell a farm and go to sea?" Then he leaped for the rigging, and I leaped after him. And that time I had no least touch of vertigo. The first time yet.

One night a flat calm fell upon the hidden sea. The ship lay still. Pitch black, and somewhere below zero. At two that morning the mate cried, "Wash the decks down!"

We fetched the deck buckets, the brooms, and we fetched sand. We hung a lantern in the icy rigging. We flung the sand upon her planks, and scrubbed the green sea slime away, making them safer to walk upon. With that green slime, they were grown treacherous. You could not move along them, unless you gripped a lifeline. Next day the hurricane was back.

Six bitter weeks we fought the blasting Horn. Forty-two days. And no man ever had a dry rag. And no man had palms that were not red and raw. And always hungry. And never rest enough. And never, never for a moment warm. And yet there was amongst us one contented one. Old One Eye'd wink his

solitary orb, and grin, and say, "More days, more dollars, b'ys!" He'd save his money now, for his old age ashore.

At last there came an evening when the sky was high. There seemed a sort of benison of peace upon the sea. We piled full sail on her at last again; the first time in six full weeks. She seemed to say, stealing all eager over that quiet untossed sea, "Give me a wind behind! Oh, do let me go!" And not far away, upon the starboard quarter, lay a small group of tiny islets.

"Diego Ramirez," the word went around. Those tiny islets lie fifty-eight miles sou'westward from the Horn. Then Stiff was left astern! We gazed at them. And then there came a sudden ringing cry from our high forecastle head where the lookout man stood: "Sail right ahead, sir!"

We had not seen a ship in many a day, and ran to see her come. The light was fading. But soon we saw her name, *Aladdin.* She hoisted flags, and we the same. And word went around that she was out from Callao. And then we saw a sailor stand upon her rail, and on her deck behind stood all her company. His voice broke out, clear-ringing over that still peaceful sea:

Goodbye, and farewell to you, fair Spanish ladies!
Goodbye, and farewell to you, ladies of Spain!
For we've received orders to sail for old England,
But we hope in a short time to see you again.

And in a moment then the crews of both tall ships were singing:

We'll rant and we'll roam across the wide ocean,
We'll rant and we'll roam o'er the waters so blue.

And then soon the *Aladdin* was gone. We saw her bright lamp winking for a little space. And, as we turned away, with darkness falling, Johansen, that huge Scandinavian sailor, said, "Vee beats der Horn, py Gott!" And all hands laughed, because he spoke so funnily. And I was glad that I had come to sea. The first time I had ever known that I was fully glad. We'd won our victory, and I'd been there. *Oh, sailor, sailor, sailor!*

FROM

Admiral Halsey's Story

WILLIAM F. HALSEY AND J. BRYAN III

On October 23, 1944, the U.S. Seventh Fleet, under Vice-Admiral Thomas C. Kinkaid, was covering the landing of General Walter Krueger's Sixth Army on Leyte in the Philippines. The U.S. Third Fleet under Admiral William F. Halsey stood ready should the Japanese Navy offer battle. The Japanese, in fact, were approaching in three divisions. Their Northern Force, built around four carriers almost denuded of aircraft, was to decoy Halsey northward. The Center and Southern forces would then hit the exposed Seventh Fleet, turning later to deal with Halsey.

The Japanese plan might have worked. Halsey was in fact lured northward to engage the Japanese decoy force, leaving Kinkaid to deal with the Japanese Center and Southern forces, whose strength Halsey had seriously underestimated. Around Halsey's decision to go north, made in the confusion and uncertainties of battle, controversy later raged. Was it the wrong decision? Let Admiral Halsey tell his own story of the Battle for Leyte Gulf.

Decision at Leyte Gulf

SHORTLY before dawn on October 23, I received a dispatch from a Seventh Fleet picket submarine, the *Darter:* MANY SHIPS INCLUDING 3 PROBABLE BBS [battleships] 08-28 N 116-30 E COURSE 040 SPEED 18 X CHASING. This position is near the southwestern tip of the Philippine group, and the course is toward Coron Bay and Manila. The main strength of the Japanese Fleet was based, we knew, at Singapore and at Brunei, in Borneo. If it stayed holed up there, we planned to go down and dig it out. On the twenty-second, however, our submarines and patrol planes had reported that enemy units were restless, and the *Darter's* dispatch was proof that a major movement was afoot.

Certain details of fleet organization are essential to an understanding of the tremendous battle that now loomed. The key point is that we had two fleets in Philippine waters under separate commands: my Third Fleet was under command of Admiral Nimitz; Tom Kinkaid's Seventh Fleet was under command of General MacArthur. If we had been under the same command, with a single system of operational control and intelligence, the Battle for Leyte Gulf might have been fought differently to a different result. It is folly to cry over spilled milk, but it is wisdom to observe the cause, for future avoidance. When blood has been spilled, the obligation becomes vital. In my opinion, it is vital for the Navy never to expose itself again to the perils of a divided command in the same area.

The Third and Seventh Fleets also differed in functions and weapons. The Seventh Fleet was defensive; having convoyed MacArthur's transports to Leyte, it stood by to protect them with its cruisers, destroyers, old battleships, and little escort carriers. The Third Fleet was offensive; it prowled the ocean, striking at will with its new battleships and fast carriers. These powerful units were concentrated in Pete Mitscher's Task Force 38, which was made up of four task groups, commanded by Vice Admiral Slew McCain and Rear Admirals Gerald F. Bogan, Ted Sherman, and Ralph E. Davison. The task groups were not uniform, but they averaged a total of twenty-three ships, divided approximately as follows—two large carriers, two light carriers, and two new battleships, with a screen of three cruisers and fourteen destroyers. My flagship, the *New Jersey*, was in Bogan's group; Mitscher's flagship, the *Lexington*, was in Sherman's.

The morning of October 23 found McCain's group on its way to Ulithi for rest and replenishment. The other three were standing eastward of the Philippines, awaiting their turn to retire, and meanwhile preparing further strikes in support of MacArthur. On the basis of the *Darter's* report, I ordered them to close the islands and to launch search teams next morning in a fan that would cover the western sea approaches for the entire length of the chain. Experience had taught us that if we interfered with a Jap plan before it matured, we stood a good chance of disrupting it. The Jap mind is inelastic; it cannot adapt itself to an altered situation.

The three task groups reached their stations that night—Sherman, off the Polillo Islands; 140 miles southeast of him, Bogan, off San Bernardino Strait; 120 miles southeast of Bogan, Davison, off Surigao Strait. Their search teams flew out at daybreak on the twenty-fourth. At 0820, one of Bogan's teams reported contact with five battleships, nine cruisers, and thirteen destroyers south of Mindoro Island, course 050, speed 10 to 12 knots. (This force, the Central Force, was the same that had been dimly sighted by the *Darter*; she and a sister sub, the *Dace*, had already sunk two of its heavy cruisers and damaged a third.)

My log summarizes the events of the next few minutes:

At 0822, I rebroadcast Bogan's report at the top of my radio voice.

At 0827, I ordered Sherman and Davison to close on Bogan at their best speed.

At 0837, I ordered all task groups by TBS, "Strike! Repeat: Strike! Good luck!"

And at 0846, I ordered McCain to reverse course and prepare to fuel at sea. If the battle developed as I expected, we would need him.

Our planes hit the Central Force again and again through the day and reported sinking the battleship *Musashi* (Japan's newest and largest), three more cruisers, and a destroyer, and inflicting severe damage on many other units. These seemed to mill around aimlessly, then withdrew to the west, then turned east again, as if they had suddenly received a do-or-die command from Hirohito himself. (A year later I learned that our guess was close. Vice Admiral Kurita, commanding the Central Force, had strongly considered retiring, but had received this dispatch from Admiral Toyoda, Commander in Chief of the Japanese Combined Fleet: WITH CONFIDENCE IN HEAVENLY GUIDANCE, THE ENTIRE FORCE WILL ATTACK.)

That they might attempt to transit San Bernardino Strait, despite their fearful mauling, was a possibility I had to recognize. Accordingly, at 1512 I sent a preparatory dispatch to all task-force commanders in the Third Fleet and all task-group commanders in TF 38, designating four of their fast battleships (including the *New Jersey*), with two heavy cruisers, three light cruisers, and fourteen destroyers, and stating that these ships WILL BE FORMED AS TF 34 UNDER VADM [Willis A.] LEE, COMMANDER BATTLE LINE X TF 34 WILL ENGAGE DECISIVELY AT LONG RANGES.

This dispatch, which played a critical part in next day's battle, I intended merely as warning to the ships concerned that *if a surface engagement offered,* I would detach them from TF 38, form them into TF 34, and send them ahead as a battle line. It was definitely *not* an executive dispatch, but a battle plan, and was so marked. To make certain that none of my subordinate commanders misconstrued it, I told them later by TBS, "If the enemy sorties [through San Bernardino], TF 34 will be formed *when directed by me.*"

Meanwhile, at 0943, we had intercepted a message from one of Davison's search teams, reporting that it had sighted the enemy's Southern Force—two old battleships, three heavy cruisers, one light cruiser, and eight destroyers, southwest of Negros Island, course 060, speed 15 knots—and had scored several damaging hits with bombs and rockets. We did not send a strike against this comparatively weak force for two reasons: it was headed for Surigao Strait, where Kinkaid was waiting with approximately three times its weight of metal—six old battleships, four heavy cruisers, four light cruisers, and twenty-six destroyers, plus thirty PT's; second, Davison's planes, the only ones able to reach it, were more urgently needed at the Central Force, now that Sherman's group was under violent attack by shore-based planes from Luzon. He shot down 110 of them, but they succeeded in bombing the light carrier *Princeton.* The fires reached her magazines and fuel tanks, and late that afternoon he had to order her abandoned and sunk—the first fast carrier that the Navy had lost since the *Hornet* was torpedoed at the Battle of Santa Cruz two years before, almost to the day.

(The captain of the *Princeton* was Capt. William H. Buracker, who had been my operations officer at the beginning of the war. He would have been detached in a few days, and his relief was already aboard—Capt. John M. Hoskins. The bomb that gave the *Princeton* her deathblow nearly gave Hoskins his;

it mangled one foot so badly that the ship's medical officer, himself wounded, cut it off with a sheath knife. Hoskins was then put into a stretcher and carried through the flames to the fo'c'sle, but before letting himself be lowered to a whaleboat standing by, he smiled, saluted Bill Buracker, and asked, "Have I your permission to leave the ship, sir?" Later, fitted with an artificial foot, he requested command of the new *Princeton* and recommended himself as being "one foot ahead of the other applicants"; further, he said, he could beat them all turning out for general quarters, because he was already wearing a sock and a shoe. I am happy to say that Hoskins put the new *Princeton* in commission and is now a rear admiral.)

The discovery of the Southern Force buttressed my conviction that the Japs were committed to a supreme effort, but the final proof was still lacking—their carriers. Neither our submarines nor search planes had found them yet, but we were dead certain that they would appear; our only doubt was from what direction. Mitscher thought from the China Sea. My staff thought from Empire waters. I agreed with my staff and ordered a thorough search northward. While we waited for a report, Doug Moulton must have pounded the chart fifty times, demanding, "Where the hell *are* they, those goddam carriers?" At 1730 our guess was proved correct. Sherman informed me, 3 CARRIERS 2 LIGHT CRUISERS 3 DESTROYERS 18-32 N 125-28 E COURSE 270 SPEED 15.

This position, 200 miles east of Cape Engaño, the northeastern tip of Luzon, was too far for us to reach, even if dusk had not already fallen. But now we had all the pieces of the puzzle. When we put them together, we noticed that the three forces had a common factor: a speed of advance so leisurely—never more than 15 knots—that it implied a focus of time and place. The crippled Central Force's dogged second approach to San Bernardino, and the weak Southern Force's simultaneous approach to Surigao against overwhelming strength, were comprehensible only if they were under adamant orders to rendezvous with the carriers—the Northern Force—off Samar next day, the twenty-fifth, for a combined attack on the transports at Leyte.

We had no intention of standing by for a test of our theory.

Our intention was to join battle as quickly as possible. Three battles offered. The Southern Force I could afford to ignore; it was well within Kinkaid's compass. The Central Force, according to our pilots, had suffered so much topside damage, especially to its guns and fire-control instruments, that it could not win a decision; it, too, could be left to Kinkaid. (The pilots' reports proved dangerously optimistic, but we had no reason to discredit them at the time.) On the other hand, not only was the Northern Force fresh and undamaged, but its carriers gave it a scope several hundred miles wider than the others. Moreover, if we destroyed those carriers, our future operations need fear no threat from the sea.

We had chosen our antagonist. It remained only to choose the best way to meet him. Again I had three alternatives:

1. *I could guard San Bernardino with my whole fleet and wait for the Northern Force to strike me.* Rejected. It yielded to the enemy the double initiative of his carriers and his fields on Luzon and would allow him to use them unmolested.

2. *I could guard San Bernardino with TF 34 while I struck the Northern Force with my carriers.* Rejected. The enemy's potential surface and air strength forbade half-measures; if his shore-based planes joined his carrier planes, together they might inflict far more damage on my half-fleets separately than they could inflict on the fleet intact.

3. *I could leave San Bernardino unguarded and strike the Northern Force with my whole fleet.* Accepted. It preserved my fleet's integrity, it left the initiative with me, and it promised the greatest possibility of surprise. Even if the Central Force meanwhile penetrated San Bernardino and headed for Leyte Gulf, it could hope only to harry the landing operation. It could not consolidate any advantage, because no transports accompanied it and no supply ships. It could merely hit and run.

My decision to strike the Northern Force was a hard one to make, but given the same circumstances and the same information as I had then, I would make it again.

I went into flag plot, put my finger on the Northern Force's charted position, 300 miles away, and said, "Here's where we're going. Mick, start them north."

The time was about 1950. Mick began to scribble a sheaf of

dispatches: McCain to close us at his best speed; for Bogan and Davison, COURSE 000 [due north] SPEED 25; Sherman to join us as we dashed by; for Kinkaid, CENTRAL FORCE HEAVILY DAMAGED ACCORDING TO STRIKE REPORTS X AM PROCEEDING NORTH WITH 3 GROUPS TO ATTACK CARRIER FORCE AT DAWN; for the light carrier *Independence*, which was equipped with night fighters, AT 2400 LAUNCH 5 PLANES TO SEARCH SECTORS 320-010 [roughly, from northwest to north-by-east] TO 350 MILES; finally, at 2330, for Mitscher, SLOW DOWN TO 16 KNOTS X HOLD PRESENT COURSE UNTIL 2400, THEN PROCEED TOWARD LAT 16 LONG 127 [northeastward].

The purpose of this was to avoid overrunning the Northern Force's "daylight circle," the limit which it could reach by dawn from its last known position. If the enemy slipped past my left flank, between me and Luzon, he would have a free crack at the transports. If he slipped past my right flank, he would be able to shuttle-bomb me—fly from his carriers, attack me, continue on to his fields on Luzon for more bombs and fuel, and attack me again on the way back. I had to meet him head-on, and I was trusting the *Independence's* snoopers to set my course.

They began to report at 0208: CONTACT POSIT 17-10 N 125-31 E X 5 SHIPS 2 LARGE 2 SMALL 1 SIZE UNREPORTED.

At 0214: CORRECTION X 6 SHIPS 3 LARGE 3 SMALL COURSE 110 SPEED 15.

At 0220: ANOTHER GROUP 40 MILES ASTERN OF FIRST.

At 0235: SECOND GROUP 6 LARGE SHIPS.

We had them!

Later sightings, in daylight, established the composition of the Northern Force as one large carrier, three light carriers, two hermaphrodite battleships with flight decks aft (a typical gimcrack Jap makeshift), three light cruisers, and at least eight destroyers.

I ordered TF 34 to form and take station 10 miles in advance, and my task-group commanders to arm their first deckload strike at once, launch it at earliest dawn, and launch a second strike as soon afterward as possible. Our next few hours were the most anxious of all. The pilots and aircrewmen knew that a terrific carrier duel was facing them, and the ships' companies were sure that a big-gun action would follow.

The first strike took off at 0630. An hour and a half passed without a word of news. . . . Two hours. . . . Two hours and a quarter. . . . God, what a wait it was! (Mick admitted later, "I chewed my fingernails down to my elbows.") Then, at 0850, a flash report reached me: ONE CARRIER SUNK AFTER TREMENDOUS EXPLOSION X 2 CARRIERS 1 CL [light cruiser] HIT BADLY OTHER CARRIER UNTOUCHED X FORCE COURSE 150 SPEED 17.

We had already increased our speed to 25 knots. If the enemy held his course and speed, he would be under our guns before noon. I rubbed my hands at the prospect of blasting the cripples that our planes were setting up for us.

Now I come to the part of this narrative that I can hardly bring myself to write, so painfully does it rankle still. I can reconstruct it best from a sequence of dispatches in my war diary:

At 0648, I had received a dispatch from Kinkaid: AM NOW ENGAGING ENEMY SURFACE FORCES SURIGAO STRAIT X QUESTION IS TF 34 GUARDING SAN BERNARDINO STRAIT. To this I replied in some bewilderment, NEGATIVE X IT IS WITH OUR CARRIERS NOW ENGAGING ENEMY CARRIERS. Here was my first intimation that Kinkaid had intercepted and misconstrued the preparatory dispatch I had sent at 1512 the preceding day. I say "intercepted" because it was not addressed to him, which fact alone should have prevented his confusion. I was not alarmed, because at 0802 I learned from him, ENEMY VESSELS RETIRING SURIGAO STRAIT X OUR LIGHT FORCES IN PURSUIT.

When the Southern Force pushed into Surigao soon after midnight of the twenty-fourth, it pushed into one of the prettiest ambushes in naval history. Rear Admiral Jesse B. Oldendorf, Kinkaid's tactical commander, waited until the enemy line was well committed to the narrow waters, then struck from both flanks with his PT's and destroyers, and from dead ahead with his battleships and cruisers. He not only "crossed the T," which is every naval officer's dearest ambition; he dotted several thousand slant eyes. Almost before the Japs could open fire, they lost both their battleships and three destroyers. The rest fled, but Kinkaid's planes caught and sank a heavy cruiser later in the morning, and Army B-24's sank the light cruiser the following noon. One of Oldendorf's PT's was sunk, and one destroyer was damaged.

At 0822, twenty minutes after Kinkaid's second dispatch, I received his third: ENEMY BBS AND CRUISER REPORTED FIRING ON TU 77.4.3 FROM 15 MILES ASTERN. Task unit 77.4.3, commanded by Rear Admiral Clifton A. F. Sprague and comprising six escort carriers, three destroyers, and four destroyer escorts, was the northernmost of three similar task units in the Seventh Fleet's TG 77.4, assigned to guard the eastern approaches to Leyte. The enemy ships were evidently part of the Central Force, which had steamed through San Bernardino during the night. I wondered how Kinkaid had let "Ziggy" Sprague get caught like this, and why Ziggy's search planes had not given him warning, but I still was not alarmed. I figured that the eighteen little carriers had enough planes to protect themselves until Oldendorf could bring up his heavy ships.

Eight minutes later, at 0830, Kinkaid's fourth dispatch reached me: URGENTLY NEED FAST BBS LEYTE GULF AT ONCE. That surprised me. It was not my job to protect the Seventh Fleet. My job was offensive, to strike with the Third Fleet, and we were even then rushing to intercept a force which gravely threatened not only Kinkaid and myself, but the whole Pacific strategy. However, I ordered McCain, who was fueling to the east, STRIKE ENEMY VICINITY 11-20 N 127-00 E AT BEST POSSIBLE SPEED, and so notified Kinkaid.

At 0900 I received his fifth dispatch: OUR CVES [escort carriers] BEING ATTACKED BY 4 BBS 8 CRUISERS PLUS OTHERS X REQUEST LEE [commanding TF 34, the battle line] COVER LEYTE AT TOP SPEED X REQUEST FAST CARRIERS MAKE IMMEDIATE STRIKE. I had already sent McCain. There was nothing else I could do, except become angrier.

Then came the sixth dispatch, at 0922: CTU 77.4.3 UNDER ATTACK BY CRUISERS AND BBS 0700 11-40 N 126-25 E X REQUEST IMMEDIATE AIR STRIKE X ALSO REQUEST SUPPORT BY HEAVY SHIPS X MY OBBS [old battleships] LOW IN AMMUNITION.

Low in ammunition! Here was a new factor, so astonishing that I could hardly accept it. Why hadn't Kinkaid let me know before? I looked at the date-time group of his dispatch, which told when it was filed. It was "242225," or 0725 local time, an hour and fifty-seven minutes ago! And when I compared it with the date-time groups of the others, I realized that this was actually his *third* dispatch, sent eighteen minutes after he had first informed me that TU 77.4.3 was under attack. What had delayed it I have never learned.

My message was on its way to him in five minutes: I AM STILL ENGAGING ENEMY CARRIERS X MCCAIN WITH 5 CARRIERS 4 HEAVY CRUISERS HAS BEEN ORDERED ASSIST YOU IMMEDIATELY, and I gave my position, to show him the impossibility of the fast battleships reaching him.

The next two dispatches arrived close to 1000, almost simultaneously. The first was from Kinkaid again: WHERE IS LEE X SEND LEE. I was impressed less by its desperation than by the fact that it had been put on the air "clear," not in code. I was certain that the enemy had intercepted it, and I was speculating on its effect, when the second dispatch drove all other thoughts out of my mind. I can close my eyes and see it today:

From: CINCPAC
To: COM THIRD FLEET
THE WHOLE WORLD WANTS TO KNOW WHERE IS TASK FORCE 34.

I was as stunned as if I had been struck in the face. The paper rattled in my hands. I snatched off my cap, threw it on the deck, and shouted something that I am ashamed to remember. Mick Carney rushed over and grabbed my arm: "Stop it! What the hell's the matter with you? Pull yourself together!"

I gave him the dispatch and turned my back. I was so mad I couldn't talk. It was utterly impossible for me to believe that Chester Nimitz would send me such an insult. He hadn't, of course, but I didn't know the truth for several weeks. It requires an explanation of Navy procedure. To increase the difficulty of breaking our codes, most dispatches are padded with gibberish. The decoding officers almost always recognize it as such and delete it from the transcription, but CINCPAC's encoder was either drowsy or smart-alecky, and his padding—"The whole world wants to know"—sounded so infernally plausible that my decoders read it as a valid part of the message. Chester blew up when I told him about it; he tracked down the little squirt and chewed him to bits, but it was too late then; the damage had been done.

The orders I now gave I gave in rage, and although Ernie King later assured me that they were the right ones, I am convinced that they were not. My flag log for the forenoon watch that day, October 25, gives the bare bones of the story: At 0835 c/s [changed speed] to 25k to close enemy. At 0919 c/c [changed course] to 000. At 1115 c/c to 180—or from due north to due south. At that moment the Northern Force, with its two remaining carriers crippled and dead in the water, was exactly 42 miles from the muzzles of my 16-inch guns, but—I quote from my war diary—

> In view of the urgent request for assistance from Commander Seventh Fleet, Commander Third Fleet directed Task Force 34 [Lee] and Task Group 38.2 [Bogan] to proceed south toward San Bernardino Strait, and directed Commander Task Force 38 [Mitscher] with Task Groups 38.3 [Sherman] and 38.4 [Davison], to continue attacks against the enemy carrier force.

(The period between 1000, when I received CINCPAC's dispatch, and 1115, when we changed course, was spent in reshuffling the task force and refueling Bogan's nearly empty destroyers for our high-speed run.)

I turned my back on the opportunity I had dreamed of since my days as a cadet. For me, one of the biggest battles of the war was off, and what has been called "the Battle of Bull's Run" was on. I notified Kinkaid, TG 38.2. PLUS 6 FAST BBS PROCEEDING LEYTE BUT UNABLE ARRIVE BEFORE 0800 TOMORROW.

While I rushed south, Sherman and Davison struck the Northern Force again and again, and late that afternoon it retired in straggling disorder, with four of our fast light cruisers in pursuit and two wolf packs of our submarines waiting across its course. When the butchery was done, the score for the Northern Force was:

Sunk	4 carriers, 1 light cruiser, 2 destroyers.
Damaged	2 battleships, 2 light cruisers, 4 destroyers.

A curious feature of this engagement is that the air duel never came off. Our strikes found scarcely a handful of planes on the enemy carriers' decks and only fifteen on the wing. We assume that the rest had ferried into Luzon and that our attack had caught them by surprise, because during the morning our radars picked up large groups of bogeys—unidentified planes—approaching from the westward, but they presently reversed course and disappeared. They must have been unarmed, expecting to arm aboard, and when they saw that their mother ships were afire, they could do nothing but fly back to Luzon again.

Meanwhile, Kinkaid had been sending me another series of dispatches: ENEMY RETIRING TO NORTHEASTWARD. Later, CVES AGAIN THREATENED BY ENEMY SURFACE FORCES. Still later, SITUATION AGAIN VERY SERIOUS X YOUR ASSISTANCE BADLY NEEDED X CVES RETIRING LEYTE GULF. Finally, at 1145: ENEMY FORCE OF 3 BB 2 CA 9 DD 11-43 N 126-12 E COURSE 225 SPEED 20.

This position was 55 miles northeast of Leyte Gulf, but the course was not toward the entrance. Moreover, the dispatch had been filed two hours before I received it, and I had no clue as to what had happened since then. The strongest probability was that the enemy would eventually retrace his course through San Bernardino Strait, and my best hope of intercepting him was to send my fastest ships in advance. The only two battleships I had that could sustain high speeds were the *New Jersey* and *Iowa*. I threw a screen of light cruisers and destroyers around them, as TG 34.5, and told them on TBS, "Proceed at 28 knots on course 195. Prepare for 30 knots. Be ready for night action," and I notified Kinkaid that we would arrive off San Bernardino at 0100 next morning, seven hours earlier than my original schedule.

I was puzzled by the Central Force's hit-and-run tactics and still more puzzled when I learned the complete story. Four battleships, six heavy cruisers, two light cruisers, and eleven destroyers had survived our air attacks on October 24 and had transited San Bernardino that night. When they were sighted next, at 0631 on the twenty-fifth, they were only 20 miles northwest of Sprague's task unit. His 17-knot escort carriers were no match for the enemy in either speed or gun power, and at 0658 he was taken under fire at a range of 30,000 yards.

Sprague immediately turned east, into the wind, launched his available planes, and ordered all ships to make smoke. The enemy formation now divided, the heavy ships advancing to his port and the light to starboard, thereby forcing him around to the southwest, in the direction of Leyte Gulf. When the cruisers had closed to 14,000 yards, Sprague ordered his screen to fall back and deliver a torpedo attack. Two destroyers, the *Hoel* and *Johnston,* and the destroyer escort *Samuel S. Roberts* reversed course, ran within 10,000 yards of the battleships, and fired a half-salvo, then fired the other half within 7,000 yards of the cruisers. Smoke concealed the effect of their torpedoes, but it lifted to show that all three of these heroic little ships had been sunk.

The enemy continued to close, and presently his fire began to take toll. If he had had the elementary intelligence not to use armor-piercing projectiles, many of which ripped through our ships' thin skins as if through a wet shoebox, without detonating, he might have annihilated Sprague's unit, since every ship in it suffered hits. As it was, except for the three ships from the screen, Sprague's only loss to the guns was the carrier *Gambier Bay*. At 0820 she dropped astern under continuous fire, and after being riddled with 8-inch shells from the murderous range of 2,000 yards, she blew up at 0900.

For these first two hours, Sprague's gallant men fought entirely alone, at such close quarters that his CVE's' single 5-inchers were registering hits on the cruisers, and with such valor that his Avengers, their bombs and torpedoes expended, were making dummy runs to distract the battleships. Oldendorf's force not only was 100 miles away, deep in Surigao Strait, but was practically impotent. Its action early that morning, following five days of shore bombardments, had severely reduced its fuel and ammunition. The other two carrier task units that made up TG 77.4 were obligated to flying support missions for the troops on Leyte. In addition, the southern unit had been shelled, and the central unit's carriers had been subjected to a violent shore-based air attack—the *Sangamon* had been damaged by a bomb, the *Suwannee* and *Santee* by suicide planes, and the *Santee* had been further damaged by a torpedo. However, planes from both these task units were able to reinforce Sprague's by 0900. One of his destroyers had already crippled a heavy cruiser; and when the combined air attacks succeeded in sinking three others, the enemy was panicked into breaking off the engagement. I opened my hand and let the bird fly away off Luzon. So did the enemy off Samar.

Now came an intermission during which the offensive passed to us, but at 1050 the enemy's shore-based air struck again, this time on Sprague's wounded, exhausted carriers. One plane plunged into the *Kalinin Bay's* flight deck, causing a small blaze; another crashed through the *Kitkun Bay's* catwalk; a third dropped a bomb on the *Saint Lo* and itself crashed close aboard. The *Saint Lo's* fires could not be controlled; she was abandoned with heavy losses. The enemy still did not exploit his overwhelming advantage, and soon it was gone forever. At 1310 McCain's planes arrived. In the emergency, he had launched them from far outside their range of return; after their attacks, they had to land and rearm at Tacloban and Dulag Fields on Leyte, which had fallen to MacArthur only a few days before. Together with planes from TG 77.4, they sank a light cruiser and a destroyer and damaged most of the other ships. Sprague had lost five of his thirteen ships. TG 77.4 had lost 105 planes.

The Central Force was in full retreat by late afternoon, and by 2200 it was re-entering San Bernardino, with my force still two hours away. However, shortly after midnight one of my van destroyers made contact with a straggler. I was able to watch the action from the *New Jersey's* bridge—the first and only surface action I saw during my entire career. The cruisers poured in their 6-inch shells, then a destroyer delivered the knockout with torpedoes. They must have touched off her magazines, because I felt the explosion distinctly, 15 miles away.

At that distance, none of us on the *New Jersey* could tell what type of ship had been sunk, so we put the query on the TBS. The roundup is a commentary on the accuracy of observation during a night engagement.

The light cruiser *Vincennes* reported, "She was a heavy cruiser of the *Aoba* or *Atago* class."

The light cruiser *Miami*, "A destroyer of the *Fubuki* or *Asashio* class."

The light cruiser *Biloxi* said cautiously, "A cruiser."

The destroyer *Miller*, which had fired the torpedoes, "A *Terutsuki*-class destroyer."

The destroyer *Owen*, "A *Fuso*-class battleship."

The commander of our destroyer squadron, "A *Yubari*-class light cruiser."

The commander of our cruiser division, "I have an open mind. I'll settle for a cruiser of any sort."

And that's as close to the truth as we ever came.

This was our last surface action. The air phase resumed at dawn next morning, the twenty-sixth, with McCain's and Bogan's planes harrying the Central Force's scattered remnants, still fleeing westward, while our ships searched east of Samar for other stragglers and for our airmen who had ditched the day before. We found no Jap ships, but Jap swimmers were as thick as water bugs. I was having breakfast when Bill Kitchell burst in and cried, "My God Almighty, Admiral, they're all over the place! Are we going to stop and pick 'em up?"

I told him, "Not until we've picked up our own boys."

We charted their position, along with wind and tide data, and when we had recovered all the Americans, I ordered our destroyers, "Bring in cooperative Nip flotsam for an intelligence sample. Noncooperators would probably like to join their ancestors and should be accommodated." (I didn't want to risk their getting ashore, where they could reinforce the garrison.) The destroyers brought in six.

Foul weather hampered McCain and Bogan, but that night they reported: 1 NAGATO-CLASS BB HIT WITH 2 TORPEDOES MANY BOMBS, LAST SEEN STOPPED AND BLAZING OFF SOUTH TIP MINDORO X 10 MILES SOUTH OF HER, 1 HOSHIRO-CLASS CL HIT WITH 1 TORPEDO 2 BOMBS X NORTHWEST OF PANAY ARE 2 BBS YAMATO- AND KONGO-CLASS HIT WITH ROCKETS AND HALF- AND QUARTER-TON BOMBS X ALSO AT THIS POSITION 1 DD WITH BOW BLOWN OFF BUT STILL UNDERWEIGH AND 1 CA [heavy cruiser] DEAD IN WATER AFTER HITS WITH BOMBS AND 2 TORPEDOES X 1 CL DAMAGED IN TABLAS STRAIT X 1 SEAPLANE TENDER HIT IN GUIMARAS STRAIT BLEW UP AND SANK X WE SHOT DOWN 40 PLANES AND LOST 11, MOSTLY TO INTENSE JAP WARSHIP AA.

Thus ended the three-day, threefold Battle for Leyte Gulf. Six of our ships had been sunk and eleven damaged. Twenty-six enemy ships had been sunk, and twenty-five damaged. In my official report, I was able to write with conviction that the results of the battle were "(1) the utter failure of the Japanese plan to prevent the reoccupation of the Philippines; (2) the crushing defeat of the Japanese fleet; and (3) the elimination of serious naval threat to our operations for many months, if not forever."

COMINCH's endorsement of my second and third claim was reluctant at first. On the night of October 25, I had radioed CINCPAC, THE JAPANESE NAVY HAS BEEN BEATEN AND ROUTED AND BROKEN BY THE THIRD AND SEVENTH FLEETS. I heard later that COMINCH had told CINCPAC that nothing in the reports he had received could justify my optimism. On the twenty-ninth, however, COMINCH was telling Kinkaid and myself, A LARGE PART OF THE ENEMY NAVY HAS BEEN EFFECTUALLY DISPOSED OF FOREVER AND THE REMAINDER FOR SOME TIME TO COME X ALL OFFICERS AND MEN OF YOUR FLEETS HAVE THE HEARTIEST ADMIRATION OF ALL HANDS X WELL DONE.

That's something, coming from Ernie!

When I reported to him in Washington the following January, my very first words were, "I made a mistake in that battle."

He held up his hand. "You don't have to tell me any more. You've got a green light on everything you did."

But I wanted to get it off my chest. I said, "I still think it was a mistake to turn south when the Japs were right under my guns."

Ernie said, "No. It wasn't a mistake. You couldn't have done otherwise."

All the bigwigs sent us congratulations. General MacArthur's message was particularly warming: WE HAVE COOPERATED WITH YOU SO LONG THAT WE EXPECT YOUR BRILLIANT SUCCESSES X EVERYONE HERE HAS A FEELING OF COMPLETE CONFIDENCE AND INSPIRATION WHEN YOU GO INTO ACTION IN OUR SUPPORT. General Marshall told us, A SPLENDID AND HISTORIC VICTORY X THE ARMY OWES YOU A DEBT OF THANKS. From Secretary Forrestal, THE THIRD FLEET HAS DONE IT AGAIN.

Such praise from such men is agreeable to read, but I would gladly forgo every word of it if I could also forgo a few words of my own. These are the ones: "At 1115 c/c to 180."

I have attempted to describe the Battle for Leyte Gulf in terms of my thoughts and feelings at the time, but on rereading my account, I find that this results in an implication grossly unfair to Tom Kinkaid. True, during the action, his dispatches puzzled me. Later, with the gaps in my information filled, I not only appreciate his problems, but frankly admit that, had I been in his shoes, I might have acted precisely as did he.

—Which urges me to re-emphasize a point I made earlier: although our naval power in the Western Pacific was such that we could have challenged the combined fleets of the world, the fact that it was not co-ordinated under any single authority was an invitation which disaster nearly accepted. What brought us victory instead was simply this: all hands thought alike. And that we did so is a tribute to our indoctrination in the United States Navy.

FROM

Two Years Before the Mast

RICHARD HENRY DANA

A Boston patrician, Richard Henry Dana went to sea after a weakness of his eyes, the result of a case of measles, had forced him to withdraw from Harvard College. He was nineteen, a sensitive, protected youth who knew nothing at all about ships and the sea, when, in August 1834, he sailed for California as a common seaman in the brig Pilgrim. *When he returned aboard the ship* Alert *two years later, he was a robust and manly twenty-one, eager to resume his conventional life but also imbued with a desire to do something to better the lot of seamen.* Two Years Before the Mast, *which he wrote while a student at Harvard Law School, was intended in part as an exposé of conditions at sea. One of the memorable incidents of Dana's story is the flogging aboard the* Pilgrim.

Flogging

For several days the captain seemed very much out of humor. Nothing went right or fast enough for him. He quarreled with the cook, and threatened to flog him for throwing wood on deck, and had a dispute with the mate about reeving a Spanish burton; the mate saying that he was right, and had been taught how to do it by a man *who was a sailor!* This the captain took in dudgeon and they were at swords' points at once. But his displeasure was chiefly turned against a large, heavy-molded fellow from the Middle States, who was called Sam. This man hesitated in his speech, was rather slow in his motions, and was only a tolerably good sailor, but usually seemed to do his best; yet the captain took a dislike to him, thought he was surly and lazy, and "if you once give a dog a bad name"—as the sailor phrase is—"he may as well jump overboard." The captain found fault with everything this man did, and hazed him for dropping a marline-spike from the main yard, where he was at work. This, of course, was an accident, but it was set down against him. The captain was on board all day Friday, and everything went on hard and disagreeably. "The more you drive a man, the less he will do," was as true with us as with any other people. We worked late Friday night, and were turned-to early Saturday morning. About ten o'clock the captain ordered our new officer, Russell, who by this time had become thoroughly disliked by all the crew, to get the gig ready to take him ashore. John, the Swede, was sitting in the boat alongside, and Mr. Russell and I were standing by the main hatchway, waiting for the captain, who was down in the hold, where the crew were at work, when we heard his voice raised in violent dispute with somebody, whether it was with the mate or one of the crew I could not tell, and then came blows and scuffling. I ran to the side and beckoned to John, who came aboard, and we leaned down the hatchway, and though we could see no one, yet we knew that the captain had the advantage, for his voice was loud and clear—

"You see your condition! You see your condition! Will you ever give me any more of your *jaw?*" No answer; and then came wrestling and heaving, as though the man was trying to turn him. "You may as well keep still, for I have got you," said the captain. Then came the question, "Will you ever give me any more of your jaw?"

"I never gave you any, sir," said Sam, for it was his voice that we heard, though low and half choked.

"That's not what I ask you. Will you ever be impudent to me again?"

"I never have been, sir," said Sam.

"Answer my question, or I'll make a spread eagle of you! I'll flog you, by G—d."

"I'm no Negro slave," said Sam.

"Then I'll make you one," said the captain; and he came to the hatchway, and sprang on deck, threw off his coat, and, rolling up his sleeves, called out to the mate: "Seize that man up, Mr. Amerzene! Seize him up! Make a spread eagle of him! I'll teach you all who is master aboard!"

The crew and officers followed the captain up the hatchway;

but it was not until after repeated orders that the mate laid hold of Sam, who made no resistance, and carried him to the gangway.

"What are you going to flog that man for, sir?" said John, the Swede, to the captain.

Upon hearing this, the captain turned upon John; but, knowing him to be quick and resolute, he ordered the steward to bring the irons, and, calling upon Russell to help him, went up to John.

"Let me alone," said John. "I'm willing to be put in irons. You need not use any force"; and, putting out his hands, the captain slipped the irons on, and sent him aft to the quarter-deck. Sam, by this time, was *seized up*, as it is called; that is, placed against the shrouds, with his wrists made fast to them, his jacket off, and his back exposed. The captain stood on the break of the deck, a few feet from him, and a little raised, so as to have a good swing at him, and held in his hand the end of a thick, strong rope. The officers stood round, and the crew grouped together in the waist. All these preparations made me feel sick and almost faint, angry and excited as I was. A man—a human being, made in God's likeness—fastened up and flogged like a beast! A man, too, whom I had lived with, eaten with, and stood watch with for months, and knew so well! If a thought of resistance crossed the minds of any of the men, what was to be done? Their time for it had gone by. Two men were fast, and there were left only two men besides Stimson and myself, and a small boy of ten or twelve years of age; and Stimson and I would not have joined the men in a mutiny, as they knew. And then, on the other side, there were (besides the captain) three officers, steward, agent, and clerk, and the cabin supplied with weapons. But besides the numbers, what is there for sailors to do? If they resist, it is mutiny; and if they succeed, and take the vessel, it is piracy. If they ever yield again, their punishment must come; and if they do not yield, what are they to be for the rest of their lives? If a sailor resist his commander, he resists the law, and piracy or submission is his only alternative. Bad as it was, they saw it must be borne. It is what a sailor ships for. Swinging the rope over his head, and bending his body so as to give it full force, the captain brought

it down upon the poor fellow's back. Once, twice,—six times. "Will you ever give me any more of your jaw?" The man writhed with pain, but said not a word. Three times more. This was too much, and he muttered something which I could not hear; this brought as many more as the man could stand, when the captain ordered him to be cut down.

"Now for you," said the captain, making up to John, and taking his irons off. As soon as John was loose, he ran forward to the forecastle. "Bring that man aft!" shouted the captain. The second mate, who had been in the forecastle with these men the early part of the voyage, stood still in the waist, and the mate walked slowly forward; but our third officer, anxious to show his zeal, sprang forward over the windlass, and laid hold of John; but John soon threw him from him. The captain stood on the quarter-deck, bareheaded, his eyes flashing with rage, and his face as red as blood, swinging the rope, and calling out to his officers, "Drag him aft! Lay hold of him! I'll *sweeten him!*" etc., etc. The mate now went forward, and told John quietly to go aft; and he, seeing resistance vain, threw the blackguard third mate from him, said he would go aft of himself, that they should not drag him, and went up to the gangway and held out his hands; but as soon as the captain began to make him fast, the indignity was too much, and he struggled; but, the mate and Russell holding him, he was soon seized up. When he was made fast, he turned to the captain, who stood rolling up his sleeves, getting ready for the blow, and asked him what he was to be flogged for. "Have I ever refused my duty, sir? Have you ever known me to hang back or to be insolent, or not to know my work?"

"No," said the captain, "it is not that that I flog you for; I flog you for your interference, for asking questions."

"Can't a man ask a question here without being flogged?"

"No," shouted the captain; "nobody shall open his mouth aboard this vessel but myself"; and he began laying the blows upon his back, swinging half round between each blow, to give it full effect. As he went on his passion increased, and he danced about the deck, calling out, as he swung the rope, "If you want to know what I flog you for, I'll tell you. It's because

I like to do it! because I like to do it! It suits me! That's what I do it for!"

The man writhed under the pain until he could endure it no longer, when he called out, with an exclamation more common among foreigners than with us: "O Jesus Christ! O Jesus Christ!"

"Don't call on Jesus Christ," shouted the captain; *"He can't help you. Call on Frank Thompson!* He's the man! He can help you! Jesus Christ can't help you now!"

At these words, which I never shall forget, my blood ran cold. I could look on no longer. Disgusted, sick, I turned away, and leaned over the rail, and looked down into the water. A few rapid thoughts, I don't know what—our situation, a resolution to see the captain punished when we got home—crossed my mind; but the falling of the blows and the cries of the man called me back once more. At length they ceased, and, turning round, I found that the mate, at a signal from the captain, had cast him loose. Almost doubled up with pain, the man walked slowly forward, and went down into the forecastle. Every one else stood still at his post, while the captain, swelling with rage and with the importance of his achievement, walked the quarter-deck, and at each turn, as he came forward, calling out to us: "You see your condition! You see where I've got you all, and you know what to expect! You've been mistaken in me! You didn't know what I was! Now you know what I am! I'll make you toe the mark, every soul of you, or I'll flog you all, fore and aft, from the boy up! You've got a driver over you! Yes, a *slave driver!* I'll see who'll tell me he isn't a slave!" With this and the like matter, equally calculated to quiet us, and to allay any apprehensions of future trouble, he entertained us for about ten minutes, when he went below. Soon after, John came aft, with his bare back covered with stripes and wales in every direction, and dreadfully swollen, and asked the steward to ask the captain to let him have some salve, or balsam, to put upon it. "No," said the captain, who heard him from below; "tell him to put his shirt on; that's the best thing for him, and pull me ashore in the boat. Nobody is going to lay-up on board this vessel." He then called to Mr. Russell to take those two men and two others in the boat, and pull him ashore. I went for one.

The two men could hardly bend their backs, and the captain called to them to "give way!" but finding they did their best, he let them alone. The agent was in the stern sheets, but during the whole pull—a league or more—not a word was spoken. We landed; the captain, agent, and officer went up to the house, and left us with the boat. I and the man with me stayed near the boat, while John and Sam walked slowly away, and sat down on the rocks. They talked some time together, but at length separated, each sitting alone. I had some fears of John. He was a foreigner, and violently tempered, and under suffering; and he had his knife with him, and the captain was to come down alone to the boat. But nothing happened; and we went quietly on board. The captain was probably armed, and if either of them had lifted a hand against him, they would have had nothing before them but flight, and starvation in the woods of California, or capture by the soldiers and Indians, whom the offer of twenty dollars would have set upon them.

After the day's work was done we went down into the forecastle and ate our plain supper; but not a word was spoken. It was Saturday night; but, there was no song—no "sweethearts and wives." A gloom was over everything. The two men lay in their berths, groaning with pain, and we all turned in, but, for myself, not to sleep. A sound coming now and then from the berths of the two men showed that they were awake, as awake they must have been, for they could hardly lie in one posture long; the dim swinging lamp shed its light over the dark hole in which we lived, and many and various reflections and purposes coursed through my mind. I had no real apprehension that the captain would lay a hand on me; but I thought of our situation, living under a tyranny, with an ungoverned, swaggering fellow administering it; of the character of the country we were in; the length of the voyage; the uncertainty attending our return to America; and then, if we should return, the prospect of obtaining justice and satisfaction for these poor men; and I vowed that, if God should ever give me the means, I would do something to redress the grievances and relieve the sufferings of that class of beings with whom my lot had so long been cast.

FROM

Men Under the Sea

EDWARD ELLSBERG

Aboard the salvage ship Falcon *on December 21, 1927, Lieutenant Commander Edward Ellsberg prepared to dive. One hundred and ten feet below lay the submarine* S-4, *accidentally rammed and sunk four days before by the Coast Guard destroyer* Paulding. *For a few days the survivors had communicated with their rescuers by code through the steel hull. Now all was silent; the* S-4 *was the tomb of forty men. In an hour, Ellsberg would come perilously close to finding his own grave on the muddy bottom of the Atlantic.*

Down to the S-4

WHAT injuries had the *S-4* suffered in that collision with the onrushing *Paulding?* Had the destroyer so knifed into her, was her back so severed by the impact that she would break in two if we tried to lift her? The *Paulding*, lying there in Provincetown with her stem smashed and crumpled and her bow so deep in the water that she seemed in danger of sinking, was evidence enough of the terrific violence of the collision. What were the effects on the *S-4?*

To determine that, while the ventilation of the forward compartment went on, I was dressed for my first dive. Cased from ankles to neck in three suits of heavy blue north woods woolen underwear and wearing three pairs of thick woolen socks, I went aft to the dressing bench looking decidedly rotund.

I seated myself on the bench on the *Falcon's* fantail—for all my clothing, chilled in the cold wind—and the dressers went expertly to work on me. First came the diving dress, a canvas-covered rubber suit. Into this stiff garment I slid thankfully, for at least its impervious texture made it an excellent windbreaker, shielding me from that piercing wind. While the dressers lifted me and the suit by its rubber collar, unceremoniously shaking me down inside, I slipped my padded toes into the feet and my bulky gloved hands down into the watertight gloves forming the ends of the diving sleeves. With a final wiggle of fingers and toes to slide everything home, I settled back again on the bench, and the rest of my ponderous regalia was hastily put on. A pair of thirty-pound lead shoes was strapped over my feet, an eighty-pound lead belt draped round my waist, a copper breastplate tightly bolted to the rubber collar of my dress to make a waterproof seal, a telephone headset buckled on over my ears, a massive diving knife hooked to my belt, and I was ready to test out. Hurriedly my telephone was checked, my air hose tried. Both worked satisfactorily, and down over my head came the helmet. A quick twist on it from the tender to lock the screw joint, and I was ready. Completely shut inside my suit, I opened the valve on my air hose a trifle to get some air to breathe, and immediately my rig ballooned out under the slight pressure.

Two husky dressers seized me, one by each shoulder, and helped me rise. Staggering under a load of two hundred pounds of lead and copper, I walked unsteadily, supported by the dressers, shuffling my heavy shoes across the deck to the *Falcon's* rail. With an effort, I lifted my bulky shoes a few inches onto a steel stage dangling from a boom overhead and gripped the steel bails of the stage to steady myself. Then the tenders let go.

A bosun's pipe shrilled, a winch rattled into action, up went the stage, out swung the boom, and the next instant I was swaying erratically, with the stage outboard of the bulwark and only the sea beneath me. Again, muffled by the noise of the air whistling through my helmet, I heard the bosun piping, and down into the sea splashed the stage. Instantly my canvas suit, which had in the air been grotesquely swelled out, collapsed like a punctured balloon, the folds of canvas-covered rubber now pressing in tightly against my frame, leaving only a little air space inside over my chest where the breastplate held it out.

Down a few feet, and the stage stopped. Peering out of my faceplate through the water, I could see, alongside me, the rounded red hull of the *Falcon* sloping away to her keel, with here and there a few barnacles and some moss. Over me was the surface, undulating like a silver sheet, sharply dividing the world I was now in from the normal world of men—a billowing sheet, crested, wrinkled, flecked with driving foam, letting through the dull December light but completely shutting off any view above as effectively as a ground-glass screen.

I was alone now and truly in another world. Gone was the sense of being crushed down by all the weights I carried. Completely immersed in the sea, I was now buoyed by it, and the lift on my helmet as it tended to float up in the water took from my shoulders the burden of my bulky belt. Quickly I adjusted my air valve and the exhaust valve on my helmet to give me some negative buoyancy, enough to prevent my floating upward off the stage, and then through the telephone transmitter I sang out:

"Topside, there! All ready! Lower away!"

I felt the lifeline and air hose tied to my suit at the breastplate tauten up as my tender took in the slack, then a faraway voice sounded through the transmitters over my ears:

"O.K. Step off the stage!"

I stepped off, the stage was promptly hoisted, and there I hung, dangling on my lifelines, with nothing below me now but the bottom of the sea, and in front of me only a Manila line tied somewhere below to the *S-4*. I grabbed the line and wound my canvas-covered legs round it. The tenders started to lower.

The light, never very good, quickly faded as I sank. A few fathoms down, the *Falcon* disappeared from view, the surface faded away, and around me was nothing but water into which, a little above me, the Manila line down which I slid seemed to dissolve, and out of which, beneath my feet, more line seemed to materialize constantly out of nothing.

Down I slid endlessly, through a world composed of nothing but dimly lighted water and a few fathoms of Manila line. The pressure increased, breathing became harder, my eardrums dilated painfully, I swallowed hard continuously to relieve them. The cold water started to strike through to my skin in spite of my many layers of protective wool, to add an intense chill to my other discomforts.

And still down I went through the seemingly bottomless depths, through an unearthly quiet broken only by the air whistling through my helmet and then out, leaving behind me a trail of air bubbles streaming from my exhaust valve, rising, expanding, breaking up in the water as they rose like huge clusters of grapes spiraling magically upward on some gigantic vine.

But I had no time for watching bubbles. My eyes were down now, always down, peering through my faceplate at the Manila descending line which was my guide. The line started to slope away more sharply toward the horizontal; I took a firmer grip with my legs to hang onto it. And then vaguely forming out of the water below me was the *S-4*, an imponderable shape at first, which, like the rope down which I slid, seemed to be materializing fantastically out of nothingness. A few more fathoms down the line, and I stopped, shouted into my telephone:

"On the bottom!"

There I was at last, on the *S-4*. There she lay before me, silent, motionless, huge in mass as I stared at her, her bulk strangely magnified by the water. I was standing on her very bow, in the thin triangle where sides and deck met stem, a precarious perch with no railing for support. A little dizzy from the pressure, I paused a moment, clinging tightly to my guide line, while I readjusted air valves to suit conditions on the bottom. Then, checking my lifelines to make sure they were not fouled around the descending line but were floating clear, I let go the Manila rope which had been my guide till now. Signaling on my lifelines for more slack, I cautiously walked aft. The deck was level, the submarine had neither heel nor trim. The visibility was fair; I could see perhaps ten feet; beyond that, like an opaque screen, the water shrouded everything.

Aft I went, pushing slowly through the water in the queer walk of the diver, resembling nothing so much as a slow motion picture gait, the clang of my lead-soled boots ringing out metallically against the steel deck. Beneath me was the torpedo room—there at my feet was the round hatch on which Eadie had first hammered, on the underside of which Lieutenant Fitch had banged out his answering signal. All was quiet inside the *S-4* now. No man, with who can say what desperate hope surging through his breast, sprang up beneath me inside that torpedo room to beat a frantic tattoo in answer to the clattering of diving boots against that sunken hull. It was too late now for anything, except, if possible, to lift that steel coffin with Fitch and his shipmates to the surface again for burial. But could we lift it, or would it break in two?

I continued aft, lifelines trailing behind me through the water, helmet bent forward, eyes fixed to the deck looking for damage. So far, nothing. The *S-4*, silent, immobile, bow diving fins still trained out, rested there on the bottom as erect, as unhurt as if she were simply bottoming for practice and might at any minute start up her motors and swim gently upward.

The deck widened still further. I was perhaps seventy feet aft and increasing my pace, when before me the deck suddenly vanished, torn completely away! In a ragged tangle of torn steel, the deck ended where the *Paulding*, evidently riding across, had ripped the superstructure and the deck clean off the submarine. Peering over the edge of the broken deck, I could see below me the cylindrical hull. Cautiously so as not to cut open my diving suit on any of those jagged plates, I clambered down to the hull below, then continued aft again, eyes glued now on that round steel shell, searching for the rupture which had flooded the inside of the submarine. But there was no opening, no gash in it anywhere, just that smooth round hull beneath my feet with the superstructure wiped clean off, except to port, where in an ugly-looking tangle lay the twisted remnants of the superstructure in which Michels had been trapped.

For twenty feet more I kept on, scanning the exposed hull. Then there rose abruptly before me, torn and jagged again, the continuation of the deck, and just abaft that, looming massively through the water, the *S-4's* forecastle gun, slewed drunkenly to port, breech high above the starboard rail, muzzle down, as the careening side of the *Paulding*, hurtling by, had twisted it from its normal fore and aft position and jammed it down on the deck.

Carefully keeping to port, I crawled up over the broken deck, dragged my cumbersome rig up on the depressed gun muzzle, holding my precious air hose high to avoid fouling it in that mass of torn steel, and slid down off the gun to land on the undamaged deck.

Inwardly thankful for the safer footing, as fast as the drag on my lifelines would permit breasting through the water, I went on aft till, standing sharply like a precipitous island, the conning tower of the *S-4* rose in my path, so far as I could see wholly undamaged and showing no definite sign of contact with the *Paulding*. Certainly there could be no damage to the boat from there aft.

Puzzled, I stopped. Where was the *hole* in the submarine which had sunk her? The damage to the deck and to the superstructure which I had seen was in no way vital. There must be a hole torn in that sub somewhere. That hole I was supposed to find, to examine carefully before the salvage operation proceeded. Certainly it must be forward of me; somehow I had missed seeing it. Signaling on my lifelines to start taking in slack, I turned, retraced my steps to look for it again.

Once more I clambered over the slewed gun, dropped down over the broken deck edge onto the cylindrical hull, and started slowly forward, staring sharply down through my faceplate at the smooth round plates below me, searching from starboard to port for that hole.

A few steps forward, and then, as if a fog had suddenly rolled in, the submarine disappeared—from my waist down I stood in a cloud of mud; in no direction was any part of the S-4 visible!

I stopped instantly, all sense of direction lost, fearful that, if I took a single step the wrong way, I should go sliding overboard from the rounding cylinder on which I stood. Where was the fore and aft line now along the hull of the sub that I must follow if I were to stay aboard her? Perplexed, I looked around. The gun and the conning tower astern of me had faded away, dissolved, so to speak, in the translucent water. They could not serve as guides. I reflected. The sub, I knew now, lay on the bottom on a north and south line. If only I could get a compass direction, that would fix it. It was late afternoon, the sun was in the west. I looked up hopefully through the water, trusting to discover which way the light of the sun was coming. Useless. Down in the depths there was only a uniform semitwilight pervading everything coming from nowhere. Another idea. Before me, starting in a long curve from my breastplate, I could see a few fathoms of my lifeline and air hose rising toward the surface and the *Falcon.* I might get my direction from that. Which way was the *Falcon,* east or west, north or south, from where I stood? I stared through my faceplate at those lines, undulating gently till, not so far above me, they also dissolved in the water. There was no answer. The *Falcon* might be in any direction.

I was completely lost. I looked down at the clouds of mud billowing there in the water like clouds in the sky, blotting out my legs, blanketing the submarine. What had happened? Apparently in my passage aft along the sub I must have stirred up a fine layer of mud with which the sea had coated the *S-4.* Now going forward again, I was caught in the resulting fog. Somewhere to port of me was the wreckage in which Michels had been trapped, to starboard the curving side of the hull. A step in any direction but the right one would land me in trouble, but which way in that mud-shrouded water was right? I stood there motionless, cursing myself for a fool. Why, when I was safely out of the Navy and through with diving forever, had I been idiot enough voluntarily to come back and get into—

And then it came. On the surface, the *Falcon* took a wide yaw among the waves, my lifelines suddenly tautened, jerked my breastplate, threw me off balance, and I felt myself going over sideways, in another instant to be sprawled face down on the submarine, sliding helplessly through the water over the curving hull of the *S-4!* Faster and faster I went, lead weights clattering, copper helmet banging against the submarine's shell, while involuntarily I tried to dig my gloved fingers into the steel plates beneath me, to get a grip on something, anything, to stop my fall. Useless. The plates were smooth and slippery, there were no projections. With increasing speed, I shot overboard and started to drop vertically, still clawing wildly. No use. Down I went.

Then suddenly in the water a projection flashed before my faceplate! Out shot my right hand, grasped it. I stopped with a jolt that nearly jerked my arm from its socket, to find that there before my face was what I had made that dive to find. Through the faceplate of my copper helmet I was staring straight into the hole punched through the *S-4's* side into her battery room! And the projection I was clinging to was part of

"Up I went, legs tearing free of the mud, and when the heaving ceased, there I was, clear at last." —*Down to the S-4* the *Paulding's* steel stem, still jammed like a broken lance into the *S-4's* death wound!

Dangling there in the water by one arm, completely forgetful of my own plight, I swiftly examined that hole where it pierced the inner hull. It was a surprisingly small gash—hardly a foot across—to have sunk that ship and killed her crew, but still, aided by the increasing pressure of the sea as the sub went down, it had been more than enough to pour into the battery room a torrent which quickly spelled complete disaster.

A second look into that hole finished my examination. The damage was insignificant as affecting the strength of the ship to stand a lift—no danger of that trifling hole causing it to break in two when our lifting gear took a strain.

With that, I swiftly forgot all about the submarine's troubles and came back to my own. We could lift the submarine all right, but how about myself? I had broken my fall; what could I now do to lift myself up on deck? I tilted back my head and looked out through the top port of my helmet. Then cold fear suddenly gripped me. A stream of bubbles was pouring upward through the water from my hand! The jagged steel to which I clung had cut open my watertight glove, and from the highest point in my suit I was rapidly losing all my air!

Frantically my lead-soled shoes beat the sides of the *S-4*, trying to get a foothold on something to support me, to allow me to drop that arm below my helmet and save my air. It was useless. On the sheer side of the submarine there wasn't the slightest toehold. I felt the sea pressing in on my chest as the air went out and breathing became more difficult. Despairingly as I dangled there I glanced up again at my cut glove, at the air bubbling away. I couldn't climb up and I couldn't hang there much longer or the sea pressure would finish me. There was nothing to do but to let go while still I had a little air left in my suit, and take my chances on the sea floor. I let go.

Down I went again through the water, faster than ever now, with little air to buoy me up, and that two hundred pounds of lead and copper dragging me into the depths. I got one last glimpse of the side of the *S-4* shooting by my faceplate and then —the light went out!

I had hit bottom, but instead of stopping, I shot completely through it to find myself buried in soft mud, engulfed in total darkness, and still sinking helplessly, dragged down by my weights!

I came to rest at last, sprawled out sideways in utter blackness, to feel mud pressing in on me from all directions while the water which had leaked into my suit from my cut glove now all poured into my helmet and half strangled me. Convulsively I tried to straighten myself, to get my feet down and my head up, but with each desperate flailing of my arms and legs I could feel myself only sinking deeper through that clinging mud, lead shoes on my feet, lead belt on my waist, copper helmet on my head all equally dragging me down again with every spasmodic struggle. Was there no bottom to that mud?

Then at last I struck something hard, quit sinking, came to rest still sprawled out on my right side. With a gasp of relief, I thrust my arm down hard, intent on getting my head up, getting that water out of my helmet, only to feel my arm go full length down again into unresisting mud. There was nothing solid under my shoulders; just my body was resting on anything.

Instinctively I began to wiggle myself along that supporting shelf, to get wholly on it, so that I might work myself erect, but after the first motion, I immediately quit moving and lay still, terror gripping me completely. All along beneath me I felt sharp points jabbing upward into my diving suit, sawtoothed steel protruding everywhere from the support beneath me. What I had come to rest on there in the mud was twisted wreckage torn from the *Paulding's* keel as she raked over the *S-4*, wreckage now sunk alongside her victim. And if I moved, those razor-edged steel plates would cut my suit wide open in a dozen places as the *Paulding's* bow had already ripped apart my glove, and drown me out of hand!

I lay still. No more struggling, no more efforts to rise. In the blackness, in the cold, in the mud twenty fathoms down, I lay quietly, not daring to move a muscle, hardly daring to breathe, desperately wondering what to do, with the one slim relief in my situation that I was resting on my right side with my cut right glove beneath me so that I could still keep air in my suit.

Then the answer came to me. Simple! No reason at all for me to worry. I should have seen it before. Inside my helmet I had a telephone; tied to my breastplate was a lifeline. All I had to do to get clear of my trouble was to call my tenders on the surface and tell them to pull on my lifeline. They would immediately heave me up off that terrifying broken steel, up through that clinging mud which was engulfing me in maddening darkness.

Carefully, slowly, I twisted my head round to bring my mouth opposite the telephone transmitter in the roof of my helmet, fortunately clear of the water lapping round my neck, and gasped out:

"Topside there!" Then I waited with straining ears for a reply. Had the water already short-circuited my telephone? With infinite relief I heard the answer from the *Falcon* in the world above me:

"Topside. What is it?"

"Heave in on my lifeline!"

"Aye, aye. Right away!"

My head dropped back thankfully. All my troubles were over. With muscles tensed and stiffened legs, I waited for the tug on my breastplate which would pivot me about my lead-clad feet, pull me erect, and then up and off that terrible bed in the mud. But the tug never came and after what seemed to me an endless wait with not the slightest pull on my lines that I could feel, in anxious tones I sang out again:

"Topside there! Are you heaving yet?"

The answer fell like a sledge-hammer blow on my strained nerves.

"Yes! Four men are heaving hard on your lines but they can't get an inch of slack. What's the matter down there?"

Four men heaving on my lines and I couldn't feel even a slight pull! And they were getting in no slack at all on deck. Then my lines must be afoul of something above me, probably tangled in the *Paulding's* broken stem, which had already pierced my glove! The strain that four men heaving hard on deck could put on my air hose, fouled on the sharp edges of that jagged stem projecting from the *S-4's* side, could easily cut my rubber air hose in two, leave me there in the mud to be asphyxiated! In a strangled voice, I screamed:

"Topside there! Avast heaving! Slack off! Slack off for God's sake!"

An agonized moment passed while I waited in suspense. Would they get that message in time, would they obey it? Then almost with a sob of relief I heard:

"We're slacking away! Do you want any help down there?"

Did I want any help? Heaven knew I needed it badly enough, but I could waste no more breath in talking. My head sagged back, I didn't bother to answer, and I heard nothing further. On the topside, I knew that they would do what they could anyway, probably dress a relief diver and send him down, but, in my position, I gave up expecting any further aid from the *Falcon.* I must rely on myself. Long before they on the topside could do anything for me, I should probably be finished. The *Falcon* and my shipmates on her might for the next few minutes just as well be on the moon so far as helping me was concerned.

Despair, black as the blinding night around, gripped me. On top of all else now, my air hose fouled and likely to be severed, leaving me loaded down with heavy ballast to choke to death! And if I moved to extricate myself, the chances were excellent that I should cut my suit to pieces and drown in a flood of mud gushing into my helmet!

I tried to think. What could I do to save myself? But on the bottom, twenty fathoms down, with the pressure of the whole Atlantic numbing my brain, thinking was next to impossible. Then that paralyzing blackness! Light, light! If I were going to die, it would be so much easier if only I could see a little! And all the time there kept obtruding into my frantic efforts to pull my thoughts together, to think coherently if only for a moment, a shattering vision, the image of that silent, motionless steel coffin, the *S-4*, whose deck short minutes before I had been treading, with forty men stretched cold in death inside her. And there I was, the forty-first, already buried in the mud alongside their tomb, ready to join them!

Silently, motionlessly, I lay there in the ooze of the ocean floor, trying to concentrate on my problem, momentarily expecting my suit to give way to that piercing steel, to feel the mud gushing in on me. No one could do anything for me in time.

What could I do to save myself? Desperately I strove to put that recurring vision of the submarine out of my mind, to concentrate on diving. What trick in diving technique that I knew or could imagine could get me safely off that broken steel beneath me, up out of the Stygian blackness of the mud enveloping me? With an effort, I canvassed every diving trick I could think of, painfully trying to fit each one to my situation, dejectedly rejecting one after another as offering no hope. The only obvious one, my lifeline, I had tried and it had failed. Nothing else seemed applicable. With body numbed from cold, nerves deadened by repeated shocks, and mind dulled by heavy pressure, I lay now in a torpor. Further struggle seemed hopeless.

Then gradually I became vaguely aware, in the utter silence and blackness of that grave beneath the ocean floor, of a persistent murmur in my helmet, of a murmur to which long familiarity had made me oblivious. A small current of air was still flowing through my helmet, escaping with a gurgle through the exhaust valve somewhere near my chin. I still had air coming through my hose from above. Suddenly across my dazed brain that brought an idea. That air could save me!

Slowly, cautiously, not to let any movement of my body saw through my suit, I dragged my left arm through the clinging mud to my breast, fumbled with frozen fingers encumbered by mittens and stiff diving glove till I found the handle of the air control valve bolted to my breastplate. Through that valve the air from the *Falcon's* compressors, coming down my air hose, entered my helmet.

Convulsively my fingers closed on the valve handle, twisted it wide open. Immediately a suddenly increased stream of compressed air roared into my helmet, started to inflate my suit. I could feel the canvas which had been pressing in on my chest ease off as if a heavy weight had been removed and begin to swell. Under the increasing buoyancy, my helmet lifted a trifle, then, as if a giant hand had seized me by the shoulders, my body started to float upward through the mud, to come erect as my suit swelled more and more. Another moment and I was free of that bed of torn steel plates, erect once more, and could feel myself dragged vertically upward through the mud by my overinflated diving suit!

A little further and my helmet burst through the ooze of the ocean floor into the water. Light! Blessed, soul-satisfying light streaming through my faceplate again! After the terrifying darkness of the mud, that dim half-twilight of the depths seemed to me as dazzling as if the sun had suddenly risen inside my helmet! I had light now; anything was possible! I gasped in relief. I was saved!

But my dangers were not yet over. Under the pull of my partially ballooned-out rig, I was still rising from the mud, excessively buoyant. If, when I tore free of that clinging ooze, I was still so light, I would go shooting upward through the water with ever-increasing speed as the sea pressure decreased and the swelling air in my suit ballooned it out further, perhaps to crash at high speed into the *Falcon* above and kill myself, or, if I missed her, to break through the surface of the sea like a salmon leaping at a fly and then fall back helplessly, immediate victim to the bends, having risen from the heavy pressure of the depths to the surface without the slow decompression which alone could avoid it.

No, thankful as I was over the light, I couldn't afford to take time giving thanks, or I should find myself "blowing up" from the depths. Instantly when my helmet popped out into the water, my still-buried fingers were clawing again through the mud for my control valve, shutting off the air before it was too late. When the excess air had blown itself off through the exhaust and my ballooned-out rig had shrunk back to more normal proportions so that I ceased rising, I found myself still buried to my waist in mud with only the upper half of my body in the water. But I dared not float myself any further up for fear of not stopping. And there, in equilibrium, half in water, half in mud, I stood suspended in the ocean floor.

I looked up. To my pleased surprise, my lifeline and my air hose were floating vertically above me with no tangles in sight. Were they still fouled, or had my rise from below permitted them to slack off and to come clear of trouble? I could quickly find out. Once more I called the *Falcon*.

"Topside there! Take an easy pull on my lines!"

A brief moment, and then I felt a gentle tug on my breastplate. My lines were free! Swiftly I bled more air from my rig to make sure I was heavy enough not to float and then:

"Topside there! Pull me up ten feet!"

My lines promptly tautened and up I went, legs tearing free of the mud, and when the heaving ceased, there I was, clear at last, a fathom off the bottom, dangling in the water from my lifelines. And now to get back on the submarine so that I could come up the descending line.

Where was the submarine? Slowly I kicked myself around in a complete circle, beating the water with arms and legs, but in no direction could I catch any glimpse of her. While I must be surely within ten feet of it, for I had fallen straight down its sheer side, yet the *S-4* had completely vanished in that translucent water.

I gave up all hope of having the tenders above land me on the sub; even more out of question was finding her myself by having them lower me to the bottom again and floundering around in that mud.

My inspection was done anyway—by a freak of fortune, successfully. My hour on the bottom was certainly up. A few more words over the telephone and I was started directly upward for the surface, on my slow and tedious rise through the icy sea, a rise broken by lengthening stops every few fathoms as the water pressure decreased, to allow the air to work itself out of my blood gradually, to decompress me and avoid the bends.

And so, step by step, I was lifted. Halfway up I clambered aboard the little steel stage lowered into the sea alongside me. Then up again till waving over my helmet I could once more see through my faceplate that foam-flecked undulating sheet, the surface, with the familiar red underwater hull of the *Falcon* nestling in it. One more last stop, and then at last the welcome message:

"Coming aboard!"

With a final heave, the stage rose and I burst through the surface, clinging tightly to the bails of the stage again to avoid collapse as my buoyancy vanished and the unsupported load of all my lead and copper ballast came suddenly down on my shoulders. Swaying violently, the stage rose over the bulwark, swung inboard, dropped with a bang on the deck. Dripping mud and water, I was seized by the tenders and dragged to a bench. My belt, shoes, and helmet were hastily stripped off, and then, without a pause, still clad in my dripping suit, I was rushed across the deck, up the passage, and unceremoniously jammed through the outer door of the recompression chamber into the first lock. Slam! went the door. A tender with me twisted open an air valve and in roared a stream of compressed air, once more to get me under pressure, to make sure that no bubbles of air formed in my veins to give me the bends.

Exhausted, I sank down on the deck. As the pressure rose, the tenders in the lock with me unbolted my breastplate and dragged me out of my mud-plastered suit. By the time that was done, the pressure had risen to balance the pressure in the inner chamber, and the round door to that swung back. In the inner lock, I would finish my decompression, surrounded by hot towels and hot drinks. Chilled and shivering, I crawled through the round door into the inner chamber.

To my surprise, I found I was not alone in that recompression tank. Stretched out on the floor of the inner chamber, clad like myself in blue diving underwear, was Bill Carr, while alongside him was Tom Eadie, rubbing his legs. I looked at them inquisitively. Carr, with his underwear half soaked and his legs blue with cold, had evidently like myself recently come up from a dive.

Queer, I thought. I didn't know any other diver was on the bottom since I went down.

"Been down, Carr?" I asked him.

"Yeh," answered Carr briefly, evidently too chilled to want to talk.

Eadie hospitably offered me a drink, one of our hot "submarine cocktails." Greedily I swallowed it, thankful for the fiery warmth that went racing through my frozen form. Eadie, as I drank, once more turned to Carr, kneading his arm muscles to warm them up. I sank down on a bench. Eadie, still working, looked up at me.

"Didn't you know Carr was down, Commander?"

"No, Tom," I muttered wearily. "I thought I was alone down on the bottom."

"Well, you weren't," said Eadie. "You hadn't been down five minutes when they sent Bill down with a fire hose to start washing a tunnel through under the port bow of that sub, so's we could get the lifting chains through under her there. You didn't see nothing of him?"

"No, Tom," I assured him. "Not a sign."

"Well, he was there," continued Eadie, his gray eyes fixed solemnly on me the while he vigorously massaged Carr. "And he was down there when you telephoned up first to heave on your lines and then yelled to quit heaving and we knew you was in trouble. So we telephoned down to him, seeing as he was already on the bottom, saying:

" 'Commander Ellsberg's in bad trouble somewhere on the sub. Leave what you're doing, Bill, and go over and help him!' "

I looked from Eadie to Carr, who, still stretched out at my feet, was apparently vigorously trying to signal to Eadie to shut up. But Eadie, ignoring him, went on:

"And d'ye know, Commander, what Bill said when we told him you were in trouble and to go over and help you?"

"No, Tom," I replied, "that's beyond me. What did Bill say?"

"Well," said Eadie, "he sings out into his telephone:

" 'Aw, tell him to go to hell! I'm stuck in the mud myself!' "

This was too much for the prostrate bosun's mate. Carr came instantly to a sitting position, almost knocking Eadie over backward in the flurry. His face, flaming red, shot one scornful look at Eadie, then turned toward mine.

"Say, Commander! Don't believe a word Tom says! You know I'd never say a thing like that about you! You wanna know what I really said?"

"Sure, Bill, don't worry. Tom's only kidding. I know you'd never throw a shipmate down like that. What did you say?"

"Well," said Carr, "there I was alongside the port bow, washin' away with the hose, when the topside phones me about you. Quick as a wink, I drops my hose, grabs my descending line, starts climbing up the port side o' that sub, thinkin' o' the argument you once gave me in New York over that letter o' commendation, because I'd never had a chance to be a hero. And when I gits on deck, I starts runnin' aft four bells lookin' for you an' shoutin' into my telephone:

"'Hooray! Here's where I gits that Navy Cross!'"

Carr paused, looked mournfully at me, then concluded sadly: "Aw, Commander, why didn't you wait till I got there to rescue you?"

FROM

Tramps and Ladies

SIR JAMES BISSET

At her launching in May 1911, the British press hailed the White Star Line's 46,000-ton superliner Titanic *as "the Wonder Ship," the most stupendous, the most luxurious, the safest ship afloat. When she left Southampton on April 10, 1912, on her maiden voyage to New York, her passenger list abounded with prominent names, leaders of business and society on both sides of the Atlantic.*

The day after the Titanic *left Southampton, the Cunard liner* Carpathia *left New York bound for the Mediterranean. Its second mate was James Bisset, who, many years later—after he himself had commanded the superliners* Queen Mary *and* Queen Elizabeth *and had retired as commodore of the Cunard fleet—would recall his part in one of the greatest maritime disasters of all time.*

The Sinking of the Titanic

At the outset of her maiden voyage, when the *Titanic* was leaving Southampton, at noon on Wednesday, April 10, 1912, the problems of undocking a leviathan liner were graphically demonstrated. After her moorings had been cast off, and her propellers had begun to turn, her forward movement caused a sudden displacement of a vast volume of water inside the restricted space of the dock. This set up a suction which caused the American liner *New York*, berthed at an adjacent quay, to strain at her moorings.

The *New York* was a vessel of 10,500 tons. The sudden strain snapped her manila mooring lines. She swung away from the quay, drawn by the suction and by the pressure of a breeze, and bore down rapidly toward the port beam of the *Titanic*, amidships. A collision appeared inevitable. The *New York* was entirely out of control, with her engines stopped and no officers on her bridge.

The commander of the *Titanic,* Captain Edward J. Smith, was on his bridge with the pilot, and all his officers were on stations. Captain Smith was one of the most experienced of the White Star shipmasters. He had commanded the *Adriatic* and the *Majestic,* and had made several crossings of the Western Ocean in command of the *Olympic* before being appointed to command the *Titanic* on her maiden voyage.

Instantly appraising the situation, he stopped the *Titanic's* engines. Though the giant ship continued under way, the surge of her propellers had ceased, and, as she glided ahead, the swinging stern of the *New York* cleared the port quarter of the *Titanic* with only inches to spare.

This narrow escape from a collision proved that the master and the pilot, and all others concerned in handling the big ship, had not yet acquired full experience of the theoretical and practical problems created by her massive bulk. The amount of water displaced by a vessel of 46,000 tons in motion is capable of mathematical calculation. As much as 60,000 tons may be pushed ahead of her and to the sides of the bow, creating an eddy or suction astern which is formidable in a narrow dock or embanked channel, its force depending on the speed at which the vessel is moving.

The *Titanic* had three screws, and it would have been advisable to use only one, at dead slow, to move her, with the aid of tugs, away from the wharf and out of the narrow mouth of the Itchen River and into Southampton Water; but even in that wider channel ships have to proceed slowly, to avoid damaging with their "wash" the embankments or other vessels at moorings.

Captain Smith or the pilot, or both of them, had underestimated this effect. The development of leviathan liners had created new problems of many kinds, requiring a new kind of seamanship. Technical progress had been too rapid for mental adjustments to it to be fully made. This is typical of progress in all fields of human effort. Mistakes are made by pioneers for the benefit of those who come after.

The *Titanic* was a "hoodoo ship" from the beginning, but

only because she was a forerunner of the gigantic superliners. Not one, but many errors brought her to disaster; but from each of those errors the necessary lesson would be learned, to make her successors safe.

Typical of the way in which mental adjustments lagged behind technical progress were the regulations of the Board of Trade for lifeboats. The *Titanic* was certified to carry a total of 3547 persons, passengers and crew. Yet the regulations for lifeboat accommodation were based on an old rule that was hopelessly out of date.

This rule, made in 1894, stipulated that "vessels over 10,000 tons" must carry sixteen lifeboats, with a total capacity of 5500 cubic feet, plus rafts or floats with 75 per cent of the capacity of the lifeboats, that is, an additional 4125 cubic feet.

As lifeboat accommodation is based on the calculation that one person requires ten cubic feet, the *Titanic* was therefore compelled by law to provide lifeboat and raft floatage for only 962 persons, while at the same time she was certified by the Board of Trade to carry 3547 persons!

Apparently no one in authority had noticed this discrepancy. The *Titanic* had sixteen wooden-planked lifeboats and four "Englehardt" patent collapsible boats or rafts. The total cubic capacity of this floatage was sufficient for 1178 persons, scarcely more than half of the 2207 persons carried in the liner on her maiden voyage.

This was in excess of the Board of Trade requirements, but no one thought that lifeboats would be needed in an "unsinkable ship." No provision was made for boat drill, or for lifeboat training of the crew. The regulations merely classified this huge vessel of 46,000 tons as "over 10,000 tons" and the tragic incompetence of that definition was not apparent until too late.

The near mishap in the dock at the outset of the voyage was considered by some of the ship's people as an ill omen. This may have been superstition, or it may have been seamanlike judgment which took the form of a whisper that she was "unlucky."

The rumor had started several days before the *Titanic* left Southampton. Newspapers for months had been printing articles extolling her wonderful qualities, but, on the morning when she was due to leave Southampton, twenty-two men who had signed on in her crew were missing. At the last moment, thirteen others were signed on as substitutes. All members of the crew were British, and most of them had their homes in Southampton.

When she reached Queenstown, one man deserted. If he was affected by the fo'c'sle rumor that she was an unlucky ship, or if he had some premonition of his own, perhaps he was "fey."

Leaving Queenstown at 2 P.M. on Thursday April 11, the *Titanic* steamed along the Irish coast in fine weather, and had Fastnet Island abeam at 5 P.M. From there she steamed on the Great Circle course southwesterly for 1634 miles, to the vicinity of the "Corner" or turning point, in long. 47 deg. W. lat. 41 deg. 30 min. N., on the usual track of vessels westward bound for New York.

At this point ships veer almost due westerly, headed for Sandy Hook at the entrance to New York Lower Bay, 1222 miles from the "Corner." (These distances are approximate, as the "Atlantic Tracks" were not defined in 1912, and shipmasters set courses at their own discretion.)

At a speed of 22 knots, she would travel 528 miles per day of twenty-four hours of elapsed time, but, as she was making a westing through thirty-seven and a half degrees of longitude between Fastnet and the "Corner," the clock was retarded two and a half hours in that transit, with a "gain" of time.

In three days traveling from Fastnet, that is, in seventy-four and one half hours elapsed time, at 22 knots, she would cover 1639 miles, and would arrive at the "Corner" at 5 P.M. on Sunday, April 14.

To travel the distance of 1222 miles from the Corner to Sandy Hook would require another 51 hours of elapsed time. Adding two and a half hours for the further westing to New York, this gain would be occupied in the slow-speed passage of the harbor channels and quarantine delays. She would therefore berth at New York at the earliest at 5 P.M. on Tuesday, April 16—an inconvenient time to arrive for publicity purposes. Moreover, a passage of six full days from Queenstown would evoke no paeans of praise for the "Wonder Ship" when the *Mauretania* was regularly making that passage in four-and-a-half days.

Any reduction of the *Titanic's* speed below 22 knots, on the passage between the "Corner" and Sandy Hook, whether in the hours of darkness or daylight, would have meant either a night arrival in New York on Tuesday, or even a morning arrival on Wednesday, the seventh day out from Southampton—a slow passage in fine weather, with no excuses to be made for such an anticlimax to tremendous publicity.

In these circumstances, the requirements of publicity, or, as a later generation would term it, "ballyhoo," took precedence over sound and safe seamanlike judgment.

Captain Smith was at the disadvantage of having on board as a passenger the Managing Director of the White Star Line, Bruce Ismay. There is testimony that Ismay urged the captain to maintain maximum speed, and dictated to him the expected time of arrival at New York.

The speed was increased to twenty-two and one half knots during the hours of darkness on Sunday. This was the greatest speed of which the *Titanic* was capable. Her average speed on the preceding three days, from Fastnet to the "Corner," had been slightly less than twenty-two knots. As with all who recklessly press on to reach a destination, regardless of risks by the way, on land as on sea or in the air, the belief is that time gained is time saved—*but what do they do with the time they save?*

At sea, the shipmaster must be in sole command. He has the duty as well as the right to ignore any orders from the owner in matters concerning navigation. If Captain Smith deferred to Ismay, that was one of the factors, but not the only one, in the *Titanic* tragedy. . . .

On Sunday morning, when the *Titanic* had not yet reached the "Corner," the *Carpathia* was plugging along at fourteen knots, eastward bound on the Great Circle course from Sandy Hook to Gibraltar. I was on the bridge in the 8 A.M. to 12 noon watch. On this third day out, covering 336 miles in a day of twenty-four hours, we were approximately 1000 miles to the eastward of New York, but we were "losing time"—that is the ship's clock was being advanced one hour for each fifteen degrees of longitude in our easting (roughly 675 miles in that latitude).

Our course was easterly, a little to the north of the fortieth parallel of N. latitude. At 9 A.M., our wireless operator, Harold Cottam, handed up to the bridge a message he had picked up from the Cunarder *Caronia,* which was westward bound from Liverpool to New York. She reported sighting ice in lat. 42 deg. N., extending from long. 49 deg. W. to 51 deg. W.

This was nothing for us to worry about, as we were to the southward of it, but I informed the captain, who remarked, "It seems to be a big field. Keep a sharp lookout. Carry on!"

The *Caronia's* message was picked up also by the *Titanic.* It was the first of several ice warnings that she received during that day.

We had only one wireless operator in the *Carpathia.* He had a "shack" on deck abaft the bridge. His apparatus had a range of not much more than 150 miles. We considered him to be of very little use. He could communicate with vessels beyond our visual range, but vessels that we could not see were of little interest and certainly no danger to us. From eye level on the bridge, fifty feet above water level, we had a view to the horizon eight miles away, and that was more than enough sea room in which to avoid collisions with any other vessels, or with icebergs.

It was a clear, sunny day, with excellent visibility, but a sparkling frostiness in the air, caused by cold currents from the ice field to our north.

I went off duty at noon, loafed around, chatted with passengers, and had a nap during the afternoon. The eight-to-twelve watch was by far the best for getting in good sleeps at "natural" hours of rest.

When I came on duty again at 8 P.M., I noticed that two more ice warnings had been picked up by Cottam. One was from the White Star *Baltic,* eastward bound, reporting ice sighted at 1:42 P.M. in long. 49 deg. 52 min. W., lat. 41 deg. 51 min. N. The other was from the Leyland Line cargo steamer *Californian,* westward bound, reporting ice at 7:30 P.M. in long. 49 deg. 9 min. W., lat. 42 deg. 3 min. N.

Cottam mentioned also that the *Titanic* was now strongly within his radio range. She was sending a large number of commercial marconigrams to Cape Race in Newfoundland for transmission by cable from there to New York or to Europe. "Busy traffic," he commented. "Stock exchange quotations and that sort of thing for the multimillionaires!"

The ice field defined by the messages sent out by the *Caronia*, the *Baltic*, and the *Californian* was directly in the *Titanic's* track. She had received all these warnings.

As the *Carpathia* carried only one wireless operator, his instrument was left unattended while he took his meals, rest, and recreation. He sent and received messages only in Morse, with earphones clamped over his head. Being an enthusiast, he was to be seen crouched over his apparatus, sending or receiving messages, for many hours throughout the day, from 7 A.M. until 11 P.M. or even midnight.

Ships equipped with wireless usually carried only one operator. It had not occurred to shipowners that three operators are required to stand watches in rotation for an efficient twenty-four-hour service per day. The main duty of the operators was to send and receive commercial marconigrams for passengers to and from shore stations, which relayed them as telegrams. Ships' messages were also transmitted as marconigrams. These included messages between ships, such as ice warnings, or between ships and the shore, with expected times of arrivals or owners' instructions and suchlike.

When marconigram business was slack, the operators in ships "gossiped" unofficially with one another, often in a joking and sometimes profane and insulting manner. The operators nearly always knew what ships were within range, and exchanged at least identification signals and brief messages of greeting. There was no systematic organization of the use of "wave lengths." The operators manipulated their crystal detectors until they heard signals, and then joined in, listening for anything of interest, or sometimes "chipping in" with a comment or their own identification. Frequently an operator transmitting marconigrams would signal to another in his neighborhood Q R L, meaning "Keep quiet, I'm busy," or G T H ("Get to hell!").

Nearing the shore, on both sides of the Atlantic, conditions in the ether were made chaotic by the activities of hundreds of amateurs, known as "tin-can operators," who cut in on ships' messages with their own comments, sometimes frivolous or sarcastic. These pests "faded" 150 miles from the shore, but, even in midocean, there were usually half a dozen or more ships within range of one another at any time, and many of the operators, having met on shore or in training schools, were personally acquainted. They were a fraternity of pioneers, considered to be cranks, and had the curious habit of addressing one another as OM ("Old Man"). A common signal exchanged between them was GTHOMQRL ("Get to hell, old man, shut up, I'm busy!"), or ASOM ("Wait a minute, old man!"). Acknowledgment of an identification was often TUOMGN ("Thank you, old man, good night").

At 9:40 P.M., Cottam handed up to the bridge a message he had just received from a westward bound steamer, *S.S. Messaba*, reporting an extensive ice field sighted from long. 49 deg. W. to 50 deg. 30 min. W., between lat. 41 deg. 25 min. N. and lat. 42 deg. N.

This was only a confirmation of the warnings we had received earlier in the day from the *Caronia*, the *Baltic*, and the *Californian*. On our course we had not sighted any ice. We were thirty miles to the southward of this field, which according to the various warnings received during the day appeared to be slowly drifting southwards from lat. 42 deg. N., and now had its southern limit in lat. 41 deg. 25 min.

Captain Rostron came onto the bridge, and I told him of the latest ice warning. He called the Wireless Operator and asked him what ships were within his range.

"The *Titanic*, sir," said Cottam, "coming in very strong. She seems to be only thirty or forty miles away, but may be more, as she has a powerful transmitter. She's sending marconigrams to Cape Race. Then there's the *Californian*. She's stopped her engines for the night because she's surrounded by ice."

"It must be thick, then," commented the Captain quickly. "I suppose that the *Titanic* will have to slow down, or steer a more southerly course than the usual track. She'll be late in

New York. It's hard luck on her maiden voyage! Any other ships near?"

Cottam told him that he had identified four others within his 150-mile range radius of our position—the Norddeutscher Lloyd *S.S. Frankfort;* the Canadian Pacific *S.S. Mount Temple;* the Allan Liner *S.S. Virginian;* and a Russian cargo-steamer, *S.S. Birma.* These were in addition to the *Messaba,* the White Star *Baltic,* and the Cunarder *Caronia* identified earlier in the day. He had picked up faint signals also from the *Olympic,* now eastward bound out of New York, 500 or 600 miles to the westward of our position. She, like the *Titanic,* had a powerful transmitter, and carried two operators.

"Thank you," said the captain. "I suppose you'll be turning in presently for the night?"

"Yes, sir," said Cottam. "I may listen in to Cape Race for a while, in case there is any news of the coal strike in England."

I walked with the captain in the darkness to the port wing of the bridge. The weather was calm, the sea smooth, with no wind. The sky was clear, and the stars were shining. There was no moon, but the aurora borealis glimmered like moonbeams shooting up from the northern horizon. The air was intensely cold.

Though visibility was good, the peculiar atmospheric conditions, caused partly by the melting of the large ice field to our northward in the waters of the Gulf Stream, made the sea and sky seem to blend into one another, so that it was difficult to define the horizon.

Captain Rostron stood silently gazing ahead, and to the sky, and then turned to the north, watching the play of light from the aurora borealis. I knew better than to interrupt his meditations. Presently he raised his cap a few inches from his forehead, and uttered a silent prayer, moving his lips soundlessly.

After this he turned to me, and said, in a matter-of-fact voice, "You may sight the *Titanic* if she bears southward to avoid the ice. I don't suppose she'll try to run through it, when the growlers and bergs are so thick that the *Californian* has stopped for the night. Wonderful thing, wireless, isn't it? The ice has come south very early this year. There must have been an early thaw on the Labrador Coast. We're in clear water here, but keep your eyes peeled, all the same!"

"We'll soon be into the warmer weather," I remarked.

"Who knows what's ahead?" he said quietly, then added, "I'm sorry for Smith of the *Titanic*. After all the newspaper boasting, she's proved a slow coach on her maiden voyage, and now this ice field will make him lose more time if he steers to the southward around it, as I suppose he will! She must be a wonderful ship, but all their newspaper bragging seems a kind of blasphemy, claiming that she's 'unsinkable' and all that kind of thing."

Aware of the captain's piety, and respecting it, I murmured agreement. He changed the subject briskly. "The night's clear, and I'll turn in." Going into the chartroom, he wrote out his night orders, handed them to me, and, in his usual crisp manner, said, "Good night!" and went to his cabin below the bridge.

The quartermaster at the wheel struck four bells for 10 P.M., repeated by the lookout man in the crow's nest on his bigger bell with the cry, "All's well and lights burning brightly."

The promenade decks of the *Carpathia* were deserted on this chilly night, and the ship gradually became silent as the passengers turned in to their bunks, free of care. At six bells (11 P.M.) all was quiet, except for the throbbing of the engines; and most of the lights on deck and in the passenger compartments and saloons had been put out.

There was a light in the wireless shack. Cottam was listening to the stream of marconigrams sent out by Operator Jack Phillips of the *Titanic*. He heard Operator Cyril Evans, of the *Californian*, trying to cut in with an ice warning, "We are stopped, blocked by ice."

At that time (11 P.M.) the *Titanic* was not more than twenty miles from the *Californian*. The mammoth ship was driving on, at her utmost speed of twenty-two and one half knots, trying to make up time, and headed toward the ice field. Cottam smiled as he heard the curt reply from Phillips to Evans, "Shut up, old man, I'm busy!"

After that, Evans closed down for the night and went to bed. Cottam also hung up his earphones and got ready to retire. He had every right to do so, as Evans had. The *Titanic's* big-business marconigrams to Cape Race were not worth listening to.

At 11:40 P.M., the *Titanic* struck an iceberg, ten miles southward from where the *Californian* lay at a standstill, and approximately fifty miles NW by N of the *Carpathia's* position at that time. The collision had been a glancing blow on the starboard bow, and the big liner proceeded half a mile or more before she was stopped for investigations of the damage.

The wireless distress call was not sent out immediately. I had heard nothing new from Cottam at midnight, when I was relieved on the bridge by First Officer Dean. I handed over the *Carpathia's* course and details to him, and went to my cabin below the bridge. Captain Rostron's cabin was in darkness. He had gone to bed two hours previously.

There was a light in the wireless shack. I saw Cottam unlacing his boots, getting ready to turn in. He had taken the headphones off his ears.

I undressed and got into bed. Not feeling very sleepy, I picked up a book and began reading. At 00:15 A.M., the *Titanic* sent out her first distress call: "CQD CQD CQD (six times) MGY (*Titanic's* call sign). Have struck an iceberg. We are badly damaged. Lat. 41.46 N., long. 50.14 W."

Cottam was not listening at that moment. Ten minutes later, at 00:25 A.M., he idly picked up the headphones. At that time nothing was being transmitted. Instead of switching off and going to bed, he decided to call up Phillips of the *Titanic*. On getting the curt response—from Phillips—"K" ("Go ahead"), he began affably tapping out "GMOM (Good morning, old man). Do you know that there are despatches for you at Cape Cod?"

To his utter amazement Phillips broke in: "CQD CQD SOS SOS CQD SOS. Come at once. We have struck a berg. CQD OM. Position 41.46 N., 50.14 W. CQD SOS."

This was the first time in history that the internationally agreed signal of distress was sent out from a liner at sea.

Cottam, half dressed, sprang up to the bridge, told Dean of the message, and then woke the captain.

By this time it was 00:30 A.M., and I was dozing off to sleep. Suddenly I heard the captain's voice, singing out orders up to the bridge, "Stop her. Send for the chief engineer. Send for the chief officer. Call all the officers. Call all hands on deck and get ready to swing out the boats."

This last order particularly brought me out of my bunk on the jump. I flung on my clothes and overcoat, pulled on my boots and sprang up the bridge ladder to find out what was what. Dean tersely informed me in an excited voice, "The *Titanic* has struck a berg and has sent out the distress signal."

Already the *Carpathia* was being turned around. The captain was in the chartroom, working out the course. He came out onto the bridge and said briskly to the helmsman, "North 52 West! Full ahead!"

"Aye aye, sir, North 52 West!"

The other officers, including the chief engineer, were now on the bridge. The captain beckoned us into the chartroom and said, "The *Titanic* has struck a berg and is in distress fifty-eight miles from here on the bearing N. 52 W. We will make our utmost speed in going to her rescue. Call out an extra watch in the engine room and raise every ounce of steam possible. We may reach her in four hours. All seamen on deck for sharp lookout and to swing out the boats. We may have to pick up 2000 or more people. All stewards on duty to prepare blankets, hot coffee, tea, and soup. The doctors to stand by in the dining rooms. All gangway doors to be opened. Boatswain's chairs slung at each gangway. Pilot ladders overside. Forward derricks to be rigged and steam on winches. Oil to be got ready to quiet the sea if needed. Rockets to be got ready. Everything must be done as quietly as possible so as not to alarm our own passengers."

All this, quickly spoken in Captain Rostron's clear and steady tones within less than a minute, roused men still drowsy to a pitch of intense alertness. The chief engineer hurried below. The chief officer attended to details on deck, telling us off for the various duties, while more and more orders flowed from the captain.

Within a few minutes the engines increased the tempo of their thudding, and presently we were belting along at sixteen knots: the greatest speed that old lady had ever done in her life. The captain called me to the starboard wing of the bridge. "Station yourself here, Mister, and keep a special lookout for lights or flares—*and for ice!* I will remain on the bridge. In this smooth sea it's no use looking for white surf around the base of the bergs, but you will look for the reflection of starshine in the ice pinnacles. We'll be into the ice field at 3 A.M., or perhaps earlier. Extra lookouts will be posted on the bows and in the crow's nest, and on the port wing of the bridge, but I count on you, with your good eyesight, and with God's help, to sight anything in time for us to clear it. Give that all your attention!"

"Aye aye, sir!"

As the *Carpathia* thrust on into the night, Captain Rostron stood silently beside me for a minute, his cap raised a little from his brow, and his lips moving in silent prayer.

Then, like an electric spark, he was hurtling around, galvanizing everybody to activity.

On the captain's instructions, our wireless operator (Cottam) had signaled to the *Titanic* at 00:45 A.M.: "We are coming as quickly as possible and expect to be there within four hours." This was acknowledged by Phillips: "T U O M (Thank you, old man)."

After that Cottam did not send any more signals. He refrained from doing anything which would interfere with the transmissions from the *Titanic*. He heard her signals answered by other ships—the *Frankfort*, the *Mount Temple*, and, at 1:25 A.M., from a great distance (400 to 500 miles to the westward), by the *Olympic*. But there was no signal from the *Californian*, which lay only ten miles from the *Titanic's* position. Her wireless operator had shut down for the night and gone to bed before the first distress signal was sent out.

The land station at Cape Race had heard the distress signal and was relaying it to ships at sea and to other stations on land. It was from this source that the news first reached New York, picked up by amateur wireless operators.

At 1:25 A.M., Cottam heard the *Titanic* signaling to the *Olympic*, "We are putting the women off in the boats." At 1:45, the *Titanic* called up the *Carpathia*: "Come as quickly as possible. Engine room filling up to the boilers. T U O M G N."

When these two messages were handed to Captain Rostron, he envisaged for the first time the possibility that the *Titanic* might actually be foundering. Until then, he had assumed that she was seriously damaged—otherwise she would not have sent out a distress signal—but he expected that she would remain afloat, and that possibly the whole of her passengers, crew, and mails would have to be transferred to the *Carpathia*, or to other steamers which might hasten to the rescue.

It seemed incredible that the great "unsinkable ship" could actually sink. At 1:45 A.M., her wireless signals became faint. This indicated that the electric power plant had failed, and that the reserve batteries were being used. At 2:05 A.M., her wireless signals ceased entirely. At this time the *Carpathia* had run twenty-four miles at the forced speed of sixteen knots. We were thirty-four miles from the *Titanic's* position.

At 2:40, when we had twenty-five miles to go, we sighted a green light on the horizon ahead. For a moment this was disconcerting. It looked like the starboard navigation light of a steamer, perhaps of the *Titanic* herself, unaccountably nearer than we had thought, but then the light vanished, and we knew that it had been a pyrotechnic rocket, flaring at five hundred feet above sea level, to appear to us to be on the horizon from our distance of twenty-five miles away.

Though the night was cloudless, and stars were shining, the peculiar atmospheric conditions of visibility intensified as we approached the ice field with the greenish beams of the aurora borealis shimmering and confusing the horizon ahead of us to the northward. My face was smarting in the frosty air as I stood on the wing of the bridge, keeping a lookout for icebergs.

When the green flare was sighted ahead, Captain Rostron ordered a rocket to be fired in reply, followed by the Cunard identification rockets of colored balls of fireworks ("Roman candles"), and these were repeated every fifteen minutes, to let the *Titanic* people know our position. The sudden bursts of light from our rockets added to the difficulties of lookout, but they were an imperative procedure in the circumstances.

At 2:45 I sighted the glimmer of a star beam in an iceberg three-quarters-of-a-mile ahead of us on the port bow. I immediately reported it by singing out to the captain, who was standing by the helmsman. He reacted promptly in a seamanlike manner, altering course to starboard and reducing to half speed.

Then he strode out to the port wing of the bridge to make his own observations, and, when he had sighted the berg and saw that we had avoided it with ample clearance, and that no other obstruction was in sight, he brought the ship back to her former course and moved the engine-telegraph handle again to full speed ahead.

I may remark now, in the retrospect of the years, that, in this incident, and what followed it, my own feelings and senses were concentrated to a rare pitch of intensity. I dare say that every man on the bridge and on lookout in the *Carpathia* felt likewise that his nerves were as taut as violin strings, attuned by the hand of a master player.

Arthur Rostron, responsible for the safety of 1035 souls in his own ship, but knowing that more than 2000 people were in peril twenty miles away, and that every minute was precious, drove the *Carpathia* at forced full speed, in darkness, into the ice field in which the *Titanic* had met with disaster!

In taking this calculated risk, he relied on seamanship and sharp lookout, which had apparently been neglected in the *Titanic*. He knew—as every shipmaster of experience gained in the North Atlantic, and to the south of Cape Horn, knew—that icebergs are visible by starlight half-a-mile ahead in clear weather. That allows sufficient sea room in which to avoid them.

In the *Carpathia* we had a dozen pairs of eyes on the lookout for bergs. It happened that I sighted the first one we met with, because I had been specially told off for that purpose, and I had keen eyesight, and I knew what to look for, and I was keyed up to abnormal alertness; but, if I had not sighted it, the men in the crow's nest, or on the bows, or on the other wing of the bridge, would assuredly have done so in time to sing out a warning to the men in the wheelhouse who were standing on the alert for that very warning.

The fact that the *Titanic* had struck a berg in calm weather on a clear night meant one of three things—insufficient lookout; responses too slow from her bridge; or that the big vessel at her full speed had not quickly enough answered her helm to avoid a collision.

Despite her extensive electrical installations, the *Titanic* either did not have a searchlight or did not use it. We in the *Carpathia* did not have a searchlight, but as our track was to the southward of ice limits, we did not need one. In fact, very few merchant ships used searchlights, except in the passage of the Suez Canal.

The disaster of the *Titanic* was due to a combination of exceptional circumstances, and not to any one factor for which any individual could be blamed. The calm sea and the absence of wind to whip a surf around the base of the berg made sighting unusually difficult; the ice had come farther south than usual at that time of the year; finally, the berg was not isolated, but was part of an extensive field which greatly increased the mathematical chances of collision. Yet these were only some of the many exceptional elements that combined to produce the *Titanic* disaster. . . .

Within a few minutes we sighted another berg. We steered around it as before, and then sighted another, and another.

Captain Rostron later stated his earnest belief that the "hand of God was on the helm of the *Carpathia*" during that half hour when, in eight more miles at forced full speed, we zigzagged among the bergs, clearing them with sufficient room as we sighted them one after the other.

At 3:15 we were within twelve miles of the *Titanic's* wirelessed position. At intervals we sighted green flares, and our course was steered now on bearings from these, but we could not sight the big liner's masthead lights, or any other lights of her superstructure or hull. At 3:30 there were numerous bergs surrounding us, and small growlers of ice grinding along our hull plates.

Captain Rostron reduced speed to half, and then to slow, as the *Carpathia* was steered cautiously toward a green flare sighted low in the water, at a distance difficult to judge in the continuing peculiar conditions of visibility. It appeared likely, but at first was not certain, that this flare was from a lifeboat.

We were longing for daylight. I glanced at the deck of the bridge, and to my joy could see the holes in the gratings. Daylight was coming in. The light of the green flare toward which we were steering had burned out. Captain Rostron ordered the engines to be stopped. It was 4 A.M. We had arrived in three and a half hours.

Powerful is the force of routine. As eight bells sounded for the change of the watch, the lookout man in the crow's nest sang out the long-drawn wailing cry, "A-a-all's WELL and LIGHTS burning BRIGHTLY . . ."

First Officer Dean was relieved on the bridge by Chief Officer Hankinson. At that moment, in the dim gray light of dawn, we sighted a lifeboat a quarter of a mile away. She was rising and falling in the ocean swell, and now, as so often happens at dawn, a breeze sprang up and whipped the surface of the water to choppy seas.

The boat was laboring toward us. In her stern sheets stood a man wearing officer's cap and uniform, steering with the tiller. Only four other men were in the boat, each of them with an oar, but rowing feebly, as though they were inexperienced, and also utterly exhausted. Huddled in the boat were twenty-five women and ten children.

With the breeze that had sprung up, the boat was on our windward side, and drifting toward us. It was not practicable to maneuver the *Carpathia* to windward of the boat, so that she could make fast on our lee side in the smoother water there, as correct seamanship required. A large iceberg was ahead of us, which would have made that maneuver difficult when time was the chief consideration. If the boat had been well manned, she could have passed under our stern to the leeward side; but, as she drifted down toward us, the officer sang out, "I can't handle her very well. We have women and children and only one seaman."

Captain Rostron gave me an order, "Go overside with two quartermasters, and board her as she comes alongside. Fend her off so that she doesn't bump, and be careful that she doesn't capsize."

I hurried with two seamen to the rail of the foredeck, where rope ladders were hung overside. As the boat came alongside, we climbed quickly down and sprang onto her thwarts, and, by dint of much balancing and fending off, succeeded in steadying the boat and dropping her astern to an open side door on "C"

Deck, where we made her fast with her painter to lines lowered by willing hands from the doorway.

Many of the women and children castaways were seasick from the sudden choppy motion of the boat caused by the dawn breeze. All were numbed with cold, as most of them were lightly clad. Some were quietly weeping.

As they were in no fit condition to climb safely up the short Jacob's ladder to the side door, bosun's chairs were lowered, also canvas bags into which we placed the children, and, one at a time, they were all hauled to safety.

During this operation, we were occupied with allaying the fears of the women and children, and getting them safely out of the boat. They behaved well, waiting their turns to be hauled up to the door.

As we fastened one of the women into a bosun's chair, I noticed that she was wearing a nightdress and slippers, with a fur coat. Beneath the coat she was nursing what I supposed was a baby, but it was a small pet dog! "Be careful of my doggie," she pleaded, more worried about her pet's safety than her own.

When the women and children had been sent up, the four oarsmen and the officer climbed up the ladder—the officer being the last of the castaways to leave the boat. I followed him up, leaving our two seamen in charge of the boat, to hook her onto number-one derrick, ready to be hoisted to our foredeck.

The officer was a young man, Joseph Boxhall, Fourth Officer of the *Titanic*. I took him up to the bridge to report to our captain.

Without preliminaries, Rostron burst out excitedly, "Where is the *Titanic?*"

"Gone!" said Boxhall. "She sank at 2:20 A.M."

In the moment of stunned silence that followed, every man on the bridge of the *Carpathia* could envisage the appalling reality, but not yet to its fullest extent. It was now 4:20 A.M.

Boxhall added in a voice of desperation, "She was hoodoo'd from the beginning. . . ."

Captain Rostron took the young officer by the arm, and said quietly and kindly to him, "Never mind that, m'son. Tell me, were all her boats got away safely?"

"I believe so, sir. It was hard to see in the darkness. There were sixteen boats and four collapsibles. Women and children were ordered into the boats. She struck the berg at 11:40. The boats were launched from 12:45 onwards. My boat was cleared away at 1:45, one of the last to be lowered. Many of the boats were only half full. People wouldn't go into them. They didn't believe that she would sink . . ."

"Were many people left on board when she sank?"

"Hundreds and hundreds! Perhaps a thousand! Perhaps more!" Boxhall's voice broke with emotion. "My God, sir, they've gone down with her. They couldn't live in this icy cold water. We had room for a dozen more people in my boat, but it was dark after the ship took the plunge. We didn't pick up any swimmers. I fired flares . . . I think that the people were drawn down deep by the suction. The other boats are somewhere near. . . ."

"Thank you, Mister," said Rostron. "Go below and get some coffee, and try to get warm."

Our immediate task was only too clear—to search for the people in boats or rafts, and any other survivors. The increasing daylight revealed dozens of icebergs within our horizon. Among them were four or five big bergs, towering up to two hundred feet above water level. One of these was the one that the *Titanic* had struck. Dozens of smaller "calves" or growlers drifted sluggishly on the choppy seas. To the northward was a field of pack ice extending westward for many miles.

On all sides we could see lifeboats making laboriously toward us, some dangerously overcrowded, some half empty. A mile away was a mass of wreckage, like an island, marking the spot where the *Titanic* had gone down. Captain Rostron decided that we must give priority to picking up the people in the boats. They were in danger of perishing from exposure to the cold, or perhaps of capsizing; and among them were a large number of women and children. They at least were living, and could be rescued; but it was unlikely that any swimmers could have survived in water that was almost at freezing point, among those chunks of melting ice.

In four and a quarter hours, from 4:15 A.M. to 8:30 A.M., we picked up 703 survivors from the sixteen wooden lifeboats and four "Englehardt" collapsible boats. After 6 A.M., the *Car-*

pathia's deck rails were lined with our own passengers, joined by increasing numbers of rescued people, anxiously watching each boat arrive. The rescue operations proceeded in a deathly silence. Except for an occasional working order, no one was capable of saying anything that would be adequate to the occasion.

The *Titanic* lay in Davy Jones's locker, two miles deep below us. With her plunge to those deeps, fifteen hundred people had been drawn down to death in the icy waters, to perish in a vortex hundreds of fathoms deep. Their bodies, with the added buoyancy of the cork lifebelts which most of them wore, would gradually rise again to the surface. If any strong swimmers had got clear of the down suction, or had clung to wreckage in the darkness, they would surely have perished of cold within two hours after being immersed. The surface temperature of the water, by thermometer readings, was 33° F.—only one degree above freezing point. This was due to the large quantity of ice floating in small pieces from the disintegrating bergs.

The dead bodies were *there,* totally or partially submerged, but, in the choppy seas, it was now almost impossible to sight them, as white life jackets would have an appearance similar to that of the thousands of small pieces of floating ice or white-painted wreckage. A dead body floats almost submerged.

The water had a sinister greenish crystal tinge. People lining the decks of the *Carpathia* stared overside in shocked fascination and horror; for here, a thousand miles from land, the elemental ocean was, in truth, a watery grave in which, as a quick count and calculation indicated, the lives of fifteen hundred human beings had been extinguished almost without warning —plunged from warmth, light, and gaiety to icy doom.

Captain Rostron ordered the *Carpathia's* house flag to be lowered to half mast. The ship was in mourning.

At 8 A.M., when eight bells were struck, the lookout man's wailing cry of "A-a-all's WELL!" resounded like a ghostly sardonic lamentation, mocking the truth. But it had a meaning, beyond routine. In the midst of death we were in life.

Though so many had perished, many, too, had been saved. For them, at least, all was as well as could now be expected.

I took over the watch on the bridge from Chief Officer Hankinson. It was of no importance that I had gone without sleep all night, and that I had already been on duty for twelve hours; for, like all the other officers and members of the crew, I was keyed up to the tenseness of action in which fatigue is unnoticed.

Now the morning sunlight rippled on the slight seas. The last of the *Titanic's* lifeboats was laboring toward the *Carpathia.* She was crowded with seventy-five survivors, and her gunwales were within three inches of the water; but a good seaman was at her tiller. He was Charles Lightoller, Second Officer of the *Titanic.* He had gone down with the ship, and had been picked up by Boat Number Twelve. He had taken command of her, and had picked up other survivors. We maneuvered the *Carpathia* to windward, and drifted down to him, so that he was able to make fast alongside in our lee, and all the people in the boat were got safely on board.

Besides Lightoller and Boxhall, two other officers of the *Titanic* were saved. They were Third Officer Herbert Pitman and Fifth Officer Harold Lowe. All these officers had done grand work in launching the boats and handling them.

When Lightoller arrived with the last of the possible survivors, the best and worst were known. We had then received on board 493 passengers of the *Titanic,* comprising 315 women,

52 children, and 126 men. The rule when her lifeboats were lowered had been "women and children first."

We had also picked up 210 of the crew, comprising 189 men and 21 women. In all, we had 703 survivors on board, and the bodies of four men who had died of exposure in the lifeboats.

According to later published official estimates, a total of 1503 persons had perished. These were 661 men, 101 women, and 53 children of the passengers, and 686 men and 2 women of the crew.

Of the women and children who had perished, some had timidly refused a chance to go into the lifeboats. Others in the confusion had been unable to reach the lifeboat stations from below decks.

The final roll call of the dead and of the living, of both passengers and crew, revealed that 1347 men, 103 women, and 53 children had perished; while 315 men, 336 women, and 52 children had been saved.

These figures indicated the supreme sacrifice made by the men who had stood aside on the *Titanic's* decks to allow women and children to enter the lifeboats.

There was no reflection of wrong conduct on the men who had survived in the boats. Some, including crew members, had been ordered to go to handle the boats. Others had been allowed to go or had jumped in when boats were being lowered only partly filled with women and children. Others had been picked up from the water.

Among the men who had perished were the master of the *Titanic*, Captain Smith; her chief officer, H. F. Wilde, and First Officer Murdock, who had been on watch on the bridge when the collision occurred.

Her first wireless operator, J. G. Phillips, had gone down, but the junior operator, Harold Bride, was saved.

The passengers who had perished included the millionaires Jacob Astor, Benjamin Guggenheim, Martin Rothschild, Isidor Straus, Charles Hays, William Dulles, Frederick Hoyt, Clarence Moore, Emil Taussig, J. B. Thayer, Washington Roebling, and Harry Widener; the famous journalist W. T. Stead; the theatrical manager Henry Harris; President Taft's adviser, Major Archie Butt; the artist Frank Millet . . . and many more . . .

Among the survivors were Bruce Ismay, who, according to evidence, had jumped into a boat that was being lowered half empty; Henry Harper, the publisher; Sir Cosmo Duff Gordon; Baron von Drachstedt; Colonel Archibald Gracie; and others who had taken a proper opportunity to jump into boats, or had been picked up from the water.

The survivors were given immediate care and attention by our three doctors and by the stewards and passengers. Intense activity was going on, as the stewards found berths for the survivors.

Our first- and second-class passengers, and all the officers in the *Carpathia,* willingly gave up their cabins to women and children, and moved below to the third-class cabins.

In the meantime the *Titanic's* boats were being hauled up to the *Carpathia.* Our own boats, which were swung out on davits, had not been lowered. They were now returned to the chocks. Six of the *Titanic's* boats were hoisted up to the *Carpathia's* foredeck, and seven were carried slung overside in davits. This was all that we could conveniently hoist and stow. The others were set adrift.

When Lightoller's boat came alongside, the survivors previously taken on board knew finally the extent of their bereavements. If their loved ones were not in that boat, they had perished. At that moment seventy-five of the married women among the survivors, who had dared to cling to hope, had to face the fact that they were widowed, and that their children were orphaned. Others learned that a son or a father had gone. The extinction of hope came as a shock too terrible for the relief of weeping. The minds of the bereaved were numbed. There were no words that could comfort them. Anguish was silent. There was no hysteria. There was only a pall of unutterable grief, and a dazed staring from eyes of bewildered incredulity.

FROM

South

ERNEST SHACKLETON

After drifting for nine months in the pack ice of the Weddell Sea, the Endurance, *in October 1915, was finally crushed, leaving the Imperial Trans-Antarctic Expedition stranded on the ice two hundred miles from the nearest land and one thousand miles from any settlement. During the next six months the expedition, led by Sir Ernest Shackleton, made its way by sledge and boat to bleak, inhospitable Elephant Island. There, huddled in the island's narrow ice-free area, the men contemplated the approach of another Antarctic winter. No one would look for the shipwrecked party there, they knew. If they were to be saved, some of them would have to go in search of help.*

Ernest Shackleton here describes the eight hundred mile voyage to South Georgia Island in a twenty foot long open boat that resulted in the rescue of the expedition.

The Boat Journey

I HAD all sails set, and the *James Caird* quickly dipped the beach and its line of dark figures. The westerly wind took us rapidly to the line of pack, and as we entered it I stood up with my arm around the mast directing the steering. The pack thickened and we were forced to turn almost due east, running before the wind toward a gap which I had seen in the morning from the high ground. At 4 P.M. we found the channel, and, dropping sail, we rowed through without touching the ice, and by 5:30 P.M. we were clear of the pack with open water before us. Soon the swell became very heavy, and when it was time for our first evening meal we had great difficulty in keeping the Primus lamp alight and preventing the hoosh from splashing out of the pot.

Three men were needed to attend to the cooking, and all their operations had to be conducted in the confined space under the decking, where the men lay or knelt and adjusted themselves as best they could to the angles of our cases and ballast. It was uncomfortable, but we found consolation in the reflection that without the decking we could not have used the cooker at all.

The tale of the next sixteen days is one of supreme strife amid heaving waters, for the sub-Antarctic Ocean fully lived up to its evil winter reputation. I decided to run north for at least two days while the wind held, and thus get into warmer weather before turning to the east and laying a course for South Georgia.

We took two-hourly spells at the tiller. The men who were not on watch crawled into the sodden sleeping-bags and tried to forget their troubles for a period. But there was no comfort in the boat, indeed the first night aboard the boat was one of acute discomfort for us all, and we were heartily glad when dawn came and we could begin to prepare a hot breakfast.

Cramped in our narrow quarters and continually wet from the spray, we suffered severely from cold throughout the journey. We fought the seas and the winds, and at the same time had a daily struggle to keep ourselves alive. At times we were in dire peril. Generally we were encouraged by the knowledge that we were progressing toward the desired land, but there were days and nights when we lay hove to, drifting across the storm-whitened seas, and watching the uprearing masses of water, flung to and fro by Nature in the pride of her strength.

Nearly always there were gales. So small was our boat and so great were the seas that often our sail flapped idly in the calm between the crests of two waves. Then we would climb the next slope, and catch the full fury of the gale where the wool-like whiteness of the breaking water surged around us. But we had our moments of laughter—rare, it is true, but hearty enough.

On the third day out the wind came up strong and worked into a gale from the northwest. We stood away to the east, but the increasing seas discovered the weaknesses of our decking. The continuous blows shifted the box lids and sledge-runners so that the canvas sagged down and accumulated water. Then

icy trickles, distinct from the driving sprays, poured fore and aft into the boat. We did what we could to secure the decking, but our means were very limited, and the water continued to enter the boat at a dozen points.

Much bailing was necessary, but nothing could prevent our gear from becoming sodden. The searching runnels from the canvas were really more unpleasant than the sudden definite douches of the sprays. There were no dry places in the boat, and at last we simply covered our heads with our Burberrys and endured the all-pervading water. The bailing was work for the watch.

None of us, however, had any real rest. The perpetual motion of the boat made repose impossible; we were cold, sore, and anxious. In the semidarkness of the day we moved on hands and knees under the decking. By 6 P.M. the darkness was complete, and not until 7 A.M. could we see one another under the thwarts. We had a few scraps of candle, but we preserved them carefully so that we might have light at mealtimes. There was one fairly dry spot in the boat, under the solid original decking at the bows, and there we managed to protect some of our biscuit from the salt water. But I do not think any of us got the taste of salt out of our mouths during the voyage.

The difficulty of movement in the boat would have had its humorous side if it had not caused so many aches and pains. In order to move along the boat we had to crawl under the thwarts, and our knees suffered considerably. When a watch turned out I had to direct each man by name when and where to move, for if all hands had crawled about at the same time the result would have been dire confusion and many bruises.

Then there was the trim of the boat to be considered. The order of the watch was four hours on and four hours off, three men to the watch. One man had the tiller ropes, the second man attended to the sail, and the third bailed for all he was worth. Sometimes, when the water in the boat had been reduced to reasonable proportions, we could use our pump, which Hurley had made from the Flinders' bar case of our ship's standard compass. Though its capacity was small this pump was quite effective.

While the new watch was shivering in the wind and spray,

the men who had been relieved groped hurriedly among the soaking sleeping bags and tried to steal some of the warmth created by the last occupants, but it was not always possible to find even this comfort when we went off watch. The boulders which we had taken aboard for ballast had to be shifted continually in order to trim the boat and give access to the pump, which became choked with hairs from the molting sleeping bags and finneskoe.

The moving of the boulders was weary and painful work. As ballast they were useful, but as weights to be moved about in cramped quarters they were simply appalling. They spared no portion of our poor bodies. Another of our troubles was the chafing of our legs by our wet clothes, and our pain was increased by the bite of the salt water. At the time we thought that we never slept, but in fact we dozed off uncomfortably, to be roused quickly by some new ache or by another call to effort. My own share of the general discomfort was increased by a finely developed bout of sciatica, which had begun on the floe several months earlier.

Our meals were regular in spite of the gales. Attention to this was essential, since the conditions of the voyage made ever-increasing calls upon our vitality. The meals, which consisted chiefly of Bovril sledging ration, were the bright beacons in these cold and stormy days. Finding ourselves in need of an oil lamp to eke out our supply of candles, we emptied one of our two tins of Virol in the manner which most appealed to us, and fitted it with a wick made by shredding a bit of canvas. This lamp was of great assistance to us at night. Since we had six and a half gallons of petroleum, we were fairly well off for fuel.

A severe southwesterly gale on the fourth day out forced us to heave to. The delay was vexatious, since up to that time we had been making sixty to seventy miles a day, good going with our limited sail area. We hove to under double-reefed mainsail and our little jigger, and waited for the gale to blow itself out. The weather, however, did not improve, and on the fifth day we were obliged to take in the double-reefed mainsail and hoist our small jib instead.

We put out a sea-anchor to keep the boat's head up to the sea. This anchor consisted of a triangular canvas bag fastened to the end of the painter and allowed to stream out from the bows. The boat was high enough to catch the wind, and, as she drifted to leeward, the drag of the anchor kept her head to windward. Thus our boat took most of the seas more or less end on, but even then we shipped a great deal of water, which necessitated unceasing bailing and pumping. A thousand times it seemed as if the *James Caird* must be engulfed, but the boat lived.

The gale had its birthplace above the Antarctic Continent, and its freezing breath lowered the temperature far towards zero. The spray froze upon the boat and gave bows, sides and decking a heavy coat of mail. This ice reduced the buoyancy of the boat, and to that extent was an added peril, but from one point of view it possessed a notable advantage. The water ceased to drop and trickle from the canvas, and the spray came in solely at the well in the afterpart of the boat. We could not allow the load of ice to increase beyond a certain point, and in turn we crawled about the decking forward, chipping and picking at it with what tools we had.

When daylight came on the sixth day we saw and felt that the *James Caird* had lost her resiliency. She was not rising to the oncoming seas. The weight of the ice was having its effect, and she was becoming more like a log than a boat. The situation called for immediate action. First of all we broke away the spare oars, which were encased in ice and frozen to the sides of the boat, and threw them overboard. We kept two oars for use when we got inshore. Then two of the fur sleeping bags went over the side, weighing probably 40 lb. each. We still had four bags, three in use and one in reserve should a member of the party permanently break down. The reduction of weight relieved the boat to some extent, and vigorous chipping and scraping, by which we got rid of a lot of ice, helped more. The *James Caird* lifted to the endless waves as though she lived again.

About 11 A.M. the boat suddenly fell off into the trough of the sea. The painter had parted and the sea-anchor had gone. This was serious. The boat went away to leeward, and we had no chance to recover the anchor and our valuable rope, which had been our only means of keeping the boat's head up to the sea without the risk of hoisting sail in a gale. Now we had to set the sail and trust to its holding. While the *James Caird* rolled in the trough, we beat the frozen canvas until the bulk of the ice had cracked off it, and then we hoisted it. The frozen gear worked protestingly, but after a struggle our little craft came up to the wind again, and we breathed more freely.

Skin frostbites were troubling us, and we had developed large blisters on our fingers and hands, but we held the boat up to the gale during the day, enduring as best we could discomforts amounting to pain. Our thoughts did not embrace much more than the necessities of the hour. Every surge of the sea was an enemy to be watched and circumvented. Night fell early, and in the lagging hours of darkness we were cheered by an improvement in the weather. The wind dropped, the snow squalls became less frequent, and the sea moderated.

When the morning of the seventh day dawned there was not much wind, and we shook the reef out of the sail and laid our course once more for South Georgia. The sun came out bright and clear, and presently Worsley got a snap for longitude. We hoped that the sky would remain clear until noon so that we could get the latitude, for we had been six days out without an observation, and our dead reckoning naturally was uncertain.

The boat on that morning must have presented a strange appearance. All hands basked in the sunshine. We hung our sleeping bags to the mast, and our socks and other gear were spread all over the deck. Porpoises came blowing round the boat, and Cape pigeons wheeled and swooped within a few feet of us. These little black-and-white birds have an air of friendliness which is not possessed by the great circling albatross.

We reveled in the warmth of the sun during that day. Life, after all, was not so bad. Our gear was drying, and we could have a hot meal in more or less comfort. The swell was still heavy, but it was not breaking, and the boat rode easily. At noon Worsley balanced himself on the gunwale and clung with one hand to the stay of the mainmast while he got a snap of the sun. The result was more than encouraging. We had done over 380 miles and were getting on for halfway to South Georgia. It looked as if we were going to get through.

During the afternoon the wind freshened to a good stiff breeze, and the *James Caird* made satisfactory progress. I had not realized until the sunlight came how small our boat really was. So low in the water were we that each succeeding swell cut off our view of the skyline. At one moment the consciousness of the forces arrayed against us would be almost overwhelming, and then hope and confidence would rise again as our boat rose to a wave and tossed aside the crest in a sparkling shower. My gun and some cartridges were stowed aboard the boat as a precaution against a shortage of food, but we were not disposed to destroy our little neighbors, the Cape pigeons, even for the sake of fresh meat. We might have shot an albatross, but the wandering king of the ocean aroused in us something of the feeling that inspired, too late, the Ancient Mariner.

The eighth, ninth, and tenth days of the voyage had few features worthy of special note. The wind blew hard during these days, and the strain of navigating the boat was unceasing, but we kept on advancing toward our goal and felt that we were going to succeed. We still suffered severely from the cold, for our vitality was declining owing to shortage of food, exposure, and the necessity of maintaining our cramped positions day and night. I found that it was now absolutely necessary to prepare hot milk for all hands during the night, in order to sustain life until dawn. This involved an increased drain upon our small supply of matches, and our supply already was very small indeed. One of the memories which comes to me of those days is of Crean singing at the tiller. He always sang while he was steering, but nobody ever discovered what the song was.

On the tenth night Worsley could not straighten his body after his spell at the tiller. He was thoroughly cramped, and we had to drag him beneath the decking and massage him before he could unbend himself and get into a sleeping bag.

A hard northwesterly gale came up on the eleventh day (May 5), and in the late afternoon it shifted to the southwest. The sky was overcast and occasional snow squalls added to the discomfort produced by a tremendous cross sea—the worst, I thought, which we had encountered. At midnight I was at the tiller, and suddenly noticed a line of clear sky between the south and southwest. I called to the other men that the sky was clearing, and then, a moment later realized that what I had seen was not a rift in the clouds but the white crest of an enormous wave.

During twenty-six years' experience of the ocean in all its moods I had never seen a wave so gigantic. It was a mighty upheaval of the ocean, a thing quite apart from the big white-capped seas which had been our tireless enemies for many days. I shouted, "For God's sake, hold on! It's got us!" Then came a moment of suspense which seemed to last for hours. We felt our boat lifted and flung forward like a cork in breaking surf. We were in a seething chaos of tortured water, but somehow the boat lived through it, half full of water, sagging to the dead weight and shuddering under the blow. We bailed with the energy of men fighting for life, flinging the water over the sides with every receptacle which came into our hands; and after ten minutes of uncertainty we felt the boat renew her life beneath us. She floated again, and ceased to lurch drunkenly as though dazed by the attack of the sea. Earnestly we hoped that never again should we encounter such a wave.

The conditions of the boat, uncomfortable before, were made worse by this deluge of water. All our gear was thoroughly wet again, and our cooking-stove was floating about in the bottom of the boat. Not until 3 A.M., when we were all chilled to the limit of endurance, did we manage to get the stove alight and to make ourselves hot drinks. The carpenter was suffering particularly, but he showed grit and spirit. Vincent, however, had collapsed, and for the past week had ceased to be an active member of the crew.

On the following day (May 6) the weather improved, and we got a glimpse of the sun. Worsley's observation showed that we were not more than one hundred miles from the north-west corner of South Georgia. Two more days, with a favorable wind, and we should sight the promised land. I hoped that there would be no delay, as our supply of water was running very low. The hot drink at night was essential, but I decided that the daily allowance of water must be cut down to half a pint per man. Our lumps of ice had gone some days before; we were dependent upon the water which we had brought from Elephant Island, and our thirst was increased by the fact that we were at this time using the brackish water in the breaker which had been slightly stove in when the boat was being loaded. Some sea water had entered it.

Thirst took possession of us, but I dared not permit the allowance of water to be increased, because an unfavorable wind might have driven us away from the island and have lengthened our voyage by several days. Lack of water is always the most severe privation which men can be condemned to endure, and we found that the salt water in our clothing and the salt spray which lashed our faces made our thirst quickly grow to a burning pain. I had to be very firm in refusing to allow any one to anticipate the morrow's allowance, which sometimes I was begged to do.

I had altered the course to the east so as to make sure of striking the island, which would have been impossible to regain if we had run past the northern end. The course was laid on our scrap of chart for a point some thirty miles down the coast. That day and the following day passed for us in a sort of nightmare. Our mouths were dry and our tongues were swollen. The wind was still strong and the heavy sea forced us to navigate carefully. But any thought of our peril from the waves was buried beneath the consciousness of our raging thirst. The bright moments were those when we each received our one mug of hot milk during the long, bitter watches of the night.

Things were bad for us in those days, but the end was approaching. The morning of May 8 broke thick and stormy, with squalls from the northwest. We searched the waters ahead for a sign of land, and, although we searched in vain, we were cheered by a sense that the goal was near. About 10 A.M. we passed a little bit of kelp, a glad signal of the proximity of land. An hour later we saw two shags sitting on a big mass of kelp, and we knew then that we must be within ten or fifteen miles of the shore. These birds are as sure an indication of the proximity of land as a lighthouse is, for they never venture far to sea.

We gazed ahead with increasing eagerness, and at 12:30 P.M., through a rift in the clouds, McCarthy caught a glimpse of the black cliffs of South Georgia, just fourteen days after our departure from Elephant Island. It was a glad moment. Thirst-ridden, chilled, and weak as we were, happiness irradiated us. The job was nearly done.

We stood in toward the shore to look for a landing place, and presently we could see the green tussock grass on the ledges above the surf-beaten rocks. Ahead of us, and to the south, blind rollers showed the presence of uncharted reefs along the coast. The rocky coast appeared to descend sheer to the sea. Our need of water and rest was almost desperate, but to have attempted a landing at that time would have been suicidal.

Night was approaching and the weather indications were unfavorable. We could do nothing but haul off until the following morning, so we stood away on the starboard tack until we had made what appeared to be a safe offing. Then we hove to in the high westerly swell. The hours passed slowly as we awaited the dawn; our thirst was a torment and we could scarcely touch our food, the cold seemed to strike right through our weakened bodies.

At 5 A.M. the wind shifted to the northwest, and quickly increased to one of the worst hurricanes any of us had ever experienced. A great cross sea was running and the wind simply shrieked as it converted the whole sea scape into a haze of driving spray. Down into the valleys, up to tossing heights, straining until her seams opened, swung our little boat, brave still but laboring heavily. We knew that the wind and set of the sea were driving us ashore, but we could do nothing.

The dawn revealed a storm-torn ocean, and the morning passed without bringing us a sight of the land; but at 1 P.M., through a rift in the flying mists, we got a glimpse of the huge crags of the island and realized that our position had become desperate. We were on a dead lee shore, and we could gauge our approach to the unseen cliffs by the roar of the breakers against the sheer walls of rock. I ordered the double-reefed mainsail to be set in the hope that we might claw off, and this attempt increased the strain upon the boat.

The *James Caird* was bumping heavily, and the water was pouring in everywhere. Our thirst was forgotten in the realization of our imminent danger, as we bailed unceasingly and from time to time adjusted our weights; occasional glimpses showed that the shore was nearer.

I knew that Annewkow Island lay to the south of us, but our small and badly marked chart showed uncertain reefs in the passage between the island and the mainland, and I dared not trust it, though, as a last resort, we could try to lie under the lee of the island.

The afternoon wore away as we edged down the coast, and the approach of evening found us still some distance from Annewkow Island; dimly in the twilight we could see a snow-capped mountain looming above us. The chance of surviving the night seemed small, and I think most of us felt that the end was very near. Just after 6 P.M., as the boat was in the yeasty backwash from the seas flung from this iron-bound coast, just when things looked their worst, they changed for the best; so thin is the line which divides success from failure.

The wind suddenly shifted, and we were free once more to make an offing. Almost as soon as the gale eased, the pin which locked the mast to the thwart fell out. Throughout the hurricane it must have been on the point of doing this, and if it had nothing could have saved us. The mast would have snapped like a carrot. Our backstays had carried away once before, when iced up, and were not too strongly fastened. We were thankful indeed for the mercy which had held the pin in its place during the hurricane.

We stood offshore again, tired almost to the point of apathy. Our water had long been finished. The last was about a pint of hairy liquid, which we strained through a bit of gauze from the medicine chest. The pangs of thirst attacked us with redoubled intensity, and I felt that at almost any risk we must make a landing on the following day. The night wore on. We were very tired and longed for day. When at last dawn came there was hardly any wind, but a high cross sea was running. We made slow progress toward the shore.

About 8 A.M. the wind backed to the northwest and threatened another blow. In the meantime we had sighted a big indentation which I thought must be King Haakon Bay, and I decided that we must land there. We set the bows of the boat toward the bay and ran before the freshening gale. Soon we had angry reefs on either side. Great glaciers came down to the sea and offered no landing-place. The sea spouted on the reefs and thundered against the shore. About noon we sighted a line of jagged reef, like blackened teeth, which seemed to bar the entrance to the bay. Inside, fairly smooth water stretched eight or nine miles to the head of the bay.

A gap in the reef appeared, and we made for it, but the fates had another rebuff for us. The wind shifted and blew from the east right out of the bay. We could see the way through the reef, but we could not approach it directly. That afternoon we bore up, tacking five times in the strong wind. The last tack enabled us to get through, and at last we were in the wide mouth of the bay.

Dusk was approaching. A small cove, with a boulder-strewn beach guarded by a reef, made a break in the cliffs on the south side of the bay, and we turned in that direction. I stood in the bows, and directed the steering as we ran through the kelp and made the passage of the reef. The entrance was so narrow that we had to take in the oars, and the swell was piling itself right over the reef into the cove. But in a minute or two we were inside, and in the gathering darkness the *James Caird* ran in on a swell and touched the beach.

I sprang ashore with the short painter, and held on when the boat went out with the backward surge. When the boat came in again three men got ashore and held the painter while I climbed some rocks with another line. A slip on the wet rocks twenty feet up nearly closed my part of the story, just when we were achieving safety. A jagged piece of rock held me and also sorely bruised me. I, however, made fast the line, and in a few minutes we were all safe on the beach, with the boat floating in the surging water just off the shore.

We heard a gurgling sound which was sweet music in our ears, and, peering round, we found a stream of fresh water almost at our feet. A moment later we were down on our knees drinking the pure, ice-cold water in long draughts which put new life into us. It was a splendid moment.

FROM

A Voyage Round the World

RICHARD WALTER

In 1741, during the War of Jenkins's Ear, Commodore George Anson, in the sixty-gun Centurion, *led a squadron of British warships around Cape Horn and into the "South Sea," there to attack the Spanish colonies on the west coast of South America. While the squadron was crossing the Atlantic, scurvy, that mysterious and dreaded disease, made its appearance. It recurred with heightened fury during the difficult rounding of Cape Horn. For seven terrible weeks, the* Centurion's *exhausted men battled winter gales and mountainous waves. When at last they emerged into the Pacific, they found the squadron scattered and themselves alone. Fatigue and despair added new virulence to the murderous disease. With his crew sick and dying, Anson steered for pre-established rendezvous points, first on the coast of Chile and then at Juan Fernández Island, in the hope of reassembling his squadron. Richard Walter, chaplain aboard the* Centurion, *here describes the ship's desperate course to Juan Fernández Island.*

Scurvy

SOON after our passing Streights Le Maire, the scurvy began to make its appearance among us; and our long continuance at sea, the fatigue we underwent, and the various disappointments we met with had occasioned its spreading to such a degree that at the latter end of April there were but few on board who were not in some degree afflicted with it, and in that month no less than forty-three died of it on board the *Centurion*. But though we thought that the distemper had then risen to an extraordinary height, and were willing to hope that as we advanced to the northward its malignity would abate, yet we found, on the contrary, that in the month of May we lost nearly double that number. And as we did not get to land till the middle of June, the mortality went on increasing, and the disease extended itself so prodigiously, that after the loss of about two hundred men, we could not at last muster more than six foremast men in a watch capable of duty.

This disease so frequently attending all long voyages, and so particularly destructive to us, is surely the most singular and unaccountable of any that affects the human body. For its symptoms are inconstant and innumerable, and its progress and effects extremely irregular; for scarcely any two persons have the same complaints, and where there hath been found some conformity in the symptoms, the order of their appearance has been totally different. However, though it frequently puts on the form of many other diseases, and is therefore not to be described by any exclusive and infallible criterions; yet there are some symptoms which are more general than the rest, and therefore, occurring the oftnest, deserve a more particular enumeration. These common appearances are large discoloured spots dispersed over the whole surface of the body, swelled legs, putrid gums, and above all, an extraordinary lassitude of the whole body, especially after any exercise, however inconsiderable; and this lassitude at last degenerates into a proneness to swoon on the least exertion of strength, or even on the least motion.

This disease is likewise usually attended with a strange dejection of the spirits, and with shiverings, tremblings, and a disposition to be seized with the most dreadful terrors on the slightest accident. Indeed it was most remarkable, in all our reiterated experience of this malady, that whatever discouraged our people, or at any time damped their hopes, never failed to add new vigour to the distemper; for it usually killed those who were in the last stages of it, and confined those to their hammocks who were before capable of some kind of duty, so that it seemed as if alacrity of mind, and sanguine thoughts, were no contemptible preservatives from its fatal malignity.

But it is not easy to compleat the long roll of the various concomitants of this disease; for it often produced putrid fevers, pleurisies, the jaundice, and violent rheumatick pains, and sometimes it occasioned an obstinate costiveness, which was gener-

ally attended with a difficulty of breathing; and this was esteemed the most deadly of all the scorbutick symptoms: At other times the whole body but more especially the legs were subject to ulcers of the worst kind, attended with rotten bones, and such a luxuriancy of funguous flesh, as yielded to no remedy. But a most extraordinary circumstance, and what would be scarcely credible upon any single evidence is that the scars of wounds which had been for many years healed, were forced open again by this virulent distemper: Of this, there was a remarkable instance in one of the invalids on board the *Centurion*, who had been wounded above fifty years before at the battle of the Boyne; for though he was cured soon after, and had continued well for a great number of years past, yet on his being attacked by the scurvy, his wounds, in the progress of his disease, broke out afresh, and appeared as if they had never been healed: Nay, what is still more astonishing, the callous of a broken bone, which had been compleatly formed for a long time, was found to be hereby dissolved, and the fracture seemed as if it had never been consolidated. Indeed, the effects of this disease were in almost every instance wonderful; for many of our people, though confined to their hammocks, appeared to have no inconsiderable share of health, for they eat and drank heartily, were chearful, and talked with much seeming vigour, and with a loud strong tone of voice; and yet on their being the least moved, though it was only from one part of the ship to the other, and that in their hammocks, they have immediately expired; and others, who have confided in their seeming strength, and have resolved to get out of their hammocks, have died before they could well reach the deck; and it was no uncommon thing for those who were able to walk the deck, and to do some kind of duty, to drop down dead in an instant, on any endeavours to act with their utmost vigour, many of our people having perished in this manner during the course of this voyage.

With this terrible disease we struggled the greatest part of the time of our beating round Cape Horn; and though it did not then rage with its utmost violence, yet we buried no less than forty-three men on board the *Centurion,* in the month of April, as hath been already observed, but we still entertained hopes, that when we should have once secured our passage round the Cape, we should put a period to this and all the other evils which had so constantly pursued us. But it was our misfortune to find that the Pacifick Ocean was to us less hospitable than the turbulent neighbourhood of Terra del Fuego and Cape Horn: For being arrived, on the 8th of May, off the Island of Socoro, which was the first rendezvous appointed for the squadron, and where we hoped to have met with some of our companions, we cruized for them in that station several days. And here we were not only disappointed in our hopes of being joined by our friends, and were thereby induced to favour the gloomy suggestions of their having all perished; but we were likewise perpetually alarmed with the fears of being driven on shore upon this coast, which appeared too craggy and irregular to give us the least hopes, that in such a case any of us could possibly escape immediate destruction. For the land had indeed a most tremendous aspect: The most distant part of it, and which appeared far within the country, being the mountains usually called the Andes or Cordilleras, was extremely high, and covered with snow; and the coast itself seemed quite rocky and barren, and the water's edge skirted with precipices. In some places indeed there appeared several deep bays running into the land, but the entrance into them was generally blocked up by numbers of little islands; and though it was not improbable but there might be convenient shelter in some of those bays, and proper channels leading thereto; yet as we were utterly ignorant of the coast, had we been driven ashore by the western winds which blew almost constantly there, we did not expect to have avoided the loss of our ships and of our lives.

And this continued peril, which lasted for above a fortnight, was greatly aggravated by the difficulties we found in working the ship; as the scurvy had by this time destroyed so great a part of our hands, and had in some degree affected almost the whole crew. Nor did we, as we hoped, find the winds less violent, as we advanced to the northward; for we had often prodigious squalls which split our sails, greatly damaged our rigging, and endangered our masts. Indeed, during the greatest part of the time we were upon this coast, the wind blew so hard, that in another situation, where we had sufficient sea-room, we should certainly have lain to; but in the present exigency we were necessitated to carry both our courses and top-sails, in order to keep clear of this lee-shore. In one of these squalls, which was attended by several violent claps of thunder, a sudden flash of fire darted along our decks, which, dividing, exploded with a report like that of several pistols, and wounded many of our men and officers as it passed, marking them in different parts of the body: This flame was attended with a strong sulphurous stench, and was doubtless of the same nature with the larger and more violent blasts of lightning which then filled the air.

It were endless to recite minutely the various disasters, fatigues, and terrors which we encountered on this coast; all these went on encreasing till the 22d of May, at which time, the fury of all the storms which we had hitherto encountered, seemed to be combined, and to have conspired our destruction. In this hurricane almost all our sails were split, and great part of our standing rigging broken; and, about eight in the evening, a mountainous overgrown-sea took us upon our starboard-quarter, and gave us so prodigious a shock, that several of our shrouds broke with the jerk, by which our masts were greatly endangered; our ballast and stores too were so strangely shifted, that the ship heeled afterwards two streaks to port. Indeed it was a most

tremendous blow, and we were thrown into the utmost consternation from the apprehension of instantly foundering; and though the wind abated in a few hours, yet, as we had no more sails left in a condition to bend to our yards, the ship laboured very much in a hollow sea, rolling gunwale to, for want of sail to steady her: So that we expected our masts, which were now very slenderly supported, to come by the board every moment. However, we exerted ourselves the best we could to stirrup our shrouds, to reeve new lanyards, and to mend our sails; but while these necessary operations were carrying on, we ran great risque of being driven on shore on the Island of Chiloe, which was not far distant from us; but in the midst of our peril the wind happily shifted to the southward, and we steered off the land with the main-sail only, the Master and myself undertaking the management of the helm, while every one else on board was busied in securing the masts, and bending the sails as fast as they could be repaired. This was the last effort of that stormy climate; for in a day or two after, we got clear of the land, and found the weather more moderate than we had yet experienced since our passing Streights Le Maire. And now having cruized in vain for more than a fortnight in quest of the other ships of the squadron, it was resolved to take the advantage of the present favourable season and the offing we had made from this terrible coast, and to make the best of our way for the Island of Juan Fernandes. For though our next rendezvous was appointed off the harbour of Baldivia, yet as we had hitherto seen none of our companions at this first rendezvous, it was not to be supposed that any of them would be found at the second: Indeed we had the greatest reason to suspect, that all but ourselves had perished. Besides, we were by this time reduced to so low a condition, that instead of attempting to attack the places of the enemy, our utmost hopes could only suggest to us the possibility of saving the ship, and some part of the remaining enfeebled crew, by our speedy arrival at Juan Fernandes; for this was the only road in that part of the world where there was any probability of our recovering our sick, or refitting our vessel, and consequently our getting thither was the only chance we had left to avoid perishing at sea.

Our deplorable situation then allowing no room for deliberation, we stood for the Island of Juan Fernandes; and to save time, which was now extremely precious, (our men dying four, five and six in a day) and likewise to avoid being engaged again with a lee-shore, we resolved, if possible, to hit the Island upon a meridian. And, on the 28th of May, being nearly in the parallel upon which it is laid down, we had great expectations of seeing it: But not finding it in the position in which the charts had taught us to expect it, we began to fear that we had got too far to the westward; and therefore, though the Commodore himself was strongly persuaded, that he saw it on the morning of the 28th, yet his Officers believing it to be only a cloud, to which opinion the haziness of the weather gave some kind of countenance, it was, on a consultation, resolved to stand to the eastward, in the parallel of the Island; as it was certain, that by this course we should either fall in with the Island, if we were already to the westward of it; or should at least make the mainland of Chili, from whence we might take a new departure, and assure ourselves, by running to the westward afterwards, of not missing the Island a second time.

On the 30th of May we had a view of the Continent of Chili, distant about twelve or thirteen leagues; the land made exceeding high and uneven, and appeared quite white; what we saw being doubtless a part of the Cordilleras, which are always covered with snow. Though by this view of the land we ascertained our position, yet it gave us great uneasiness to find that we had so needlessly altered our course, when we were, in all probability just upon the point of making the Island; for the mortality amongst us was now encreased to a most dreadful degree, and those who remained alive were utterly dispirited by this new disappointment, and the prospect of their longer continuance at sea: Our water too began to grow scarce; so that a general dejection prevailed amongst us, which added much to the virulence of the disease, and destroyed numbers of our best men; and to all these calamities there was added this vexatious circumstance, that when, after having got a sight of the Main, we tacked and stood to the westward in quest of the Island, we were so much delayed by calms and contrary winds, that it cost us nine days to regain the westing, which, when we stood to the eastward, we ran down in two. In this desponding condition, with a crazy ship, a great scarcity of fresh water, and a crew so universally diseased, that there were not above ten fore-mast men in a watch capable of doing duty, and even some of these lame, and unable to go aloft: Under these disheartening circumstances, I say, we stood to the westward; and, on the 9th of June, at day-break, we at last discovered the long-wished-for Island of Juan Fernandes. And with this discovery I shall close this chapter and the first book, after observing (which will furnish a very strong image of our unparalleled distresses) that by our suspecting ourselves to be to the westward of the Island on the 28th of May, and, in consequence of this, standing in for the Main, we lost between seventy and eighty of our men, whom we should doubtless have saved had we made the Island that day, which, had we kept on our course for a few hours longer, we could not have failed to have done.

FROM

Blow the Man Down

JAMES H. WILLIAMS

During the nineteenth century, a handful of American writers with firsthand experience of the sea—notably Richard Henry Dana and Herman Melville—sought to awaken their readers to the hardships and exploitations suffered by sailors. At a time when working conditions were universally harsh, no workingmen were more at the mercy of their employers and masters, less protected by legislation and unions, than seamen.

Late in the century, this handful of writers was joined by James H. Williams. A Negro, Williams had gone to sea in 1876 at the age of twelve. His education, as he liked to say, was acquired in the forecastles of a hundred ships. For many years Williams worked to arouse the public's interest in the problems of seamen. He was active in the organization of the Atlantic Coast Seamen's Union. But none of his efforts was more effective than the tales of his own life under sail that appeared in the magazine The Independent *between 1897 and 1921. One of these, reprinted here, recounts his escape from the "blood packet"* Inquisition.

Escape from the Inquisition

IN the latter part of the year 1884, I was paid off and legally discharged from the *Ramirez* in Honolulu. My share of the eightieth lay had netted me $180 in gold. Of course, I was entitled to considerably more, but why complain? A sailor's wages are always what he gets, not what he earns. According to maritime usage under the circumstances, I was also entitled to a passage to the nearest American port where we could be reshipped. But what's the use of going home when you can go anywhere else? I was only a little over twenty years old and the world is wide.

So I carefully sewed up my money in a canvas belt, strapped it securely around my waist next to my skin, and went off in search of another ship. I finally secured a berth in a Nova Scotia bark, the *Redwood*, which was "cleared for Guam," that is to say, she was free to go to any part of the world in ballast where she might secure a charter.

After a rather tiresome and aimless quest, we brought up in Kobe, Japan, where I promptly paid myself off with the jib downhaul [Williams deserted] and went to lodge with Madame Otome in Kita Nagasa Dori Chicome, No. 18. A day or two later, my old frigate sailed, and I was left a free agent again. So I crawled out of my erstwhile place of concealment and boldly surveyed the town.

There were a number of fine sailing ships lying in Kobe Bay at the time and I elected to ship in one of them, the *Inquisition.* I preferred her to any of the other ships because she had just been chartered to trade on the Asiatic coast for three years and I thought it would afford me a fine opportunity to visit a wide variety of ports and broaden my sphere of experience. So it did, greatly to my ultimate sorrow and regret.

From Kobe, we went to Nagasaki and loaded coal for Iloilo in the Philippine Islands; from thence we went to Hong Kong in ballast for orders. That short voyage was a drill to be remembered. I had already been to sea about eight years but was now to have my eyes opened to the real character of tyrannical skippers and "bucko" mates and Yankee "hell ships," of which I had heard so often and so much. No language is severe enough to depict adequately the outrages I witnessed on that short coasting trip. We were continually hazed and hounded like wild beasts, driven like dumb cattle, beaten like mules, and worked like galley slaves. We were never allowed even to speak, to pass even the most casual remarks to each other while at work. We were deprived of our watches below, kept on our bare whack of food on a coast where fresh food was both abundant and cheap, reviled and cursed from morning to night, and constantly watched over by half a dozen burly, brutal, irresponsible lynx-eyed monsters who called themselves *officers.*

The slightest inadvertence on the part of any member of crew—to drop a spot of tar or paint on deck or even to ask a shipmate for a chew of tobacco—was always considered an infraction of the rules, and the unfortunate offender would be promptly attacked with a perfect hail of blows delivered with any article of hardware that might come to hand, accompanied by the vilest of epithets and the most frightful of curses.

Why did we meekly submit to such inhuman abuse? Because even the least word of protest or sign of resistance was insubordination punishable by "tricing up," chaining down, or imprisonment in the lazarette on hard bread and water as the master might direct. Open self-defense was mutiny, punishable by years of imprisonment in the penitentiary. United action was piracy and carried a death penalty. To beat or wound or starve or overwork a seaman was not even a crime under the then existing medieval maritime law—it was only discipline. Such was the substance of the law; resistance was out of the question.

The *Inquisition* was a large, stately clipper: a perfect specimen of that most graceful, elegant, and beautiful of all sailing craft, the American East Indiaman. In every detail of her construction and equipment she showed, in its highest development, the subtle cunning and wondrous skill of the shipbuilder's art—light, lofty, tapering masts and spars towering majestically on high above her snow-white decks; erect in stays, symmetrical in design, correct in rake and alignment, perfect in general proportions, and complete in artistic finish, with sheer, high, graceful bows and gilded scrollwork on her classically carved "fiddlehead"; broad and ornate overhanging stern and neatly molded run to emphasize the even contour of her exquisitely rounded ends. What a pity that such an inspiring marvel of elegant perfection, delicate grace, usefulness, and majestic power should be made a floating torture house, a "blood packet," a beautifully sculptured shelter for human misery, grief, and despair, inhuman, fiendish cruelty, and wanton, unrestricted barbarities.

Our skipper's name was Gammon, and no man in the American merchant marine was ever more widely known, more sincerely hated, or more thoroughly detested by honest seamen the world over than he. He was a spare-built, wiry man about fifty years of age with thin, iron-gray hair, cold, cunning, heartless, ferret-like eyes, a flaming brandy knob on the end of his nose, and a face so sharp you could have split kindling wood with it. He had a shrill, squeaking, querulous voice entirely in keeping with his features. An irascible, peevish temper and a strong weakness for Three Star brandy rounded out his personality. The word honor was not in his vocabulary. He proudly and frequently boasted that he had "never paid off a son of a —— of a sailor yet," and he'd be damned if he ever would.

The chief mate, Mr. Roarer, was a big, rawboned, iron-faced giant with a roar like a lion, arms like capstan bars, and fingers like belaying pins. He was a Canadian, quite as unprincipled as the captain in his way, and he could always be depended upon to do the latter's dirty work without question. His chief claim to distinction was that he had "never seen a —— —— sailor yet" that he couldn't lick.

The second mate, whose name was Prettyman, was a tall, lanky, loose-jointed, squint-eyed "Bluenoser" from the wilds of Nova Scotia. His features were not in his favor, for he had a low beetling forehead surmounted by a mop of bristling, fiery red hair, a broken nose, and a deeply scarred face. His claim to fame lay in his truculent, overbearing disposition, his incessant flow of naval profanity, the amazing dexterity and accuracy with which he could hurl belaying pins about, and his wonderful ability to kick with both feet. All these useful and highly professional accomplishments greatly endeared him to the heart of the hatchet-faced little skipper, so that he really was considered somebody on board in spite of his repulsive features and ungainly appearance.

There were also a third mate, a bos'n, a carpenter, and some other inferior supernumeraries, but they are not worth mentioning. All were domineering bullies, bull drivers, and brutes selected by the Old Man for their detestable characters rather than for their ability to work.

Our crew was composed of the usual mixed and motley crowd of vagrant unfortunates commonly assembled to fill out the complement of a deepwater ship. Nearly every nationality and tribe among the human race was represented. Only two were native Americans, myself and a young Gloucester fisherman named Al Staples, who had been enticed into a crimping den while on a spree in Boston. He had been fleeced and robbed and subsequently shanghaied for one year's service in the *Inquisition.* Staples was the only member of the original crew which had sailed from Boston. All the rest had deserted to a man, and the present crew had been recruited, just as I had been, among the different ports touched at since.

From Hong Kong, the *Inquisition* was ordered to Saigon in French Cochin China to load teakwood timber for export. While there, we were never allowed a moment's respite from hard, bone-racking labor. It was midsummer, with long twilights at each end of the day, and the weather was terribly hot as well as very unhealthy. Yet we were turned to with lamps in the hold every morning and knocked off by lamplight every night. On the Sabbath, we were given special consideration. We did not begin work in the morning until daylight and we were permitted to quit at dusk. We were usually allowed half an hour for meals and ten minutes for our early coffee at four in the morning.

After the coal dirt from the previous cargo had been removed, we had to wash out the hold as clean as a housewife's kitchen floor. Then came the painful, excruciating job of dry holystoning the 'tween decks, a performance as unnecessary and useless as it was difficult and laborious. For two long, tedious weeks we were kept constantly at work on our knees with those damnable holystones and infernal "prayerbooks" until we were all practically cripples. It was the refinement of inquisitorial torture.

Then came the timber—great, massive, square-cut monoliths of solid teak. Thereafter, four men were told off every day to stow cargo below decks, and the remainder of the crew was kept at work aloft or anywhere else about the ship. The hold gang was changed every morning, so that, by turns, we all worked at the delicate operation of stowing timber under the gentle objurgations and persuasive caresses of Mr. Prettyman and a big stick.

We lay offshore and, of course, the timber had to be lightered off to us. When the lower hold began to fill up so as to make it necessary to jam the top courses under the deck beams, we found it impossible for four men to stow the timber as fast as a horde of howling coolies could heave it through the side ports. Therefore, it was decided one morning at breakfast time to ask for more help below. The hold gang for that day consisted of an old Irish sailor named Paddy, the oldest man in the ship; a young Swede named Lars; a Dane whom we had nicknamed "Dutchy"; and my special chum, Edward Murray.

No sooner had we bolted our frugal breakfast of lobscouse and hardtack, washed it down with "patent marine coffee" sweetened with "long lick," and got a hasty five minutes' session with our pipes, than we heard our ever alert and energetic bos'n, Jack Bender, roaring at the top of his stentorian voice: "Turn to, there, for'ard; look alive there, now, you d—d loafers!"

Then, before the echo of the bos'n's summons had ceased to reverberate among the spars, the second mate thrust his hideous features through the forecastle and bellowed out: "Come on here, now, you —— —— —— ——s! Comin' out like men, er yer want ter be dragged out like lazy dogs? Come, shake 'er up now, er I'll come in there an' help some o' you lazy ——s over ther stopwater!"

In response to these gentle admonitions, we all scrambled hastily on deck to resume our appointed tasks. Mr. Prettyman went down the hatch, as usual, to bully the hold gang. It had been previously arranged among the timber Jacks and acceded to by Paddy himself that he, being the oldest man in the group, should act as spokesman for the rest in asking for extra help. Accordingly, as soon as the second mate got below, Paddy, addressing him with all possible civility, said: "Mr. Purttyman, she's gittin' that full agin th' bames now we can't shtow th' logs as fasht as the' divils o' nagurs do be stevin' thim in, an' we nades a few more min down here ter kape up wid 'em."

"More help ye want, is it, yer —— —— lazy old stiff; I'll gie yer more help, plenty uv it!" And with these words, he struck old Paddy a terrific blow between the eyes, knocking him prostrate. But the old man, though hurt and dazed, was still game and as soon as he could regain his feet he bravely attempted to retaliate on his tormentor. It was then the real cowardly nature of the unprincipled brute became manifest, for, instead of trying to repel the old man's feeble attack in the natural way, which he could easily have done, he whipped out a murderous-looking dirk from his belt.

But the instant the second mate attempted to use the knife on old Paddy, Edward Murray, who stood directly behind him, struck him a powerful blow on the head with a slice bar and knocked him senseless. Then the four men, maddened beyond endurance by months of constant hazing and unmerited abuse, all leaped upon the prostrate form of the fallen bucko and beat him unmercifully. They only desisted when they believed him dead, and Murray told me afterward it was their united determination at the time to kill him. Had they suspected that there still remained a single vestige of the spark of life in his detestable carcass, they would never have left him until it had been stamped out.

The noise of the fracas, however, had attracted the ever vigilant attention of the fallen bully's buckos up on deck and they soon came swarming below, all armed to the teeth with shooting irons and various kinds of cutlery. The four men were soon secured and brought on deck. There they were quickly triced up to the forward boat skids by stout loops of tarred spun yarn tightly seized around their thumbs.

We had a Chinese cook named Me-Chow, one of the "whitest" men I ever knew. Shortly after the men had been strung up, Me-Chow, unable to bear their agonizing screams, ran out of the galley with a carving knife with the humane intention of cutting them down. But he was quickly frustrated in his Christian intentions by the alert third mate and bos'n, who were mounting guard for the express purpose of preventing just such a plot on the part of any members of the crew. Divining his charitable purpose, the two ruffians quickly pounced upon the poor Chinaman, and in a jiffy the unfortunate Mongolian was strung up by his pigtail beside the four seamen he had tried to rescue.

And so the five unfortunate men were left hanging in the broiling sun with the tips of their toes barely touching the planks beneath them from nine in the forenoon until two in the afternoon. Their shrieks could be heard all over the harbor, but there was none to succor them. At frequent intervals, they became unconscious; then, they would be lowered until they revived, probably on the principle that an unconscious man is cheating his persecutors because he is insensible to pain; then, the moment they revived they would be promptly strung up to the gallows once more. Their prayers for mercy were as unavailing as their supplications for water.

While in a paroxysm of delirious anguish, Edward Murray began to call down all manner of insane curses upon Captain Gammon and his fiendish mates. Whereupon, the bos'n seized an oaken heaver from a gypsy winch and struck the poor, writhing wretch a terrible blow in the mouth, knocking out all his front teeth. Such was one phase of disciplinary punishment as practiced on some of our stately, ornate clippers in the palmy days of our glorious and incomparable merchant marine.

After this frightful spectacle had been enacted in the presence of all beholders in the harbor of Saigon, every precaution was taken to prevent any authentic tidings of it from getting ashore. No one was allowed to leave the ship under any pretext whatsoever. No sampans were allowed alongside except the official bumboat. Every evening Captain Gammon and his group of official ruffians would sit together for hours on the poop deck shooting at the "jolly boat" sampans to keep them at a respectful distance from the vessel; and every night as soon as the crew had quit work we were all locked in the stifling superheated forecastle for the night lest any of us should try to escape.

It was the most terrible experience mortal men ever endured and survived. When we returned to Hong Kong a few weeks later, the tortured were still unable to resume work. Their hands and arms were still terribly swollen and discolored from the long-sustained compression of their thumbs while triced up, and the cook's scalp had been nearly torn from his pate by the long spell of suspension he had endured.

Yet none of them had received any medical relief or other attention from aft. At Hong Kong, as at Saigon, no one was allowed ashore. The only change in the previous regime was that we were no longer locked in the forecastle at night, for Hong Kong, as a British port, had laws governing maritime practices and protecting seamen which were more strictly observed there than in other parts of China.

While the ship lay in Hong Kong, young Staples' term of service expired and he demanded his money and discharge. But this request the weasel-faced skipper wrathfully refused to consider and told Staples that he might get paid off when the ship returned to the United States, if he ever lived to see it.

That night, Staples slacked himself quietly over the side and swam ashore. He hung around the waterfront until morning and then went to the American consul's office, reported his own situation, pressed his demand for wages and discharge, and told of the crucifixion at Saigon. The American consul at Hong Kong at that time was a Southerner, an ex-Confederate army officer notoriously unfavorable toward seamen, however meritorious their cause, but doubly so if they happened to be Northerners. He could not very well overlook Staples' claim to wages, but he could shirk his duty toward the injured seamen on the technical ground of lack of jurisdiction, and that is precisely what he did.

Later in the day, the skipper, after receiving a summons, arrived and talked with the consul for some time. When they came out they persuaded young Staples to take a sampan and go off to the ship for his pay, as, it was explained to him, this arrangement would be more convenient since the captain had all his money and papers locked up in his cabin on board.

In youthful innocence, Staples foolishly agreed to this plan, went off to the ship, packed up his bag, and waited for the captain's return. As soon as the Old Man came on board, he ordered Staples aft to receive his pay. Staples found the captain seated at the cabin table with a bag of money and the ship's papers before him.

The young fellow had ninety dollars in gold due him, and this the Old Man counted out in shining gold pieces with rare good will, as Staples thought. He then turned the shipping articles and a prepared receipt for ninety dollars toward the seaman and pointed out to him where to sign "clear" and sign "off." The moment Staples affixed his signature to both papers, Captain Gammon sprang up, covered the little pile of shiners with one hand, pressed a loaded revolver against the boy's head with the other, and yelled: "Now, you ——————, git out of my cabin an' jump over the side quicker'n greased lightnin'! I'll teach you, you —— skunk, to sneak up to the consulate an' make complaints ag'in me and my ship." So the lad was chased up the companion way at the point of the captain's gun and driven ashore bareheaded and penniless.

"There ye are," sneered the skipper derisively, leaning over the taffrail and waving the articles exultantly at the poor hoodwinked sailor as the sampan shoved off for the beach, "there ye are; you've got yer pay fer makin' complaints, an' I've got yer receipt fer ther money. Now ye kin go ashore an' complain an' be damned. That's how I pay all my men. Me, ol' Cap'n Gammon. T'ell wi' yer."

The next day, the crucified men were taken ashore and given a mock hearing at the consulate. But, as already intimated, the case was officially set aside on the convenient point of maritime jurisdiction. All the afterguard, excluding the third mate, who was left in charge of the ship, went as witnesses for the master, but not one of the crew was taken to testify for the aggrieved seamen.

As soon as the captain had made his statement to the effect that these four men had mutinied, made an unprovoked attack on the second mate with intent to murder him, and had afterward run amuck in an effort to induce the entire crew to mutiny and take charge of the ship, the consul formally and finally dismissed the complaint against the captain and officers and ordered the four injured seamen back to the ship without even hearing a word of their testimony in rebuttal. When the poor fellows revealed their still helpless and distorted hands, and when Edward Murray pointed to his battered mouth and broken teeth and mumbled an almost unintelligible plea for justice, the only reply he received from the "dignified" United States representative was: "Tut! Tut! Say another word and I'll give you six months' shot drill! Go back to your ship and do your duty like men, and the captain may feel disposed to forgive you. I've no jurisdiction in this matter. If I had I'd send you all up for mutiny and attempted piracy."

As a matter of fact and of justice, and in accordance with the established and accepted principles of admiralty law the world over, he did have jurisdiction, for the men had been arbitrarily denied the right of recourse or appeal either to the local consul or to port authorities at Saigon. This was a fair sample of consular justice as meted out to American seamen in the early 1880's.

After the affair at the consul's office, we were granted a little more freedom and treated with a little more leniency by the afterguard. This was simply a matter of policy, of course, on the skipper's part, but we accepted it for what it was worth and made the most of it.

One fine morning, just after breakfast, we were all astounded by the sudden announcement that the port watch was ordered aft to receive liberty money and go ashore for the day. We naturally thought that such welcome news was a hoax, but started aft with palpitating hearts to investigate.

But sure enough, there stood the Old Man at the coach-house door, where he doled out five Mexican dollars to each of us, telling us to go ashore and be good and be sure to return on board before turn-to time next morning. He also added that we should have free sampan fare both ways if we were on time.

Then, with the generous, forgiving dispositions of deepwater sailors, we promptly forgot all our recent sufferings and sorrows and tribulations in our exuberant, overwhelming gratitude for one day's respite from our hardship and toil. So we left the ship's side as lighthearted and jubilant as schoolboys released for recess, with three ringing cheers for the *Inquisition* as though she had been a prince consort to the famous missionary ship *Morning Star*.

The little diversions we enjoyed that day are not a part of this story, but one incident of my own experience is significant in view of what followed after. In Typhooshang, in Hong Kong, I met a quartermaster from an English steamer lying at one of the docks in front of the city. During our conversation, I told him of what had occurred on board the *Inquisition* and of my present anxiety to leave her.

There is a feeling of tacit freemasonry among deepwater sailors which always bids them help each other in distress and which does not take race, nationality, or color into account. The young Englishman fully understood my plight and volunteered to assist me or any of my shipmates who could reach his steamer after midnight or any time during her stay in port. As he always went on watch at midnight, he said he would try to find means of stowing us away until sailing time; after that there would be nothing to fear. On that particular night, he explained, he would not be on duty as he was ashore on twenty-four hours' leave. The steamer's name, he told me, was the *Sandon*, of Sunderland; like our own ship, she was chartered for a term of years on the coast, and she was scheduled to lay at Hong Kong three days longer. We parted late that evening with many expressions of friendship, and I went directly on board my own ship and turned in.

Next morning, all our boys showed up punctually at turn-to time with the exception of one or two laggards who were brought out later in the police boat and charged three dollars apiece for their ride. That day, the starboard watch went ashore and all went smoothly.

The idea of deserting grew upon me with the passing hours, and the more I thought about it the more determined I became to chance it. Of course, I could slip over the side unobserved in the darkness and swim ashore, but where would I hide? The captain would undoubtedly offer a reward for my apprehension and return. For this reason, I also considered it unwise to swim to the *Sandon* and take my friendly quartermaster at his word to stow me away, for once the hue and cry was raised every policeman and coolie in Hong Kong would be alert for my recapture and every ship in port would be thoroughly searched.

Moreover, I had a splendid outfit of clothes, the result of eight years of hard gathering and worth at least one hundred American dollars, which I hated to leave behind. A sailor without dunnage in a foreign port is in a hopeless position.

But I had long since decided that the *Inquisition* was no place for me. I felt sure that the sudden show of kindness exhibited toward us by Captain Gammon was only the merest pretense, a temporary truce which would be ended as soon as we left Hong Kong and got out of earshot of the port authorities.

The more I became possessed with the idea of desertion, the more determined I was to act. According to the universal custom in Far Eastern ports, Captain Gammon assigned a bumboat to the ship to supply us with such articles as we needed or wanted, such as clothes, small stores, tobacco, and food, rather than give us the opportunity to buy where we pleased.

The bumboat man, of course, took full advantage of his situation and charged the sailors three prices for his third-rate wares. He then paid the captain 50-per-cent commission for the privilege of robbing the crew.

Our bumboat man was an oily-mouthed, smooth-eyed, two-faced Mongolian whom everybody detested but with whom we were obliged to deal. He was known among the sailors frequenting the port by the somewhat opprobrious cognomen of "Cumshaw," which is pidgin English for "commission." Like all of his type, he was artful and cunning, utterly unscrupulous, cruel, treacherous, and as avaricious as old Shylock himself.

When Cumshaw came on board that particular morning, I invested much more liberally in his wares than usual and craftily induced some of my unsuspecting shipmates to do the same. Cumshaw was so highly pleased with my unwonted interest in his behalf that he gave me a fine camphorwood box and a couple of small curios by way of "baksheesh."

Having thus gotten into the good graces of the crafty Cumshaw, I coaxed him aside and offered him ten Mexican dollars to scull me ashore with my belongings after midnight that night. I took pains to exhibit the money as an evidence of good faith, and I could tell by the greedy twinkle of his wicked little almond eyes that it was a bargain. He simply could not resist the sight of money; it really was his god and high joss.

So it was agreed between us that he should come after me that night at two o'clock and take me ashore. With this understanding, we parted. Cumshaw sculled ashore, and I went about my day's work as usual with a head and a heart full of plans for the impending adventure.

Punctual to the minute, Cumshaw sculled his sampan silently beneath our bows while I sat on the knightheads with my bag ready packed and slung to the end of the jib downhaul ready for immediate departure. I was soon in the boat, dun and dunnage, and we sculled away into the darkness propelled by the long, half-rotary sweeps of the Chinaman's powerful oar.

Cumshaw sculled directly up to a deserted jetty fronting the native settlement on the extreme outskirts of the coolie quarter. Making his sampan fast, he shouldered my heavy bag and piloted me through a mystic maze of narrow, crooked, dark, and filthy streets until he came to a small but neat native house with two quaint but hideous-looking wooden images standing guard in the doorway. The diabolical grimaces which distorted their graven features were accentuated and rendered more intensely repulsive by a shaft of subdued light which fell athwart them through the glazed paper window.

Here Cumshaw dropped my bag and gave a low call. The door was promptly opened by an aged Chinese woman, and we walked in. We were evidently expected, for the woman seemed in nowise surprised by our sudden intrusion at such an unearthly hour. The ground floor of the house appeared to be divided into two rooms separated by sliding partitions. Overhead was a loft which was reached by a ladder extending from the floor below to a scuttle in the floor of the tiny attic above.

The interior of the house was perfectly neat and clean. It showed consistent attention, thrift, and simple good taste. The furniture was a sort of compromise between European and Chinese designs evidently intended to suit all comers. For instance, there were European tables and chairs for the accommodation of white guests, and low tables and squat mats for the convenience of native guests. There were, likewise, common plates and cups and saucers and knives and forks for the use of white people, and chopsticks and chow bowls for native service. A Yankee clock, made in Connecticut, ornamented a small shelf in one corner of the room, and a large American lamp with an enameled bowl stood upon an ordinary drop-leaf table and shed a brilliant light over the whole scene by the illuminating properties of Standard Oil. The walls were decorated in the usual Chinese fashion with painted paper flowers, fans, birds, and dragons, and further ornamented with hand-painted pictures of the familiar Chinese conception.

On the whole, the house was quite comfortable and attractive, and to my way-weary, homesick eyes it appeared like a haven of refuge and heavenly relief from the abominable surroundings on board the *Inquisition*.

After a brief conversation with the old woman who had admitted us, the exact import of which I could not, of course, understand, Cumshaw turned to me and said, pointing to the old crone by way of introduction, "Dis my ol' mama; him velly good ooman; muchee likee sailorman; s'pose you pay two dollar, t'ree dollar, you stop two day, t'ree day; plenty eatee, plenty sleepee, mama givee plentee chow—velly good chow. By'm'by, mornin' time, my sister comee; my sister velly smart gallee, go Clistian skulee, speakee plentee Inglese, you by'm'by makee plenty chin-chin. By'm'by you s'ip go 'way, me come tellee you, you takee 'nother s'ip homeside. Savvy?"

I savvied and paid Cumshaw the promised ten dollars and gave "old mama" three dollars more for chow; then Cumshaw departed and I retired to rest on a comfortable bamboo couch in the cockloft.

Next morning, "old mama" called me to breakfast, and when I descended to the ground floor I met a young Chinese girl who might have been anywhere from ten to thirteen years old. She was seated demurely on a bamboo settee, but rose timidly to greet me as I came down the ladder. This was the alleged sister Cumshaw had referred to the night before. "Old mama" brought me clean water in an earthen basin, a ball of soap, and a large towel. After a refreshing splurge in the basin and a brisk session with the towel, I sat down to breakfast, an enjoyable repast at which "old mama" and the girl modestly declined to join me. It consisted of rice, prepared as only an Oriental can boil it, with every grain an individual tempting factor of the meal; small fishes deliciously cooked in oil, fresh duck eggs, water cress, vegetables, fresh wheat bread, and fragrant tea. After breakfast, "old mama" presented me with a package of cigarros and I proceeded to smoke and while away the time in an effort to draw the little girl out and induce her to talk about herself. She was very timid and shy at first, but by degrees her reserve melted, so that at the end of an hour or so we were on the most familiar and sociable terms.

She spoke excellent English with a very pretty accent and seemed to be in all respects entirely natural and childish. She said she had attended one of the mission schools almost from infancy, and that she was anxious to learn to teach. She also told me that she was not Cumshaw's sister (I had suspected as much), but his cousin, and that "old mama" was her grandmother and Cumshaw's aunt, not his mother, as he had intimated.

It was rather irksome sitting in the house all day with nothing to do, and I was hopeful that Cumshaw would drop in in the evening and bring me some tidings of the ship. I dared not go out for fear of being observed, for information travels fast among the Mongolians, especially when you don't want it to.

After dinner, the little girl returned to her school duties and left me more lonesome than ever, for "old mama" could neither utter nor understand a syllable of English. After a hearty supper, I got a book out of my bag and sat down to read until ten o'clock. Then I went aloft and turned in and was soon fast asleep.

I had not slept long, however, when I was suddenly awakened by the bright glare of a bull's-eye lantern shining full in my face, a rough hand shaking me by the shoulder, and a loud voice commanding me in good, vigorous Anglo-Saxon to "get up and dress."

I started up in bed and my astonished gaze fell upon two uniformed British police and Cumshaw's cunning snakelike eyes peering at me sardonically from the background. Then the whole situation dawned upon me like a flash. Cumshaw had betrayed me! I was under arrest and would be sentenced without trial to three years in purgatory on board the *Inquisition!* I got out of bed mechanically and began slowly and absent-mindedly to dress.

"What is the meaning of this, Officer?" I asked as though I didn't know.

"Hit means that you are under arrest," replied one of them, drawing a queen's warrant about a fathom long from his breast pocket, "on a charge of desertion from the American ship *Inquisition,* and we are under orders to deliver you back to that ship and its master. Do you want to hear the warrant read?"

"Yes," I replied, "you might as well do everything in regular order." I was not at all anxious to hear the warrant, but I wanted to gain time to collect my thoughts. So I let him wade through the long rigmarole of legalistic terms while in the meantime I fumbled nervously into my clothes. As soon as the officer had concluded the perusal of the warrant, I announced myself ready to go. While he was replacing the document in his breast pocket and buttoning up his coat, I asked how they came to know where I was.

"Why," said the officer, "as soon as you were missed the captain posted a reward of twenty dollars in gold with the Hamerican consul for your happrehension, and this Chink 'ere," indicating Cumshaw, "went up and hinformed on you to claim the reward; not hoften these beggars see twenty dollars in gold, you know."

"'Ow came you to leave the ship?" asked the other officer, who until now had remained silent.

"Because she was a floating hell," I answered, "like too many of our American and Nova Scotia blood packets." Then I mentioned briefly some of the horrors which had occurred on board and how poor Staples had been paid off at Hong Kong.

"Hit's a bloody houtrage," said the first officer feelingly, "an' h'I don't min' tellin' you, pore chap, as we don't 'arf like this yere job; but duty is duty, you know, an' we must hobey horders."

"I understand your position in the matter perfectly," I said, "and I sincerely thank you for your sympathy; so I'll go aboard with you without protest and face whatever is coming to me. I suppose you want to shackle me," I added, extending my hands toward them in token of humility.

"Naw!" exclaimed one officer disdainfully. "We ain't got no darbies with us and h'I wouldn't put 'em on you if we 'ad. You don't look like a troublesome chap an' you're a good lad, any'ow."

We descended the ladder and went out into the night. A drizzling rain was falling, a sort of "Scotch mist"; there was not a breath of wind. I walked silently along between the two policemen, Cumshaw preceding us with my bag on his shoulder through the maze of narrow streets leading by devious routes toward the quay.

Cumshaw's sampan was moored to the same little jetty where I had landed the previous night. The surface of the water was as placid as a millpond and the night was as dark as night ever was.

Without a word of ceremony, we entered the sampan and

cast off. My bag was placed in the bows, the two officers seated themselves together in the stern sheets, while I took my place on a thwart just in front of them. Cumshaw took his position just forward of me, shipped his long, curved, and jointed sculling oar on the little knob which held it to the gunwale and gave way with long, regular sweeps back and forth in the ancient but efficient Chinese style.

So we started upstream against a swift ebb tide, our way illumined only by the faint glow from the little colza oil lamp burning dimly on our stem. Such a tumult of passionate thoughts as assailed my mind as I sat in that swaying sampan I have never experienced before or since. I knew that to return to the ship meant three years of brutal slavery under the most barbarous taskmasters that ever wielded a lash. I would be constantly subjected to every degree of humiliating drudgery, torture, abuse, and inquisitive punishment that devilish ingenuity could devise. There would be no chance of redress and no prospect of pay at the end. I well knew the character of the men with whom I should have to deal and that for three years to come I would be entirely at their fiendish mercy without hope of succor, escape, or relief. I would be triced up, shackled down, kicked, cuffed, beaten, maimed, starved, or killed according to the whim of Captain Gammon and his horde of "buckos." At every port we touched, I would be chained to a ringbolt or locked down in the lazarette to prevent me from escaping.

This was my future if I returned on board. From what I knew of American ships in general and the *Inquisition* in particular, I felt that my mental picture did not exaggerate my probable fate. These thoughts in conjunction with my helpless, hopeless position in the sampan almost maddened me, and I began to cast about wildly for some means of escape. To leap overboard and try to get away by swimming would be useless; to attack the two big, well-armed policemen would be equally futile and even more foolhardy.

At length, as we wended our way through the assembled merchant fleet riding lazily at anchor, I could discern the outlines of the *Inquisition* swinging idly at her cables. I could tell her even in the almost impenetrable darkness, partly by her position, but

mainly by long familiarity with her long, low, sneaking hull, the graceful outline of her bows, and the exact rake and slender, tapering symmetry of her lofty spars, so different from those of other ships in the harbor.

Yes, I saw her, a black, infernal specter silhouetted against the night, and the sight aroused me to desperation and awakened within me the determination of despair.

Then my gaze rested for a moment on the dim figure of the Chinese traitor laboring strongly at his oar, as unconcerned about my future as though I had been a mad dog.

And then my blood boiled with ungovernable rage and consuming hatred toward this man who had betrayed me, who would sell me into slavery for money earned with the wringing of my own heart's blood. Then as I surveyed the swaying figure at the oar, a desperate resolve entered my brain and took possession of my whole being. "If I could get rid of him and that infernal oar," I thought, "I might have one chance."

Lying across the thwarts in the sampan was a short length of a small English oar with the blade sawed off. It was five feet of oaken shaft, a most convenient and effective bludgeon. I had noticed it several times in the sampan before I left the ship but had never been interested enough then to ask Cumshaw where he got it. I presume, however, that he had salvaged it from the flotsam and jetsam adrift in the bay.

This oar shaft was now within easy reach, and I clutched one end of it firmly with my left hand. Then, for a brief interval, having made sure of my weapon, I watched the dim figure swaying back and forth in the murky darkness with his long queue moving with pendulum-like regularity with each stroke.

Behind me, I could hear the two officers conversing in low tones, apparently satisfied that their task was to be an easy one and that it was about over. I realized that any chance of possible success must be dependent upon my own quickness of action and sureness of aim, but I was young, strong, and nimble, as well as desperate, and, therefore, ready to take a chance.

So, watching my opportunity, just as Cumshaw started on an outward stroke, I suddenly arose and struck him with crushing force on the back of the head with that oar shaft. He fairly flew over the edge of the sampan, taking the sculling oar with him in a blind, deathlike clutch. Then, before the astonished officers could interfere, I jumped quickly over the other side and swam down.

The sampan, caught in the surge of a powerful current, was swept rapidly downstream, and since the officers had nothing with which to propel or control their clumsy craft they were entirely at the mercy of the elements. As for me, I swam underwater as long as possible to make a good offing from the sampan. When I came up to blow, I could hear the officers shouting and shooting blindly into the darkness.

As soon as I arose to the surface, I made a tangent for the shore. I could tell the direction by the thousands of lights gleaming thickly along the waterfront and more thinly scattered up the slopes of the great hills overlooking the city.

As I swam toward the shore, I could hear the shouting and the shooting of the forsaken officers growing fainter and fainter as they drifted rapidly downstream. My only fear now was that the racket they made might alarm some of the harbor police and that I might be pursued and recaptured.

In order to accelerate my own movements in contending with the strong current, I stripped off and jettisoned all my clothing, retaining only the cherished money belt around my waist. Farther inshore, the tide rift slackened and I was able to strike out with long sweeping strokes direct for the port. As soon as I got near enough to the quays to locate the *Sandon,* I swam directly down to her and climbed up her gangway dripping like a half-drowned rat.

As I had surmised, it was past midnight and my friendly quartermaster was on watch.

"Good God, mate!" he exclaimed, as I stood glistening in my naked skin in the glare of the gangway lantern. "Is that you? 'Ow in 'ell did yer get hoff 'er?"

I briefly related my night's experiences.

"Come down for'ard, lad," he said, "but be quiet. We'll gi' you a passage down to the Straits, an' you'll be clear o' the blame Yankee 'ell 'ook."

Fifteen minutes later, I was clad in a dry suit of clothes, supplied with food, a pipe, and tobacco. I then turned into a good, comfortable bunk and enjoyed a sound and dreamless sleep.

Next morning, the *Sandon* cast off her shore fasts and steamed out of Hong Kong en route to Singapore, 1450 miles farther down the coast. I had escaped from the *Inquisition!*

FROM

Seven Came Through

EDWARD V. RICKENBACKER

Twenty-five years after he won fame as America's top air ace in World War I, Captain Edward V. Rickenbacker, president of Eastern Air Lines, was called back into his country's service. As a special consultant to Secretary of War Henry L. Stimson, he was dispatched in 1942 to visit combat air bases, first in England, Ireland, and Iceland, then in the South Pacific. On October 21, 1942, he left Hawaii aboard a Flying Fortress for "Island X," some 1800 miles to the southwest. He never arrived. Lost in the vast expanses of the Pacific, its fuel exhausted, the bomber crash-landed on the heaving ocean. From their three rubber life rafts, its eight crewmen and passengers watched the plane quickly sink.

Twenty-one days later, Navy planes spotted seven survivors. In these pages, Rickenbacker recalls the first eight days of that grim experience, which were the worst of the entire ordeal.

The Rafts

THE line around my waist was now put to good use. Because the wind and seas were fast sweeping the rafts apart, I called the others in and, fastening the rope to the hand lines around the rafts, we formed a line astern, twenty feet or so apart. Cherry being captain, his raft was first, mine was second, and the two-man raft brought up the rear. The arrangement had its drawbacks. In the heavy swell, as the rafts rose and fell at their different intervals, the interminable, uneven shocks on the line made rest impossible. But I shall always believe that, had we separated, few if any of us would now be alive. A strong man may last a long time alone, but men together somehow manage to last longer.

My memory of that first afternoon is not wholly clear. The spray and the green water coming over the roll of the raft kept us soaked, and I bailed for hours with my hat—my wonderful old hat. This gave me exercise, besides keeping me from thinking too much.

Some time during the afternoon we totted up our possessions. The only food was four oranges that Cherry had stuffed in his pocket just before the crash, together with the chocolate bar that I had and half a dozen more that Alex had, which an Army doctor had given him the day before. The chocolate was never eaten. Alex's was ruined by his thrashing around in the water and he had to throw it way. Next day, when I felt in the pocket for mine, it had become a green mush, which neither I nor my companions would touch.

So, except for the oranges, we started with nothing. But knowing that a man can live a long time without food or water, I was more worried over the shortage of clothing. Only Adamson and I were fully dressed. He had his uniform and cap and I had on a blue summer-weight business suit, complete with necktie, pocket handkerchief, and refillable pencil. The others, expecting to swim, had taken off their shoes and hats before abandoning ship. None had hats or sweaters, but the two pilots had their leather jackets. Several had even thrown their socks away. Bartek, in fact, was naked except for a one-piece jumper.

I may have forgotten an item or two, but these were our total possessions: a first-aid kit, eighteen flares, and one Very pistol for firing them; two hand pumps for both bailing and renewing the air in the rafts; two service sheath knives; a pair of pliers; a small pocket compass; two revolvers belonging to Cherry and Adamson; two collapsible rubber bailing buckets; three sets of patching gear, one for each raft; several pencils; and my map of the Pacific. We all had cigarettes, but the salt water got to these immediately, and they were thrown away. And, finally, Reynolds produced two fish lines, with hooks attached, which he had snatched from a parachute bag after the crash. But there was no bait, and unless we managed to shoot down a gull, our chances of "living off the country" were decidedly thin.

But that first afternoon no one was conscious of our poverty; we were too exhausted to care. Three or four of the boys were violently seasick and I didn't feel any too comfortable myself, although I never reached the point of vomiting. Adamson was in agony from his wrenched back; every jerk of the boat, he said, felt as if someone was kicking him in the kidneys. But I was more worried about Sergeant Alex, in the little raft astern. Long after the others had stopped, he continued to retch. "What's the matter with him?" I called to De Angelis. "I don't know," answered De Angelis. "He must have swallowed a lot of salt water when we tipped over."

The sun went down swiftly, a cold mist gathering on the sea, and the moon came up—a three-quarter moon—beautiful to see. The wisecracks and the small talk, which sounded pretty silly in the immensity of the night, petered out and we were beginning to realize that we were in for hard times.

Naturally, one of the first things we had to do was to work out some organization of habits. Keeping a continuous watch—what we called an alert—was an obvious necessity. That first night we arranged to stand two-hour watches, relieving each other in turn. It seems pretty silly now, but I offered $100 to the first man to see land, a ship, or an airplane. But nobody slept that night. We were wet and miserable. Although the swell moderated just before midnight, the waves kept slopping into the rafts. Both air and water were warm, yet with each splash I felt as if I was being doused with buckets of ice water. Bartek and I changed positions every hour or so, to share the comfort of the other's lee. But I was never warm, and put in most of the night bailing. Sharks followed us from the plane; the water seemed full of them.

The second day came on slowly, first a gray mist and then the sun breaking through clear. It took hours to get warm, for the night mist penetrated to the bone. As I have said, we had those four oranges, but we decided to save them against the future. By popular vote I was made their custodian, and Cherry generously handed them over. We agreed to divide the first that morning, and the others on alternate days. That way, they would last eight days.

I cut the orange in half, then halved the halves, then halved the quarters, giving each man one eighth. With seven men watching, you can be sure I made an exact division. In fact, I studied the fruit a full minute before I cut. Some sucked and ate the peel, but Cherry and I saved ours for bait.

Men have been lost at sea before; others have spent more days on rafts than we did. A good deal of what we went through was what you might expect—hunger, thirst, heat, cold, and a slow rotting away. In some respects, the period from the second to the eighth day was the worst. A glassy calm fell upon the sea; the sun beat down fiercely all day; the rafts stood still, with the lines slack between; I even imagined I smelled flesh burning, and the sweet stink of hot rubber.

Face, neck, hands, wrists, legs, and ankles burned, blistered, turned raw, and burned again. In time De Angelis and Whittaker, having darker skins, developed a protecting tan, but the rest of us cooked day after day. My hands swelled and blistered; when the salt water got into the flesh, it burned and cracked and dried and burned again. Three months later the scars still show on the knuckles. Our mouths became covered with ugly running sores. Reynolds, having no covering for his legs, turned into a sodden red mass of hurt. Even the soles of his feet were burned raw.

These first five or six days were the worst I have ever known. The night I lay in a wrecked plane near Atlanta, with a dead man half crushed under my chest, had produced its own kind of suffering. But then the pain had been dulled by delirium, and after a while I knew help was near because I could hear people moving around in the dark. But on the Pacific I was something being turned on a spit. Without my hat, I would have been badly off. I would fill it with water, then jam it down over my ears. Before our rescue, the brim was half torn away from the crown.

Some of the others, to escape the terrible heat, paddled for hours in the water. But they paid a stiff price for the relief because their flesh burned again as it dried, and the salt brine stung. Without my handkerchiefs we would have had a much harder time. I passed them around and, folded bandit-fashion across the nose, they protected the lower part of the face. But there was no sparing the eyes. The sea sent back billions of sharp splinters of light; no matter where one looked it was painful. A stupor descended upon the rafts. Men simply sat or sprawled, heads rolling on the chest, mouths half open, gasping. Reynolds, from the cut on his nose, was a horrible sight. The sun would not let the wound heal. He washed the blood off with salt water, but it soon oozed again, spreading over his face, drying in a red crust. Bartek, too, was in agony from his cut fingers. He splashed them with iodine from the first-aid kit, but the salt water ate it away.

Daytimes we prayed for the coolness of the nights; nights we craved the sun. But I really came to hate the nights. Daytimes, I could see my fellow men, the play of the water, the gulls, all the signs of life. But the night brought us all close to fear. A cold, dense mist always rose around us. The damp soaked our clothes and we pressed together for warmth. Sometimes, when the mist was very heavy, the other rafts would be hidden. If the sea was calm and the line had fallen slack, I would sometimes come out of a nightmare, and pull in the towlines until they fetched up hard, and I knew the others were still there. Other times, I would hear moans or groans, or a cry and often a prayer. Or I would see a shadow move and twist as a man tried to ease his torture.

I know I can never hope to describe the awful loneliness of the night. Perhaps it affected me more than the others. I seldom slept more than an hour or so at a time, and even then, it seemed, with one eye open and one ear cocked. That was because I was always worried that the man who was supposed to be on watch might doze off and let a ship go by. I have gotten along most of my life with a good deal less sleep than most men are accustomed to have. This habit stood me in good stead on the Pacific. But the younger men had trouble staying awake. The stupor induced by the terrific heat of the day, together with the lulling motion of the raft as it listed and fell on the swell—a motion that at times was not unlike that of a hammock—seemed to put them quickly to sleep.

What also made the night hard for me was that I could never stretch out. Someday I shall meet the man who decided these rafts could hold two men and five men each. When I do, he is either going to revise his opinions or prove them on a long voyage, under conditions I shall be happy to suggest. Adamson weighed over two hundred pounds and I was not much lighter. On our five-man raft, he and Bartek and I shared an inside room measuring six feet nine inches by two feet four inches. Counting the narrow inflated roll, on which a man could stretch out for an hour or so with his feet dangling in the water, the dimensions were nine feet by five.

Because Adamson was in such pain, Bartek and I gave him one end to himself. He lay with his bumpus on the bottom, his head against the carbon-dioxide bottle, his feet across the roll. Bartek and I lay facing each other, or back to back, with our legs crooked over the roll. This was the way it was in Cherry's boat. But Alex and De Angelis in the two-man raft, although the smallest men, were much worse off. They had to sit facing each other, one with his legs over the other man's shoulders, while he took the legs of the other under his armpits, or they sat back to back, dangling their legs in the water. And sometimes De Angelis lay sprawled out, with Alex on his chest. Imagine two men in a small, shallow bathtub, and you will have a reasonably good idea of how much room they had.

Whenever you turned or twisted, you forced the others to turn or twist. It took days to learn how to make the most of the space, at an incalculable price in misery. A foot or hand or shoulder, moved in sleep or restlessness, was bound to rake the raw flesh of a companion. With the flesh, tempers turned raw and many things said in the night had best be forgotten.

The moon was turning into full. I was awake a good part of the time, hoping to catch the loom of a ship. In those first nights of utter calm the clouds would form the most unusual pictures, beautiful women, elephants, birds. It sounds fantastic. I remember seeing one shaped like a wild boar. I saw trees, completely formed.

The first two or three nights I thought I was seeing things. Finally I mentioned it to Adamson and he agreed with me that they were there. There was some reason for them because you could see them night in and night out, particularly during the first ten days. The moonlight helped to make these forms seem more vivid. I suppose there is a scientific explanation but I don't know what it is.

The forms were so vivid, so concise, so positive that they fascinated me. This helped some; it gave me something to think about during the long hours of the night.

The stars helped also to keep our minds occupied. We were on the equator and so all the familiar stars were in different positions, the Big Dipper, the Little Dipper, the North Star. We used to talk about them. Colonel Adamson had been in charge of the planetarium in New York for a number of years and he was able to tell us a great deal about the different constellations and the movements of the stars. I kept promoting these discussions because of the good it did all of us.

What bothered us most of all was not knowing where we were. Every member of the party had his own ideas about this. I was under the impression—and later events confirmed it—that we were somewhere west or northwest of our island destination. Captain Cherry agreed with me in this.

The next day a terrible calm settled down which made the sea just like a glassy mirror. There were very little swells only and the sun was intensely hot. The glare was terrible on the eyes and most of the boys fell into a doze or sort of stupor. Most of them had injuries of one kind or another to add to their plight. I was afraid that Sergeant Reynolds had a broken nose. In getting out he had struck his head against the radio and the blood had dried on his face. He had no hat and the sun was beginning to burn him badly, and the combination made him an awesome-looking spectacle. Bartek had had all his fingers cut on the inside of the hand, two of them to the bone, and they had bled very badly. We had hauled out the iodine from the first-aid kit as soon as we settled down on the rafts and had done what we could to dress the fingers. The effect did not last long because the salt water would take it off. It would get into the little cuts and so kept him in agony for the first two or three nights. Finally, of course, it dried out and started to heal.

On the fourth morning the second orange was divided. Except for the orange on the second morning, we had then been seventy-two hours without food or liquid. Fish were all around; I could see hundreds swimming idly just below the raft. Cherry and I fished for hours with pieces of orange peel. I even borrowed Adamson's key ring, which was shiny, and tried to manipulate it as a spinner. The fish would nose the hook, fan their tails in curiosity, but they never struck.

For six days on that glassy, sizzling sea, the rafts did not seem to move. But by our watches we knew we were drifting; each morning the sun rose just a little bit later. This meant the rafts were inching west and south. We argued interminably over where we were, but it turned out only Cherry and I were right. We were positive of having overshot our island and, if our guess was true, we could count on no land nearer than certain Japanese-held islands four hundred to five hundred miles away. I studied the map two or three times a day, always returning it to my inside coat pocket, to protect it against the water. But the colors were already beginning to run.

Commencing the second night, Cherry sent up a flare every night. Having eighteen, we first decided to use three a night, the first after sundown, the second around midnight, the last before dawn. But of the first three sent aloft, one was a complete dud and the second flickered for only a few seconds. The third, swinging on its parachute, gave a scary, blinding red light, lasting perhaps a minute and a half. Next night, cutting down the expenditure to two good ones, we had another dud; this decided us to reduce the nightly allotment to a single good one.

Always, after the light had exhausted itself, my eyes strained into the darkness, hoping to catch a responding gleam—a gleam which would not settle into the steadiness of a star. It was plain that unless we soon had food or water or the terrible hot calm relented, some of us were bound to die. Adamson, being portly, felt the heat worse than the rest. Reynolds, thin anyway, was fading to skin and bones. Alex, though, was really in a bad way. His mouth was dry and frothing; he cried continually for water. He was only a boy—barely twenty-two—and thinking he was quitting, I pulled his raft in close and asked why the hell he couldn't take it? It was a brutal thing to do, yet I was determined to shock him back to his senses. I found out then what was wrong. He was only three weeks out of the hospital. In addition, he had contracted a lip disease, something like trench mouth, with a scientific name I do not remember. All this had left him with less strength than the rest from the start, and the salt water he swallowed when his raft capsized had helped to do him in.

Unfortunately for him that wasn't the only salt water Alex had had. De Angelis woke one night to find him half out of the raft, gulping salt water. Now I had admonished everybody the first afternoon out not to drink salt water, knowing that it would drive them wild with thirst. Alex admitted he had been doing this persistently. It explained the cries for water we didn't have. "I tried not to," Alex said, "but I had to. I just had to have water."

So it was only a question of time for poor Alex. He sank deeper into delirium, murmuring his "Hail Mary" and other Catholic prayers. In his wallet was a photograph of a young girl to whom he was engaged: he talked to it, prayed over it. Finally he could neither sleep nor lie down. De Angelis tried to keep the sun off him, but there was no shadow anywhere. So he burned and burned. At night in the moonlight I could see him sitting on the raft shaking as if with ague. He literally vibrated, he was so horribly cold. Yet, except to cry for water, he never really complained.

Bartek had a New Testament in his jumper pocket. As I watched him read it, the thought came to me that we might all profit by his example. I am not a religious man, but I was taught the Lord's Prayer at my mother's knee and I had gone to Sunday school. If I had any religion in my later life, it was based on the Golden Rule. Yet I have always been conscious of God.

With the New Testament as an inspiration, we held morning and evening prayers. The rafts were pulled together, making a rough triangle. Then, each in turn, one of us would read a passage. None of us, I must confess, showed himself to be very familiar with them, but, thumbing the book, we found a number that one way or another bespoke our needs. The Twenty-third Psalm was, of course, a favorite. I have always been stirred by it, but out on the Pacific I found a beauty in it that I had never appreciated. Yet there was another that we never failed to read, because it so clearly set forth what was in our minds:

Therefore take no thought, saying, What shall we eat? or, What shall we drink? or, Wherewithal shall we be clothed?

. . . For your heavenly Father knoweth that ye have need of all these things. But seek ye first the kingdom of God, and his righteousness; and all these things shall be added unto you.

Take therefore no thought for the morrow: for the morrow shall take thought for the things of itself. Sufficient unto the day is the evil thereof. (Matthew 6:31–34.)

One or two turned scornful and bitter because the answer was slow in coming, but the rest went on praying with deep-felt hope. Yet we did not neglect anything that might help us to help ourselves. Whittaker tried to make a spear from one of the aluminum oars, tearing the flat corners away with the pliers. He drove it into the back of a shark which rubbed alongside, but the hide was tougher than the point. After several tries it was so blunted as to be useless. Whittaker threw it angrily into the bottom of the raft. He had gained nothing and wasted an oar.

Also, Cherry sat all day long with a loaded revolver in his lap, hoping to knock down a gull. But none came close enough for a shot. He broke the revolver open two or three times a day and rubbed the moving parts with oil from his nose and the back of his ears, but he could not halt the sea-water corrosion. When the parts froze solid he threw the gun into the Pacific. Adamson's gun rusted in the same way and I dropped it over the side.

To keep the sick men alive, we finished the oranges faster than we had intended. We had the third on the morning of the fifth day, the last on the sixth. The last two were shrunken, much of the juice appeared to have evaporated, and the last one was beginning to rot. So long as there was that sliver of orange to anticipate, no one complained of hunger. Now, memories of food and drink began to haunt us. We tried to catch the sharks that cruised near the rafts with our hands. I actually had several small ones by the back, but the hide was too slippery for a firm grip.

The desire for food in several men became almost violent. They agonized over their hunger pains and talked constantly about food, and whether they could go on much longer without it.

Reynolds talked about how much soda pop he was going to drink the rest of his life. Cherry couldn't think about anything but chocolate ice cream. As I listened to the thirsty talk between the rafts, my own mind slowly filled with visions of chocolate malted milk. I could actually taste it, to the point where my tongue worked convulsively. The strange part is that I hadn't had a chocolate malted milk in nearly twenty-five years.

From the start I had advised against talk, as I realized how necessary it was going to be for all of us to conserve our strength in every way possible; but, looking back now, I am rather amazed at the little talking that we did.

During the first few days, while we suffered from the shock of the fall and our minds were filled with speculation as to the chances of rescue, there was much more than later. This was particularly noticeable after several days had passed and the prospect of escape was becoming dimmer. It was then we began to sing hymns after prayer meetings. The singing seemed to release something in the minds of most of us and the talk for the first time became intensely personal. As I have already stated, there was no time that I lost faith in our ultimate rescue, but the others did not seem to share this state of mind fully with me. My companions clearly began to think of what lay beyond death and to think of it in terms of their own lives.

They began to tell of what they had experienced in life: their hopes, fears, ambitions, their achievements, their mistakes. I suppose it takes the imminence of death to release one completely from inhibitions. The talk was entirely honest and, I am sure, entirely frank. What was said will always be locked up in our minds. As far as I am concerned, no hint of those long, man-to-man conversations will ever be revealed. I am sure of one thing, that it did us a great deal of good.

As the days wore on and our strength left us, we talked less and less. A drowsiness, which in the later stages amounted almost to coma, had taken possession of us. We would lie for hours in the intense heat of the sun without a single word being spoken. What I seem to remember most about the last days was the almost complete silence. If one man spoke there would be no response. We were so completely divorced from living that we had nothing to talk about, even if we had had the strength for it.

I recall no mention of the war. It was continually in my own mind because of my conviction of survival. I was sure I would live to see the struggle through, and consequently did not get away from the speculations that I would have engaged in under normal conditions. I never put them into words, however. If my companions were thinking along the same line, they observed the same reticence that I did.

All conversation during the last stages had to do with the changes of position we found necessary in the rafts and the negative results of the Very lights we set off. Sometimes our hopes would kindle when one of us mistook a low star for the light of a ship. There would be eager discussion then, dwindling off into hopeless silences when it became certain that it had been nothing more than a delusion.

Twenty-one days of it, and during all that time, I am inclined to believe, we talked less than we would have done in the course of one normal day.

The eighth day was another hot, flat calm. It did not help our stomachs any to look down and see dolphin and mackerel, sleek and fat and twelve to eighteen inches long, and thousands of smaller fish swimming in the depths. That afternoon Cherry read the service, with the usual quotation from Matthew. About an hour later, when I was dozing with my hat pulled down over my eyes, a gull appeared from nowhere and landed on my hat.

I don't remember how it happened or how I knew he was there. But I knew it instantly, and I knew that if I missed this one, I'd never find another to sit on my hat. I reached up for him with my right hand—gradually. The whole Pacific seemed to be shaking from the agitation in my body, but I could tell he was still there from the hungry, famished, almost insane eyes in the other rafts. Slowly and surely my hand got up there; I didn't clutch, but just closed my fingers, sensing his nearness, then closing my fingers hard.

I wrung his neck, defeathered him, carved up the body, divided the meat into equal shares, holding back only the intestines for bait. Even the bones were chewed and swallowed. No one hesitated because the meat was raw and stringy and fishy. It tasted fine. After Cherry had finished his piece, I baited a hook and passed it over to him. The hook, weighted with Whittaker's ring, had hardly got wet before a small mackerel hit it, and was jerked into the raft. I dropped the other line, with the same miraculous result, except that mine was a small sea bass.

All this food in the space of a few minutes bolstered us beyond words. We ate one of the fish before dark and put the other aside for the next day. Even the craving for water seemed to abate, perhaps from chewing the cool, wet flesh while grinding the bones to a pulp. Alex and Adamson ate their shares, and I was optimistic enough to believe they were immediately better. I say in all truth that at no time did I ever doubt we would be saved, but as that eighth night rose around us I was sure we could last forever. The ocean was full of fish, and we could catch them.

FROM

Passage East

CARLETON MITCHELL

"Racing a small yacht across the North Atlantic is not entirely a technical feat nor even an adventure in the classic sense," writes yachtsman Carleton Mitchell, "but it is a great emotional and physical experience for those involved." In 1952, Mitchell was a member of the nine-man crew of the yawl Caribbee, *winner of that year's Trans-Atlantic Race from Bermuda to England. These pages from Mitchell's journal communicate something of the racing yachtsman's special experience.*

Trans-Atlantic Race

FRIDAY, *July 18. 2:45* A.M.: During the night wind and sea moderated, and we are back to a comfortable but satisfying 8 to 8.5 on the Kenyon. The wind also shifted slightly. It is now about south-southwest at 12 to 15 knots. We reel off the miles. As Bunny Rigg might say if he were aboard: "Those Plymouth girls have us by a nylon towrope!"

I write this in the cockpit by flashlight. Beside my notebook lies the chronometer-watch we use on deck, and the navigator's notebook. I wait to take time when Frank can shoot the stars. He stands by the mizzen rigging, watching, occasionally squinting through the sextant to see if the horizon is yet well enough defined for a sight.

To the north more than to the east there is the first paling of the sky. While we slept the overcast cleared away, but scattered clouds lie ahead, in the east, and another mass is clustered to the southward. Directly above the sky is clear and the stars are brilliant. Nearer the horizon they are less distinct, as though a thin haze might be forming.

The ritual of morning stars is one of the most beautiful moments of the day: the navigator standing ready, at first a barely discernible silhouette as he identifies his prey by altitude and azimuth. Then an almost imperceptible glow begins to dissolve the weld of sea and sky, and gradually the line of the horizon becomes distinct. The day grows lighter, and the dimmer stars fade. The sky goes from black to gray and slowly assumes delicate shadings of yellow and pink. Patches of foam from breaking crests appear pale gray against the darker gray of the sea, as though the water is loath to give up the stored blackness of the night.

"Stand by!" suddenly calls the navigator. "Stand by!" you repeat, mumbling seconds as the hand of the watch scurries around the dial . . . "Mark!" There is urgency in the command, the sense of communication of a precise instant in the eternity of time . . . You record hour, minute, and second, and the altitude, and the musical names assigned the stars by the ancients: Vega, Kochab, Altair, Capella, Jupiter, Dubhe, Aldebaran . . . Somehow it is a wonderful way to begin a day, a combining of old mysteries and modern precision. And you always feel grateful that again you are fixed on the earth's surface in relation to all other objects: to the islands, to the continents, to the reefs. Somehow you feel less alone.

9:25 A.M.: Around the horizon is a collection of clouds that prior to this passage would have had me standing at the weather rail. Now I sit in the companionway and watch them with a somewhat jaundiced and dispassionate eye. Since Bermuda too many have cried "wolf" for us to get excited by anything not equipped with neon lights, cowcatcher, and siren. Also large red crosses painted on sides and bottom.

North Atlantic clouds come in assorted sizes, shapes, and colors, and the showcase is usually full. At the moment I have only to raise my head to see tufted silver ones ahead, ragged gray ones to starboard, funereal black ones astern, and an odd bank of purplish-blue ones to port. Meanwhile nothing special happens. The track of the barograph remains comparatively level, the breeze blows at about the same velocity from the south-southwest, and we scoot along under the same combination of sails. After a while you seem to get used to living with any sort of threat on a companionably relaxed basis—even a volcano or the atom bomb.

Going along so comfortably, our only worry is chafe. It is really amazing how quickly any two surfaces in intermittent contact can show signs of wear. The problem usually greatest when carrying a spinnaker with the wind well forward, the working of the after guy against the main shrouds, we have solved by use of a wire guy and large rollers—exactly like spools for thread, but about 5 inches in diameter—bound to the shrouds. Elsewhere we are festooned with lengths of split hose, wrappings of canvas, and just plain tape. Miles and miles of each, it seems. Every adjustment of the sheets means endless shifting of bits and pieces of chafing gear. But the funniest chafe of all is along the luff of the mizzen staysail, where a procession of overfed types from cockpit to galley to cockpit has worn away the cloth where they squeeze past. Either we have to go on shorter rations or sew leather along the luff at tummy height! Add a new chapter to hazards of the sea.

11:35 A.M.: After a half hour at the helm I am willing to admit we are overcanvased. My arms feel as though I have been trying to lift an elevator to the top of the Empire State Building with a hand crank. The breeze is back into the twenties and the sea is causing us to sheer. Yet we are going so well and there are so many minor variations of force and direction even within this consistent breeze I hate to change to a genoa. If it would blow 5 miles harder, or the breeze would go another point ahead, there would be no question. But each time I get ready to suggest the shift, the wind moderates a hair, or swings a little farther aft. So as a compromise have dropped the mizzen to ease the helm. It has helped: we still show over 9 knots and Bobby reports the wheel better.

This is glorious going. The sun is breaking through the current overhead assortment of clouds, small flannelly jobs with a warp and woof crosshatch of blue sky between, and it is almost warm. Occasionally a little crest slaps aboard forward, a tiny spatter of sparkling drops, just enough to keep the foredeck wet; and occasionally a sea races under the quarter wave to curl over the counter and run forward along the lee waterway. The spinnaker sheet fore guy is rigid enough to use as a chinning bar, you can jump up and down on the sheet, and we run down the miles for England. As Jack said a moment ago: "We don't even have a Bermuda Race-and-a-half left to go." I cautioned him against such comparisons later for fear of hurting the feelings of sensitive types, but it is true: the remaining distance seems like nothing. If this wind holds.

A trio of whales is off to leeward pacing us. They seem to be puffing mightily in an effort to keep up, but are not quite making it on a boat-for-boat basis. However, as they appear to be strictly Class B whales in over-all length I suppose we have to give them time. Which reminds me: where is *Samuel Pepys,* and what the hell is she doing?

7:40 P.M.: At 5:00 this afternoon, while I slept peacefully, *Caribbee* ran out from under a cover of clouds into brilliant sunshine. When Dick called me at 6:00 the after stateroom was brighter than it had been for days. For a few moments I lay in my bunk and looked across the cabin and through the porthole over the opposite bunk. I could tell we had been freed by the position of the main boom, and because we were standing up straighter while the water went past just as fast. As *Caribbee* rolled I would see only white rushing foam, a few feet beyond the port; then she would lift, and I would see the green-gray North Atlantic seas; and she would roll still farther and I would be looking up at a blue ellipse of cloudless sky. There would be a moment's pause as she poised on a crest, then she would shoot ahead, rolling, and the whole cycle would begin again.

The sunshine held during the cockpit cocktail session, adding a second reason for the gathering being the most noisy and cheerful in days. Gone with the calm are the long faces and quiet voices; when water bubbles under the counter, our spirits bubble in time. Now we bubble 9 knots' worth—a lot of bubbling. Both for *Caribbee* and for us.

But as our watch was finishing dinner before taking over, Dick came below and said: "There's a black cloud bank coming up from astern. I can't tell what it means but you'd better bring oilies." And when I stuck my head through the companionway slide, there it was: from horizon to horizon it stretched, flat on top, dark and ominous, extending down to the water as a solid curtain. It lacked the neon lights and the red crosses, but everything else seemed to be present.

I stood by the weather backstay and watched. It gained fast. All afternoon there had been a pronounced swell from the northwest, persistent and heavy enough to buck the waves kicked up by our present southwest breeze, and this looked as though it might be the force behind those outriders. This is it, I kept thinking; this has to be it, the northwest gale so long overdue. A boat can't cross the ocean and not take a beating somewhere; we can't go on talking about the Great Atlantic Calm of '52 and making derisive noises without Father Neptune doing something about it. . . . Now we're going to get it, we puny mortals who have been wanting wind!

Wispy clouds raced overhead, low enough to rip their bellies on the mainmast, with the denser mass close behind—and we saw we had been fooled by the low sun: the clouds were not heavy and ominous at all, but only our traveling companion of the last 2 days, the flannel sky, temporarily left behind and hurrying to catch up. Now, as I write this, its leading edge is well ahead, although I can still see a narrow band of blue at the horizon, and we are all happy: the cloud, *Caribbee*, and us, because under the flannel cloud is just the wind we want: not too little, not too much, so we continue at 9 knots as peacefully as babes riding a carriage in the park.

10:35 P.M.: I am finally convinced the true southwesterly of the middle latitudes has come in. On going over the log, I find it was at 8:10 Wednesday night I noted: "Breeze hauling. On spinnaker." Now it has been aloft for 50-odd hours. There have been only minor variations in the strength and direction of the wind during that period, and we have run down a degree of longitude every five hours or less. Up here at latitude 51 degrees, a degree of longitude is only 37.9 nautical miles in length. We have thus taken a great leap forward on the track chart.

So at last we have the winds we expected to ride all the way across, those "prevailing westerlies" of the pilot charts. Having had a little leisure during this watch, I studied the log and found some interesting things. Beginning at noon of Friday, July 4, we sailed 635 miles, the distance of the course from Newport to Bermuda, in 72 hours 53 minutes. That figure

Dawn: "To the north more than to the east there is the first paling of the sky."
—*Trans-Atlantic Race*

represents an average speed over the bottom of 8.72 knots. The Cruising Club of America yearbook lists the Bermuda Race record for the present course as 75 hours 32 minutes, set by *Bolero* in 1950. So far good enough. But then beginning at 8:00 A.M., July 8, it took us 196 hours to sail the next 635 miles, a heartbreaking average of 3.24 knots. And in the 1946 Bermuda Race, the slowest since the war, the *last* boat in the fleet whose time was recorded made it to the finish line in 178 hours! Thus in two successive stretches across the Atlantic, *Caribbee* exceeded two records for another similar stretch: the fastest and the slowest. Now, if the wind holds, we will probably better our earlier pace.

So it has been a period of mad weather, when nature sharply reminds man his attempts to catalog her are futile. We had fresh breezes where the books said we might expect the light variables of the horse latitudes, and light variables from the east when we arrived in the charted area of the prevailing westerlies. Meanwhile the radio brings reports of record heat waves around the rim of the Atlantic, both in North America and in Europe.

Also in my study of the log I was reminded of something else: how terrible was the period of aimless slatting and fruitless beating which reached its nadir on the morning of the sixteenth. Sails up, sails down, tacking endlessly on headers, getting nowhere, until Frank looked up from the chart in disgust and said: "We're going back and forth on the same damned line. It's just getting blacker and blacker from the pencil marks." Only the arrival of the first stages of this breeze in the morning kept us from a run that might have averaged less than a knot for 24 miles—1 mile per hour for working continuously, changing sails, calling them, tacking endlessly. Believe me: I have learned record passages are the pleasant ones!

As the winds have fluctuated, so have our moods. I know these notes reveal me as a person of "ups-ies" and "downs-ies." It is a characteristic for which I do not apologize; it appears even in the writings of the most outwardly stoic of the old adventurers. But this afternoon Bobby passed along a remark by Dick which shed some light on the curious rise or fall in the spirits of sailors on long passages as the speed goes up or down:

you always think of the passage as continuing at the rate you are moving at the moment. It seems to be a universal failing. If you're enjoying a fair breeze and making 8 knots, you calculate how long it will take to cover the remaining miles at 8 knots, completely forgetting that wind is the most fickle and undependable of commodities. You rub your hands and say gleefully, "We'll be in next Tuesday." Everyone is elated. But then the breeze dies, or goes ahead, and the speed drops. You're making 2 knots. Immediately there is a new calculation and faces grow long. Someone growls, "Hell, we won't get there before Christmas." You feel cheated and vow you'll never let your hopes soar again. And you don't, until the next fair slant.

Saturday, July 19. 6:45 A.M.: The midnight log entry opens with the notation: "This day commences with pleasant westerly. Carrying spinnaker, balloon forestaysail, main, mizzen staysail, and mizzen." Yet for me this past 4-hour watch, now almost ended, has been one of the most tense and wearing ones of the passage. While dressing, after being routed out of my snug bunk at 2:45, I could tell things were rugged on deck. From my difficulty in maintaining balance against the lurch and roll I knew steering would be hard, and that the wind had freshened and the sea built. There was a roaring of water along the lee deck, a feeling of burying that indicated we might be on the verge of carrying too much sail.

Deck wasn't cheering: there was a slight glimmer of light in the east, but the whole sky was leaden and gray. A fine misting rain fell, and visibility was bad. The wind had backed still farther into the south, so we were carrying the spinnaker pole as far forward as it would go, right against the headstay. The sail was constantly on edge, even so. Even in the poor light I could see it curl.

I confess my inclination was to shift to a genoa while both watches were together. But then I thought perhaps things looked worse than they really were, as is always the case when first coming into a nasty night from a deep sleep, and did not want to give way to that first-awake letdown, the old predawn loss of courage, when the tides in men are at their lowest ebb. And we would be comfortable again if only the wind would veer a couple of points to the west. Dick settled my doubts by telling me the wind had freed in the last half hour and showed signs of continuing around.

So we set ourselves at our stations and the port watch disappeared down the companionway sack-wards faster than any gophers ever popped into holes. I watched them with envy. But not for long, as there was plenty to keep us busy. Steering was particularly hard. The northwest swell still rolled in under the wind waves of our sou'wester, the same as yesterday, but both much bigger: the result was a nasty bucking sea, occasionally combining to make *Caribbee* take a violent sheer. With each sheer the spinnaker would curl deeply, and the man forward would call frantically: "Go down! Go down!" Sometimes the rudder would take effect; at other times the spinnaker would break and refill with a resounding crash. But we carried on, reluctant to do anything which might slow us, although we did strike the mizzen and mizzen staysail to ease steering.

And then we got it. We were asking for it, and we got it. I was at the wheel when suddenly there was a *ping!* from aloft, a sound like a breaking ukulele string magnified a few hundred times. The whole boat gave a jump, as though Father Neptune had given us a good swift boot in the stern. The spinnaker sagged, but then held and filled again.

At the moment of the ping I began bearing away as fast as I could grind the wheel, and as soon as we came off before the wind yelled: "What the hell happened?" For a moment no one knew, despite a cluster forward looking up the mast. Then Frank spotted the trouble: one spinnaker halyard had let go, cause for the moment unknown, and the sail had been caught by the other one. I have noted that for this race we installed twin halyards, so one backs up the other. Fortunately, it turns out.

It was a very minor accident compared to what might have happened, so we took the hint and switched to a genoa. Immediately there was an amazing change in conditions—in apparent conditions, that is. What a moment before had been a wild dawn—the break occurred at 4:50—became merely unpleasant: a fresh southerly wind thick with fine rain setting up a bobble of a sea, neither particularly vicious. Good seamanship and good sense dictated a switch. But ocean racing? We have dropped a knot on the Kenyon, and wait impatiently for more light so a man can go aloft to find what happened, and make repairs.

8:50 A.M.: After breakfast both watches assembled on deck. It was still blowing well over twenty, and the wind had moved even more to the south, putting it forward of the beam. The conflicting seas seemed more pronounced than ever, so it was almost impossible to walk along the deck without holding onto the liferail or some other stable object. Yet we rigged the bosun's chair and tied Frank in securely and up he went: up some 75 feet into the cold raw wind, the chill spitting rain. Around us the sea and the sky were gray and lonely. No gallery to applaud, no one to know or care except the knot of oilskinned shipmates hauling on the halyard; just one more unseen vignette of the countless thousands that have occurred on the empty ocean.

From amidships I watched him trace wild arcs as *Caribbee*

plunged along at better than 8 knots: he would work awhile, hold on awhile as a particularly bad combination of seas made the motion worse, and lean to leeward for a while. It took me a little time to figure that the latter gesture was for the better downwind distribution of his breakfast pancakes. But finally he signaled to come down, and was lowered away, and we found what had happened: the strain on the halyard aloft had pulled out a splice in the strap that held the block. The ends of the wire looked like steel spaghetti. Frank had transferred the block to a spare strap at the masthead, and we were back in business. But it is not altogether pleasant to contemplate what might have happened if the second halyard had not been in place, and held: a huge nylon bag suddenly collapsing under our bows, fast to the ship by 150 feet of wire halyard, a wire foreguy, and two heavy linen sheets.

As amazed as I was at the news that a splice had pulled, I was even more amazed by Frank's color when he reached the deck. On starting up, he had blended with his shipmates; on coming down he was exactly the color of pea soup—a rich green. He drank a cup of hot tea, to which I added a good slug of rum, and now sleeps. Just before dropping off he assured Henry that he was indeed the finest of cooks: the pancakes tasted as good coming up as they had going down.

10:00 A.M.: Now I have finally gotten to my bunk I am not sleepy, although while sitting on deck in the rain I could hardly wait, and a silly paraphrase from *Alice in Wonderland* kept running through my head in tuneless and monotonous repetition: "Sack of the evening, beautiful sack." As for the first time everything below is wet and clammy, perhaps I am staying awake to savor a little longer the sheer animal satisfaction of being dry and warm. Oilskins and sweaters hang throughout the cabin in odd places. Damp socks are jammed behind light bulbs and in the front of the bookcase. There isn't much difference in temperature between cockpit and main cabin, and unless the rain stops and we get some drying weather we will have to dig deep into our stock of spare gear.

Fuel is the only miscalculation we made in our advance planning. We could carry only a small supply of briquettes for the main cabin fireplace, to heat and dry the living quarters in case of necessity, but have a fair amount left despite keeping a fire going a couple of days on the Grand Banks. I will have Henry stoke up the grate before lunch. Our real shortage is in alcohol for the cooking stove. Neither Henry nor I took into consideration that on a long passage there would be more baking and midnight snacking. Or perhaps I should be more honest and say we didn't realize as a crew that we would be capable of eating 24 hours a day, less only time for sleep and a few deck chores. We began the voyage by each watch putting on a kettle of water about a half hour before calling the other, at night; after dressing, you could struggle to the galley for a mug-up of coffee, tea, soup, or cocoa. This noble practice degenerated into a kettle bubbling almost constantly, especially during the waking hours of those supermen, the port watch. So a couple of days ago, to the great sorrow of all hands, I had to decree rationing: stove on at night only at the three o'clock change in watches, a cold lunch, and no more baking. Really rugged! Shades of Thomas James and the other old searchers for the Northwest Passage! No more hot cornbread, no more apple pie! Survival does indeed become a matter of chance, and from now on *Caribbee* will be sailed with the desperation of men willing to risk all in a desperate gamble—no Plymouth, no pie. . . . But seriously, if I were ever again making a long passage in the higher latitudes I would allow double the usual consumption of cooking fuel for shorter trips in warmer climes, and add a little bit more as a reserve.

Otherwise we are in fine shape. Our planning for food was on the basis of a 3-week passage, with another 2 weeks of emergency food in reserve—real "iron rations," Coast Guard-approved survival food for use in lifeboats, the daily supply per man having less bulk than a package of cigarettes. What a comedown that would be! But Henry assures me we are in no danger of descending to such levels. While our consumption has been as great as is humanly possible there is still an ample reserve. One reason for this was the food already on the boat when the Trans-Atlantic stores came aboard in Bermuda: our planning had been done on a "bare boat" basis, so the 21-day supply was entirely in addition to canned goods left over from the Bermuda

Race, and the "just in case" extras hidden deep in lockers and bilge.

I marvel at how well we have eaten. Italian spaghetti and meat balls; German sauerkraut and wieners; Chinese chop suey and chow mein; New England codfish balls and mashed potatoes; New Orleans crawfish bisque and shimp jambalaya; Boston baked beans; Mexican chili and tamales; Scotch kippers and Dutch ham and Alaskan salmon—our menu is cosmopolitan and varied. There seems to be nothing which cannot be found in canned form, even bread. On previous passages bread has been a real problem, for there are times when even the hardiest cook cannot bake in a small boat's oven; now bread comes in neat tins, and after weeks at sea tastes almost as good as the spanking-fresh product of the corner bakery. Rye, white, or whole wheat, take your choice. And I do not believe it is only our seagoing appetites that make everything so palatable: canned food when prepared with care and imagination can compare favorably with fresh, especially when enough thought goes into planning menus so there is no feeling of repetition. *Henri du Caribbee* has done well on all counts. One hazard I did not anticipate on this passage was having to turn sideways to get up the companionway.

Dick just came down to get the balloon jib. As he stood talking, water collected in a puddle at his feet. It still rains, and the wind remains too far forward to carry a spinnaker. Hence the ballooner, in hopes of coaxing the speed back to 9 knots.

Seeing Dick cold and dripping made me feel even more snug, and suddenly sleepy. Lights out. Let her howl for somebody else—for the next 2 hours, anyway.

4:45 P.M.: We continue to be gluttons for punishment and work, but it is a form of gluttony that eats up the miles.

On deck at 1:00 to the same leaden sky and splitting rain, but found the wind trending slightly more toward the west. So all hands kept close watch on the masthead fly. By 2:00 the apparent breeze was a bit forward of the beam, by 2:30 it had come abeam, and by 2:45 the spinnaker was set and drawing. As it is now. And the wind has continued on around until we log it as a true southwester. Again the Kenyon has climbed to 9. The sea followed the wind aft, and steering is not too bad, although occasionally a big one will rise above the level of the taffrail to shoulder the stern high, bury the bow, and cause *Caribbee* to slice across the sea ahead. But this wind lacks the weight to make the process vicious.

Two hundred seven miles today, 212 yesterday. We're in the groove, really rolling. Now have less than one Bermuda Race left to go—about a Miami-Nassau plus a St. Pete-Havana. With continuing luck we could make the finish in another 3 days. "Continuing luck" of course means continuing wind and no major catastrophes to gear; by the law of averages we should get the first, and I'm not too concerned about the second.

Thinking back, I believe we have consistently gotten the maximum speed possible in the conditions we encountered. There were times when we went mighty slow—when we didn't go at all—but we can have the satisfaction of knowing we did everything possible with what we had. It is customary for a skipper to pay tribute to his crew, but in this case I feel every page of these notes tells a story that could not be summed up by any amount of flowery compliments. I can only add I do not believe there was ever a keener or more efficient crew, which let down less or remained as cheerful under trying conditions. And nothing could be more difficult than the old nightmare sensation of running like hell but staying in the same place, while in your imagination the goblins pursue like Olympic hurdlers.

7:15 P.M.: It is strange but I feel in the last few days we all have a different attitude about this race. At first there was constant speculation about the other boats, their qualities and potentials, and how they would be sailed. In a sense, for the first few days we were sailing hard because we were racing the others, a purely competitive sensation. But now I believe our concentration is solely on *Caribbee*. It has become a fetish to keep her moving as fast as possible; it has also become our greatest pleasure. She seems to us so wonderful, this supposedly inanimate object, we can do nothing else. She has carried us almost across an ocean, kept us safe and comfortable, responded to our every demand, forgiven our excesses. In return, we have learned her whims and desires, and are willing slaves to both.

It would not be accurate if I said we do not frequently speculate on the other boats—sometimes pessimistically, feeling they might have skirted the calm while we lay helpless; sometimes optimistically, thinking the light weather must have been widespread enough to trap them, too. But now such speculation is more objective and fatalistic. The race is less important than the personal fact that we have made this passage, have shared this experience. If some super-radar could suddenly show us the others either fantastically ahead or behind, so our efforts from here to the finish would make no difference to the outcome of the race, I am sure we would sail exactly the same way as we do now—as hard and well as we can.

This passage has clarified my perspective, as well as taught me more of the sea than I could have learned in another lifetime of coastal cruising. And I know, even as I calculate the miles to the finish, I would somehow be happier if it was 6000 instead of 600 miles. I know I shall be excited and delighted when we sail into Plymouth—yet sad. Even now I can remember vividly the moment almost exactly 20 years ago when the battered old ketch *Temptress* crawled into Ft. Pierce inlet ahead of an unseasonal tropical storm, 17 days out of the Chesapeake, the three of us aboard exhausted from being buffeted by a succession of gales off Cape Hatteras. It was my first passage on the open ocean. I had been frightened, I can say honestly: the deep roar of wind in the rigging, the heavy slam of seas rolling out of the night, the sheer insensitiveness and pitilessness of the ocean, not willing to quit when man had enough and begged for mercy. . . . Yet when we gained calm water beyond the roaring hell of the inlet, breaking heavily from the first swells of the advancing hurricane, I was sad. I knew something had ended that could never be had again, not in exactly the same way. And after a time even the fear and the exhaustion were part of the perfection of the memory.

As the most important memories of this crossing will remain not as a race but as a passage.

FROM

War Fish

GEORGE GRIDER

In a few short months during World War II, the U.S. submarine Wahoo *and its commander, Dudley W. "Mush" Morton, became legends among Navy men. Morton took command of the* Wahoo *in December 1942. On five daring patrols, he sank record tonnages of Japanese shipping. In October 1943, on his fifth patrol—into the Sea of Japan itself—the* Wahoo *was lost.*

George Grider was third officer aboard the Wahoo *when Morton assumed command. Later he was transferred to another boat, and in time he commanded the submarine* Flasher. *Here is Grider's account of "Mush" Morton's first patrol in the* Wahoo.

Reconnaissance at Wewak

As the year ended, the *Wahoo* was assigned a new captain. Marvin Kennedy, the red-haired perfectionist who had supervised construction, had trained us strenuously and well, and had taken us on two patrols, went on to another assignment, and our makey-learn, big, playful Lieutenant Commander Dudley W. Morton of Kentucky, was put in command. And, in the quiet January days at Brisbane before we put to sea again, we tried to decide what the change would mean.

Everybody liked Mush. He had done a thorough job of getting acquainted with the *Wahoo* and its crew during the second patrol. He was always roaming the narrow quarters, his big hands reaching out to examine equipment, his wide-set eyes missing nothing. He was largely without responsibility on that patrol, and he had been one of the boys. The tiny wardroom always brightened when Mush squeezed his massive shoulders through one of the two narrow doorways and found a place to sit. He was built like a bear, and as playful as a cub. Once he and I got into an impromptu wrestling match after our coffee, and he put a half nelson on me and bore down just a little. Something in the back of my neck popped, and my head listed to port for weeks afterward. Even today it comes back occasionally, and I always think of Mush.

The crew loved him. Submarines are perhaps the most democratic of all military units, because within their cramped confines there simply isn't room for echelons of rank and dignity. Even so, for many officers the transition from camaraderie to authority is a jerky and awkward one, so that their men are never completely at ease. It was not this way with Mush. His authority was built-in and never depended on sudden stiffening of tone or attitude. Whether he was in the control room, swapping tall tales with Rau, the chief of the boat, or wandering restlessly about in his skivvies, talking to the men in the torpedo and engine rooms, he was as relaxed as a baby. The men were not merely ready to follow him, they were eager to.

But there had been times on the second patrol when his casually expressed opinions suggested the absence of any reasonable degree of caution. It is one thing to be aggressive, and another to be foolhardy, and it would be a mistake to think that the average man in submarines was a fire-breathing buccaneer who never thought of his own hide. Most of us, in calculating the risk, threw in a mental note that we were worth more to the Navy alive than dead—and to our wives and children as well. But when Mush expressed himself on tactics, the only risk he recognized was the risk of not sinking enemy tonnage. Talking it over at Paradise Beach, Roger and I were mildly concerned.

Another thing that worried us was that Dick O'Kane, the exec, clearly had no reservations about Mush. The two were in agreement on everything. And we still weren't too sure about Dick. He talked a great deal—reckless, aggressive talk—and it was natural to wonder how much of it was no more than talk. During the second patrol Dick had grown harder to live with, friendly one minute and pulling his rank on his junior officers the next. One day he would be a martinet, and the next he would display an overlenient, carefree attitude that was far from reassuring. With Mush and Dick in the saddle, how would the *Wahoo* fare?

Nevertheless, we looked forward almost eagerly to the prospect. As many a politician has learned, when morale sags, any change is welcome. And our doubts about Mush were theoretical; our reasons to like him were real. I remember writing to Ann about the change in glowing terms.

I wrote, too, about one of those happy meetings that occur sometimes in wars. Ed Blakely, a good friend of ours, turned up at Brisbane shortly before we were to leave, and I was able to pass his good news on to Ann: he and his wife Ginger were expecting a baby the following month. I promised to get her address and pass it on to Ann. That was the last time I saw Ed. He was lost on his next patrol.

The *Wahoo* was ready for sea on January 16, 1943, and even before we left the harbor at Brisbane, the impact of our new skipper was felt. Meals in the wardroom took on the nature of parties; instead of staring at our plates and fretting over our responsibilities, as we had grown accustomed to doing, we found ourselves led along by a captain who was constantly joking, laughing, or planning outrageous exploits against the enemy. Overnight, it seemed, the photographs of Japanese ships that had been pasted all over the *Wahoo*, even in the head, came down—not by order, but through some unspoken understanding that Mush would approve—and in their places went some of the finest pin-up pictures in the U. S. Navy. Identification of silhouettes is a useful occupation, but some silhouettes are more rewarding than others.

Our instructions were to proceed to the Carolines. To this day I don't remember exactly where we were supposed to go, because we never got there. But there was one sentence, almost incidental, in our orders that was to have considerable significance. En route, we were to reconnoiter Wewak harbor.

To reach the Carolines, we would sail north from Brisbane and follow the northeast coast of New Guinea upward, past Buna, where General MacArthur's troops were even then driving back the Japanese, and on up along the enemy-held shore. And somewhere along there, reports indicated, was a harbor called Wewak that might hold enemy ships. We were to see what we could find.

If we hurried, Mush decided, we could spend more time there than our operation order had allowed. So as we moved along the New Guinea coast, we stayed on the surface for greater speed. It was a strange and unfamiliar experience to see enemy land lying black and sinister on the port hand, to feel the enemy planes always near us, and yet it was invigorating. Contrary to all tradition on the *Wahoo*, we kept to the surface during daylight hours for six days, submerging only for one quick trim dive each morning, though we were almost never out of sight of land and often within close range of enemy airports.

The *Wahoo's* combat attitude had changed in other ways. Now, instead of two officers, four lookouts and the quartermaster on the bridge when we were on the surface, we cruised with only one officer and three lookouts, but somehow we felt we had never been so well guarded. And Mush had removed the bunk previously installed for the skipper in the conning tower. When he was ready for sleep, he went down to his stateroom and slept like a baby, leaving no doubt that the officer of the deck was on his own, that he was trusted, and that he was thoroughly in command unless or until he asked for help.

Only occasionally did Mush intervene. One day he wandered up for a bit of conversation when I was on the bridge, and suddenly as we talked we sighted a plane about eight miles away. About the same time, the radar picked it up and confirmed the range. We had always dived when we sighted a plane in the past, so I turned for the hatch. Mush's big hand landed on the back of my collar just as I reached the ladder.

"Let's wait till he gets in to six miles," he said softly.

I turned and went back. Great Lord, I thought, we're under the command of a madman.

We stood and watched as the plane closed the range. At six and a half miles his course began to take him away from us, and in a few minutes he had faded from sight. By gambling that he hadn't seen us, Mush had saved us hours of submerged travel, but even though it had worked, I wasn't sure I was in favor of it.

Meanwhile, as we neared the area where Wewak should be,

the chart problem became acute. Our orders gave no hint of its position and none of our charts of the New Guinea coast showed it by name; it could have been any one of a dozen unnamed spots. How could we reconnoiter a harbor whose location we didn't know?

At first, most of us had considered this only a minor problem. If we didn't know where Wewak was, we didn't know. We could take a look at some of the more promising spots, and make our reports, and be on our way. Then one night in the wardroom a different light was put on the matter. Mush, Dick, Roger, Hank Henderson and I were looking at the charts, speculating on which tiny dent in the coast might be Wewak, when Mush asked innocently what we understood to be the meaning of the word "reconnoiter."

I may have hammed up the answer a little, but not much.

"Why," I said, "it means we take a cautious look at the area, from far out at sea, through the periscope, submerged."

Mush grinned. "No, boy," he said. "The only way you can reconnoiter a harbor is to go right into it and see what's there."

Roger and Hank and I looked at each other in sheer consternation. Now it was clear that our captain had advanced from mere rashness to outright foolhardiness. For a submarine, as anybody knew in those days, was a deep-water ship that needed broad oceans and plenty of water under its keel to operate. And harbors are often treacherous at best, even when you enter them in surface ships handled by experienced pilots equipped with the very latest charts. It would be madness for the *Wahoo* to submerge and enter an enemy harbor whose very location on the map we didn't know.

Later, submarines penetrated other harbors, but if any had done so at that time, none of us knew about it, and it was against every tradition that had been built up on the *Wahoo*. Yet here was this skipper of ours, grinning at us under his jutting nose as if he had just told a funny story, assuring us we were going to do it and we'd darned well better find out which harbor was Wewak or he'd just pick the most likely one and go in.

After word of this attitude of Mush's got out, the search for a chart of Wewak harbor increased markedly. And in the end it was Bird-Dog Keeter, the motor machinist's mate who had sighted the *Wahoo's* first victim, who came to the rescue. I was making a tour through the engine room one night when I found Keeter poring over a book. He looked up, grabbed my arm, and yelled over the roar of the engines, "Hey, Mr. Grider, is this the Wewak we're going to?"

I grabbed the book out of his hand. It was an Australian high-school geography book he had bought while we were on leave, and he had opened it to a page that showed a map of New Guinea. Sure enough, there on the northeast coast was a tiny spot marked "Wewak."

A couple of months before, the idea of entering an enemy harbor with the help of a high-school geography would have struck me as too ridiculous even to be funny. Now I almost hugged the book and charged forward to the wardroom with it as if it were the key to the destruction of the entire Japanese Navy.

Mush took one look at it and reached for our charts. The wardroom began to hum with activity.

One of our charts did have a spot that seemed to correspond with the latitude and longitude of Wewak as shown in the book, but even then we weren't much better off. On our big chart, the Wewak area covered a space about the size of a calling card—hardly the detail you need for entering a harbor. We were on the track now, though, and Mush's determination to enter Wewak, regardless, made what we had seem a lot better than nothing.

Dick O'Kane and his quartermaster, a man named Krause, took over. First, Krause made a tracing of the area from our chart onto a piece of toilet paper. Next, we took my old Graflex camera and rigged it as an enlarger, using the ship's signal lamp as the projector light. We clamped this rig to the wardroom table and projected the enlarged image onto a large sheet of paper spread on the wardroom deck. Then, with all lights turned out, Dick and Krause traced the projected lines on the new sheet, and we had a chart. It might have made a cartographer shudder, but it was a long way ahead of no chart at all.

What we saw was a rough drawing, not of a harbor, but of a protected roadstead with islands on all four sides. And there was a name for one of the islands: Mushu. In the general triumph, this was taken as a positive omen of good hunting. And as I reassembled my Graflex, I could not help reflecting that it, too, was an omen. It was a camera that had been used in World War I by my father and his friend and fellow flier Elliott Springs. My father had been killed in action, and Elliott had saved the camera and given it to me as a memento. I had always treasured it as something special and had got myself named ship's photographer in order to bring it along on the *Wahoo*. When I thought that a chart fashioned with the help of an ancient camera used by my father more than a quarter of a century before on another side of the world in another war would lead us into Wewak harbor, I too began to believe there was some kind of guiding destiny behind the *Wahoo's* third patrol.

So, in the limited time remaining, we planned and discussed and prepared. Every scrap of information we had been able to get about Wewak was transferred to our chart. From what we assembled, it appeared that it might be plausible after all to penetrate the harbor. There was plenty of room; the harbor was about two miles across in most places, and we believed the depth might be as much as two hundred feet in most areas. Mush was delighted. He ignored the uncertainties and concentrated on the fact that we would have deep water, if we stayed where it was, and unmistakable landmarks, if we could spot them in time to use them.

It was summer in that hemisphere, and the sun rose early. We adjusted our speed to arrive at Wewak just before dawn on January 24. At three-thirty in the morning, just as the eastern horizon was beginning to gray, we dived, two and a half miles off the entrance, and proceeded submerged toward Wewak harbor.

Actually, there were several entrances, but we were sure of only one. The harbor extended about nine miles in from this point, making a dogleg that obstructed the view. We approached around the western end of one of the islands to investigate the bay beyond, but before Dick could see anything else, he spotted two torpedo boats in the periscope, headed in our direction. This was no time to be seen by small boats, so we ducked down, waited awhile, and tried again.

This time the torpedo boats were gone. There was a small tug in the distance with a barge alongside, but no other shipping in sight. We poked around into another area, a strait between two of the islands, and Dick saw something that may have been radio masts on the far side of a third island. Mush suggested we go around for a better look, but this time a reef showed up to block our way.

We spent the entire morning nosing around that harbor, trying to find out what was in it and where the safe water was. As Dick spotted light patches of water in the scope, he called off their locations and we noted them on our chart as shallows. From time to time we could pencil in landmarks. One of these we called Coast Watcher Point.

A strong southward current had been complicating our problems ever since we entered the harbor, and it was this current that was responsible for the naming of Coast Watcher Point. It swept us so close to the point that all of us in the conning tower, taking turns at the periscope, could see a Japanese lookout, wearing a white shirt, sitting under a coconut tree right on the point. We saw him so clearly, in fact, that I am sure I would recognize him if I passed him on the street tomorrow.

Except for this chance the rest of us had to look, Dick O'Kane had made all the periscope observations. Mush had a unique theory: he believed the executive officer, not the captain, should handle the periscope throughout an approach and attack. This, he explained, left the skipper in a better position to interpret all factors involved, do a better conning job, and make decisions more dispassionately. There is no doubt it is an excellent theory, and it worked beautifully for him, but few captains other than Mush ever had such serene faith in a subordinate that they could resist grabbing the scope in moments of crisis.

Right now, Mush was in his element. He was in danger, and he was hot on the trail of the enemy, so he was happy. For all the tension within us, we managed to reflect his mood. The atmosphere in the conning tower would have been more appropriate to a fraternity raiding party than so deadly a reconnaissance. Mush even kept up his joking when we almost ran aground.

This happened because of the dual nature of a periscope.

It is a very precise instrument with two powers of magnification: a low power that magnifies objects one and a half times, to give you about the same impression you would get with the naked eye, and a six-power magnification to bring things in very close. So everyone was concerned when, on one of his looks, Dick called from the periscope, "Captain, I believe we're getting too close to land. I have the periscope in high power, and all I can see is one coconut tree." If only one coconut tree, even magnified six times, filled his scope, then we were dangerously close.

"Dick," said the captain in a tone of mild reproof, "you're in *low* power."

In the electric silence that followed, Dick flipped the handle to high power and took an incredulous look.

"Down periscope!" he yelped. "All back emergency! My God, all I can see is one *coconut!*" We backed away from there in record time.

By early afternoon, Mush was beginning to lose his good humor. We had spent half a day looking for a target worth shooting at, and none had showed up. But we had got a good idea of the harbor, and now we went in farther, to where we could get a good look around the dogleg and down the bight, and there at the very end of the dogleg Dick saw what appeared to be the superstructure of a ship. At first sight, he reported it looked like a freighter or a tender of some sort, at anchor.

"Well, Captain," somebody in the conning tower said, "we've reconnoitered Wewak harbor now. Let's get cracking out of here and report there's a ship in there." We all knew it was a joke, however much we wished it weren't.

"Good grief, no," said Mush, coming to life. "We're going to go in and torpedo him."

Dick asked him to come over and help identify the potential target, and the two of them stood there like a couple of schoolboys, peering through the scope each time it was raised, trying to decide what kind of vessel lay ahead. At last they agreed, and Mush looked happily around the conning tower.

"It's a destroyer," he said.

Much has been written about the changes great fighters undergo in battle. It has been said that when General Nathan Bedford

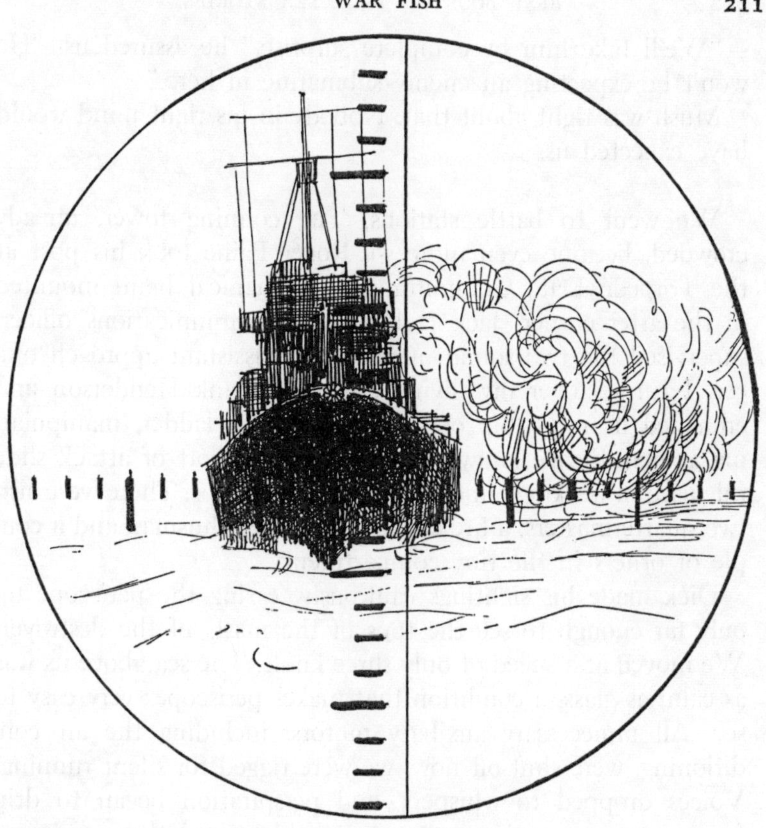

Forrest, the great Confederate cavalry officer, went into battle, his face became a deep, mottled red, his voice altered, becoming shrill and high-pitched, and his whole countenance took on a look of indescribable fierceness. Mush Morton changed, too, but in a wholly different way. Joy welled out of him. His voice remained the same, but his eyes lit up with a delight that in its own way was as fearful as Forrest's countenance must have been. Here, we were to realize before the *Wahoo's* third patrol ended, was a man whose supreme joy was literally to seek out and destroy the enemy. It was to drive him to terrifying magnificence as a submarine commander, to make him a legend within a year, and to lead eventually to his death.

Now, as the rest of us worried about the depth of the water, the pull of the unknown currents, the possibility of reefs between us and our target, he smiled at us again.

"We'll take him by complete surprise," he assured us. "He won't be expecting an enemy submarine in here."

Mush was right about that. Nobody in his right mind would have expected us.

We went to battle stations. The conning tower, already crowded, became even more so. Roger Paine took his post at the Torpedo Data Computor, the mechanical brain mounted in the after corner. Jack Jackson, the communications officer, supervised the two sound operators. As assistant approach officer, I turned over my diving duties to Hank Henderson and crouched near the top of the control-room ladder, manipulating a small device known as an "is-was"—a sort of attack slide rule used in working out distances and directions. There were also two quartermasters, a fire controlman, the helmsman and a couple of others in the tiny compartment.

Dick made his sightings cautiously, easing the periscope up only far enough to see the tops of the masts of the destroyer. We moved at a speed of only three knots. The sea above us was as calm as glass, a condition that makes periscopes very easy to see. All unnecessary auxiliary motors, including the air conditioning, were shut off now; we were rigged for silent running. Voices dropped to whispers, and perspiration began to drip from our faces as the temperature rose toward the 100-degree mark. We had the element of surprise on our side, and nothing else. We were now six miles inside an uncharted harbor, with land on three sides of us, and in a minute or so the whole harbor would know we were there.

The outer doors on our six forward torpedo tubes were quietly opened. We were approaching the range Mush had decided on, three thousand yards. It was a little long, but it should keep us in deep water.

"Stand by to fire One."

Dick O'Kane, crouched around the periscope barrel, flipped his thumbs up to indicate he wanted the scope raised one last time. The long cylinder snaked up. Dick rode the handles, clapping his eye to the eyepiece as soon as it was clear of the floorboards. He let the scope get about two inches out of water and took a quick look around.

"Down scope." There was an urgency in his whisper that brought tension to the breaking point. "Captain, she's gotten under way, headed out of the harbor. Angle on the bow ten port."

Now our plan to catch this sitting duck was gone a-glimmering. She was not only under way, she was headed almost directly at us. The only reasonable thing to do was to get out. Later, perhaps, we could get a shot at her in deep water. But Mush was in no mood to be reasonable.

"Right full rudder!"

Without a moment's pause, he was shifting to a new plan of attack. Now we would run at right angles to the destroyer's course and fire our stern tubes at her as she passed astern.

The conning tower burst into action. Periscope down . . . Roger twirling knobs on the TDC . . . Mush crouched in the middle of the conning tower, breathing heavily, spinning the disks on the is-was . . . orders being shouted now rather than whispered. The destroyer's speed, increasing as she got under way, could only be guessed at. Roger cranked a reading on the TDC, which would automatically generate the correct angles for the gyros. The ship swung hard to the right. Within one minute we were ready to fire.

"Up periscope. . . . Mark! . . . Target has zigged. . . . Angle on the bow forty starboard." Now the destroyer was heading across our bow. More frantic grinding of knobs, another quick guess at his speed—fifteen knots this time.

"Ready. . . . Stand by to fire. . . . Fire One. . . . Fire Two. . . . Fire Three."

The boat shuddered as the three torpedoes left the forward tubes.

"All ahead standard." The bow had begun to rise under the loss of weight forward.

Steam torpedoes leave a wake as wide as a two-lane highway and a lot whiter. There was no point now in lowering the periscope, for at that range the enemy could simply look down the wakes to where *x* marked the spot. Dick brought the periscope up to full height and watched. After a couple of centuries, he spoke.

"They're headed for him."

Torpedoes run at about fifty knots, but the interval between firing and hitting seems endless.

"The first one missed astern. . . . The second one missed astern. . . . The third one missed astern."

Groans sounded in the conning tower. We had guessed too low on his speed.

"Get another setup!" There was a fierce urgency in Mush's voice. "Use twenty knots."

"Ready."

"Fire Four!"

Again the boat shuddered, and Dick's eyes remained glued to the scope. And again the news, given to us piecemeal between long pauses, was bad.

"Target turning away."

"Damn!"

"The fourth missed. . . . She's swinging on around. . . . Now she's headed right at us."

The situation had changed drastically. Warned by the wakes of the first three torpedoes, the destroyer had begun a fast, determined turn away from us, continuing it for 270 degrees until now she was headed toward us, ready for revenge. A destroyer is named for its ability to destroy submarines, and this one was coming at us now with a deck full of depth charges. We had fired four of our six forward fish. We had four more in our stern tubes, but it would take too long to swing to fire them, and even longer to reload our forward tubes.

"All right," said Mush. "Get set for a down-the-throat shot."

We had talked about down-the-throats in wardroom bull sessions, but I doubt if any of us had ever seriously expected to be involved in such a shot. It is what the name implies, a shot fired at the target while he is coming directly toward you. No one knew for sure how effective it would be, because as far as I know there was then no case in our submarine records of anyone's having tried it. But it had one obvious virtue, and two staggering disadvantages. On the one hand, you didn't have to know the target's speed if the angle was zero; on the other hand, the target would be at its narrowest, and if you missed, it would be too late to plan anything else. In this particular case, we would be shooting a two-ton torpedo at a craft no more than twenty feet wide, coming toward us at a speed of about thirty knots.

A few minutes before, I had been thinking fatuously what a fine story I would have to tell Ann and Billy on my leave. Now I remembered with relief that I had left my will ashore at the beginning of the patrol.

"Ready." From Roger, at the TDC.

"Stand by to fire."

"Range eighteen hundred."

"Fire Five!"

"Periscope is under water. Bring me up."

Hank had momentarily lost control, under the impact of the firing, and we had dropped below periscope depth with that destroyer boiling down on us. "Bring her up, Hank, boy, bring her up," the skipper called down the hatch. An agonizing wait, then, with Dick clinging to the periscope.

"Captain, we missed him. He's still coming. Getting close."

It is strange how, in such situations, some portion of your mind can occupy itself with coolly impersonal analyses of factors not directly connected with your own hide. I found part of myself marveling at the change that had come over Dick O'Kane since the attack had begun. It was as if, during all the talkative, boastful months before, he had been lost, seeking his true element, and now it was found. He was calm, terse, and utterly cool. My opinion of him underwent a permanent change. It was not the first time I had observed that the conduct of men under fire cannot be predicted accurately from their everyday actions, but it was the most dramatic example I was ever to see of a man transformed under pressure from what seemed almost adolescent petulance to a prime fighting machine.

"Stand by to fire Six."

"When shall I fire, Captain?"

"Wait till she fills four divisions in low power."

"Captain, she already fills eight."

Even Mush was jarred. "Well, for heaven's sake," he yelled, "*fire!*"

"Fire Six!" From Dick. Mush echoed him with, "Take her deep!"

We flooded negative and started down, and I went down the ladder and took over from Hank. I couldn't take her really deep, because we had no idea what the depth of the water there was, and it wouldn't help to strike an uncharted reef. But I took her as far down as I dared, to ninety feet, and we rigged for depth-charge attack.

We were no longer the aggressor. Now our time as well as our torpedoes had run out, and we were helpless to fight back. All we could do was grab onto something and stand by for the final depth-charging of the U.S.S. *Wahoo*. Our time had come, and we waited for the end almost calmly.

The first explosion was loud and close. A couple of light bulbs broke, as they always do on a close explosion, and I remember watching in a detached way as the cork that lined the inside of the *Wahoo's* hull began to flake off in little pieces.

We waited for the second blast, each man lost within himself, looking at objects rather than at other men, no eyes meeting, as is appropriate for the final moments of life.

And the silence continued. Ten, twenty, thirty seconds, until I looked up and saw other eyes coming into focus, faces taking on expressions of wonderment. It was a voice from the pump room that broke the spell.

"Jeez," it said. "Maybe we hit *him!*"

There was something ridiculous, almost hilariously so, about the voice. Up in the conning tower Mush heard it, and laughed.

"Well, by God, maybe we did," he responded, his voice now a roar. "Bring her back up to periscope depth, George."

Almost frantically, we wrestled her back up.

Again, Mush left the scope to Dick. He took a long look.

"There she is. Broken in two."

Bedlam broke loose on the *Wahoo*.

I waved to Hank to take over in the control room, grabbed my Graflex, and shot up the ladder. Mush had named me ship's photographer, and I was going to get a shot of that target one way or another.

It wasn't easy. Even Mush wanted to take a look at this, and every man in the crowded conning tower was fighting for a turn by the time the skipper turned aside. But at last my chance came.

The destroyer was almost beam to, broken in two like a matchstick, her bow already settling. Apparently, her skipper had lost his nerve when he saw our last torpedo heading toward him and put the rudder over to try to miss it, and by swinging himself broadside to it he had signed the destroyer's death warrant. Now, as she began to sink, her crew swarmed over her, hundreds of men, in the rigging, in the superstructure, all over her decks. As we struggled for positions at the periscope, some of the destroyer's crew returned to their places at the forward deck gun and began firing at our periscope. They continued it as she sank slowly beneath the waves.

Somehow I got a few pictures and moved out of the way. And now Mush, who was almost a tyrant when it came to imposing his will on us in emergencies, returned to the democratic spirit he always showed when something good happened. "Let everybody come up and take a look," he called.

The whole crew came up by turns, overflowing every inch of the control room and the conning tower, each man shoving his way to the scope and bracing himself there for a long, unbelieving look before turning away with whatever word represented the extreme limit of his vocabulary. I heard some remarkable expletives that day.

We were still celebrating when a bomb went off close aboard, and it dawned on us that there was a long way to go before we were out of the woods. Down we went again to ninety feet, realizing there was an airplane up there on lookout for us, and started to pick our way out.

In a moment we began to hear the propellers of small boats, buzzing around the water above us like waterbugs as they searched for us, and we realized the only way to get out of Wewak harbor safely was to keep our periscope down. In addition to the unknowns of current and depth, we had another unknown. Now we must run silent, which meant even the gyrocompass had to be turned off. The only compass we could use was the magnetic compass, never too reliable inside all that steel. We had to make four miles, take a turn to the right, and go about two more miles before we got to the open sea, and if we turned too soon, we were going to run into the island where we had seen the coast watcher sitting under the coconut tree.

If we didn't turn soon enough, we were going to hit the reef ahead.

On the way down the dogleg before the attack, I had noticed a young sailor on the sound equipment, listening with great intensity, though he wasn't particularly needed at the time. Now he spoke to Mush.

"Captain," he said, "as we were coming in, I could hear beach noises on that island. I think I can tell from them when it's abeam."

None of us in the conning tower knew exactly what beach noises were. Since then, I have read that oceanographers say that all sorts of things, particularly shrimp, make noises in the ocean, and shrimp in large beds are common in shallow water in that area. Whatever it was, if the man on the sound gear thought he could help, we were ready to listen.

So, relying on him, we prepared for our turn. We waited until he reported the sounds were abaft the beam, then we made our turn, holding our breaths and hoping, and it worked.

We surfaced after dark, about two miles outside the harbor, and looked back. The Japanese had built bonfires on almost every point, on the shore and on the islands, all along the roadstead. They must have been sure we were still in there, and waiting for us to surface. I have always been grateful, mistakenly or otherwise, to the shrimp along Mushu Island and Coast Watcher Point for getting us safely out after our reconnoitering of Wewak harbor.

FROM

Captain Canot, or Twenty Years of an African Slaver

THEODORE CANOT AND BRANTZ MAYER

For three and a half centuries, the Atlantic Ocean was the highway for a lucrative commerce in human beings. During that time more than fifteen million African slaves were transported to the Western Hemisphere. Many millions more died chained together in packed, suffocating, pestilential ships' holds on the terrible "middle passage."

Long after Great Britain, the United States, and other nations outlawed the slave trade in the early years of the nineteenth century, a contraband traffic continued between Africa and those countries where slavery itself survived. Swift ships built especially for this illegal trade—many of them in Yankee shipyards—slipped through British and U.S. naval patrols off the African coast to deliver their human cargoes to eager purchasers in the Americas.

The most famous of the illegal slavers was Captain Theodore Canot. Born in Italy, he was fluent in four languages and sailed under a dozen flags. He was shrewd, adventurous, courageous—and completely amoral. This is his story of the voyage of La Estrella.

Black Cargo

My finances were at low-water mark, when I strolled one fine morning into Matanzas, and, after some delay, again obtained command of a slaver, through the secret influence of my old and trusty friends. The new craft was a dashing schooner, of one hundred and twenty tons, fresh from the United States, and intended for Ayudah on the Gold Coast. It was calculated that we might bring home at least four hundred and fifty slaves, for whose purchase, I was supplied plentifully with rum, powder, English muskets, and rich cottons from Manchester.

In due time we sailed for the Cape de Verds, the usual "port of dispatch" on such excursions; and at Praya, exchanged our flag for the Portuguese, before we put up our helm for the coast. A British cruiser chased us fruitlessly for two days off Sierra Leone, and enabled me not only to test the sailing qualities, but to get the *sailing trim* of *La Estrella,* in perfection. So confident did I become of the speed and bottom of my gallant clipper, that I ventured, with a leading wind, to chase the first vessel I descried on the horizon, and was altogether deceived by tri-color displayed at her peak. Indeed, I could not divine this novel nationality till the speaking trumpet apprised us that the lilies of France had taken triple hues in the hands of Louis Philippe! Accordingly, before I squared away for Ayudah, I saluted the *royal republican,* by lowering my flag thrice to the new divinity.

I consigned *La Estrella* to one of the most remarkable traders that ever expanded the African traffic by his genius.

Señor Da Souza—better known on the coast and interior as Cha-cha—was said to be a native mulatto of Rio Janeiro, whence he immigrated to Dahomey, after deserting the arms of his imperial master. I do not know how he reached Africa, but it is probable the fugitive made part of some slaver's crew, and fled from his vessel, as he had previously abandoned the military service in the delicious clime of Brazil. His parents were poor, indolent, and careless, so that Cha-cha grew up an illiterate, headstrong youth. Yet, when he touched the soil of Africa, a new life seemed infused into his veins. For a while, his days are said to have been full of misery and trouble, but the Brazilian slave trade happened to receive an extraordinary impetus about that period; and, gradually, the adventurous refugee managed to profit by his skill in dealing with the natives, or by acting as broker among his countrymen. Beginning in the humblest way, he stuck to trade with the utmost tenacity till he ripened into an opulent factor. The tinge of native blood that dyed his complexion perhaps qualified him peculiarly for this enterprise. He loved the customs of the people. He spoke their language with the fluency of a native. He won the favor of chief after chief. He strove to be considered a perfect African among Africans; though, among whites, he still affected the graceful address and manners of his country. In this way, little by little, Cha-cha advanced in the regard of all he dealt with, and secured the commissions of Brazil and Cuba, while he was regarded and protected as a prime favorite by the warlike king of Dahomey. Indeed, it is alleged that this noted sovereign formed a sort of devilish compact with the Portuguese factor, and supplied him with everything he desired during life, in consideration of inheriting his wealth when dead.

But Cha-cha was resolved, while the power of enjoyment was still vouchsafed him, that all the pleasures of human life accessible to money should not be wanting in Ayudah. He built a large and commodious dwelling for his residence on a beautiful spot, near the site of an abandoned Portuguese fort. He filled his establishment with every luxury and comfort that could please the fancy or gratify the body. Wines, food, delicacies and raiment were brought from Paris, London, and Havana. The finest women along the coast were lured to his settlement. Billiard tables and gambling halls spread their wiles, or afforded distraction for detained navigators. In fine, the mongrel Sybarite surrounded himself with all that could corrupt virtue, gratify passion, tempt avarice, betray weakness, satisfy sensuality, and complete a picture of incarnate slavery in Dahomey.

When he sallied forth, his walk was always accompanied by considerable ceremony. An officer preceded him to clear the path; a fool or buffoon hopped beside him; a band of native musicians sounded their discordant instruments, and a couple of singers screamed, at the top of their voices, the most fulsome adulation of the mulatto.

Numbers of vessels were, of course, required to feed this African nabob with doubloons and merchandise. Sometimes, commanders from Cuba or Brazil would be kept months in his perilous nest, while their craft cruised along the coast, in expectation of human cargoes. At such seasons, no expedient was left untried for the entertainment and pillage of wealthy or trusted idlers. If Cha-cha's board and wines made them drunkards, it was no fault of his. If *rouge et noir,* or *monte,* won their doubloons and freight at his saloon, he regretted but dared not interfere with the amusements of his guests. If the sirens of his harem betrayed a cargo for their favor over cards, a convenient fire destroyed the frail warehouse after its merchandise was secretly removed!

Cha-cha was exceedingly desirous that I should accept his hospitality. As soon as I read my invoice to him—for he could not do it himself—he became almost irresistible in his *empressement.* Yet I declined the invitation with firm politeness, and took up my quarters onshore, at the residence of a native *manfuca,* or broker. I was warned of his allurements before I left Matanzas, and resolved to keep myself and property so clear of his clutches that our contract would either be fulfilled or remain within my control. Thus, by avoiding his table, his "hells," and the society of his dissipated sons, I maintained my business relations with the slaver and secured his personal respect so effectually that, at the end of two months, four hundred and eighty prime Negroes were in the bowels of *La Estrella.*

I have always regretted that I left Ayudah on my homeward voyage without interpreters to aid in the necessary intercourse with our slaves. There was no one on board who understood a word of their dialect. Many complaints from the Negroes that would have been dismissed or satisfactorily adjusted, had we comprehended their vivacious tongues and grievances, were passed over in silence or hushed with the lash. Indeed, the whip alone was the emblem of *La Estrella's* discipline; and in the end it taught me the saddest of lessons.

From the beginning there was manifest discontent among the slaves. I endeavored at first to please and accommodate them by a gracious manner; but manner alone is not appreciated by untamed Africans. A few days after our departure, a slave leaped overboard in a fit of passion, and another choked himself during the night. These two suicides, in twenty-four hours, caused much uneasiness among the officers, and induced me to make every preparation for a revolt.

We had been at sea about three weeks without further disturbance, and there was so much merriment among the gangs that were allowed to come on deck, that my apprehensions of danger began gradually to wear away. Suddenly, however, one fair afternoon, a squall broke forth from an almost cloudless sky; and as the boatswain's whistle piped all hands to take in sail, a simultaneous rush was made by the confined slaves at all the after gratings, and amid the confusion of the rising gale, they knocked down the guard and poured upon deck. The sentry at the *fore hatch* seized the cook's ax, and sweeping it round him like a scythe, kept at bay the band that sought to emerge from below him. Meantime, the women in the cabin were not idle. Seconding the males, they rose in a body, and the helmsman was forced to stab several with his knife before he could drive them below again.

About forty stalwart devils, yelling and grinning with all the savage ferocity of their wilderness, were now on deck, armed with staves of broken water-casks, or billets of wood, found in the hold. The suddenness of this outbreak did not appall me, for, in the dangerous life of Africa, a trader must be always admonished and never off his guard. The blow that prostrated the first white man was the earliest symptom I detected of the revolt; but, in an instant, I had the arm chest open on the quarter-deck, and the mate and steward beside me to protect it. Matters, however, did not stand so well forward of the mainmast. Four of the hands were disabled by clubs, while the rest defended themselves and the wounded as well as they could with handspikes, or whatever could suddenly be clutched. I had always charged the cook, on such an emergency, to distribute from his coppers a liberal supply of scalding water upon the belligerents; and, at the first sign of revolt, he endeavored to baptize the heathen with his steaming slush. But dinner had been over for some time, so that the lukewarm liquid only irritated the savages, one of whom laid the unfortunate "doctor" bleeding in the scuppers.

All this occurred in perhaps less time than I have taken to tell it; yet, rapid as was the transaction, I saw that, between the squall with its flying sails, and the revolt with its raving blacks, we would soon be in a desperate plight, unless I gave

the order *to shoot*. Accordingly, I told my comrades *to aim low and fire at once.*

Our carbines had been purposely loaded with buckshot, to suit such an occasion, so that the first two discharges brought several of the rebels to their knees. Still, the unharmed neither fled nor ceased brandishing their weapons. Two more discharges drove them forward among the mass of my crew, who had retreated toward the bowsprit; but, being reinforced by the boatswain and carpenter, we took command of the hatches so effectually, that a dozen additional discharges among the ebony legs, drove the refractory to their quarters below.

It was time, for sails, ropes, tacks, sheets, and blocks were flapping, dashing, and rolling about the masts and decks, threatening us with imminent danger from the squall. In a short time, every thing was made snug, the vessel put on our course, and attention paid to the mutineers, who had begun to fight among themselves in the hold!

I perceived at once, by the infuriated sounds proceeding from below, that it would not answer to venture in their midst by descending through the hatches. Accordingly, we discharged the women from their quarters under a guard on deck, and sent several resolute and well-armed hands to remove a couple of boards from the bulkhead that separated the cabin from the hold. When this was accomplished, a party entered, on hands and knees, through the aperture, and began to press the mutineers forward toward the bulkhead of the forecastle. Still, the rebels were hot for fight to the last, and boldly defended themselves with their staves against our weapons.

By this time, our lamed cook had rekindled his fires, and the water was once more boiling. The hatches were kept open but guarded, and all who did not fight were suffered to come singly on deck, where they were tied. As only about sixty remained below engaged in conflict, or defying my party of sappers and miners, I ordered a number of auger holes to be bored in the deck, as the scoundrels were forced forward near the forecastle, when a few buckets of boiling water, rained on them through the fresh apertures, brought the majority to submission. Still, however, two of the most savage held out against water as well as fire. I strove as long as possible to save their lives, but their resistance was so prolonged and perilous, that we were obliged to disarm them *for ever* by a couple of pistol shots.

So ended the sad revolt of *La Estrella*, in which two of my men were seriously wounded, while twenty-eight balls and buckshot were extracted, with sailors' skill, from the lower limbs of the slaves. One woman and three men perished of blows received in the conflict, but none were deliberately slain except the two men, who resisted unto death.

I could never account for this mutiny, especially as the blacks from Ayudah and its neighborhood are distinguished for their humble manners and docility. There can be no doubt that the entire gang was not united or concerned in the original outbreak, else we should have had harder work in subduing them, amid the risk and turmoil of a West Indian squall.

There was very little comfort on board *La Estrella* after the suppression of this revolt. We lived with a pent-up volcano beneath us, and, day and night, we were ceaselessly vigilant. Terror reigned supreme, and the lash was its scepter.

At last, we made land at Porto Rico, and were swiftly passing

its beautiful shores, when the inspector called my attention to the appearance of one of our attendant slaves, whom we had drilled as a sort of cabin-boy. He was a gentle, intelligent child, and had won the hearts of all the officers.

His pulse was high, quick and hard; his face and eyes red and swollen; while, on his neck, I detected half a dozen rosy pimples. He was sent immediately to the forecastle, free from contact with anyone else, and left there, cut off from the crew, till I could guard against pestilence. It was small-pox!

The boy passed a wretched night of fever and pain, developing the malady with all its horrors. It is very likely that I slept as badly as the sufferer, for my mind was busy with his *doom.* Daylight found me on deck in consultation with our veteran boatswain, whose experience in the trade authorized the highest respect for his opinion. Hardened as he was, the old man's eyes filled, his lips trembled, and his voice was husky, as he whispered the verdict in my ear. I guessed it before he said a word; yet I hoped he would have counselled against the dread alternative. As we went aft to the quarter-deck, all eyes were bent upon us, for every one conjectured the malady and feared the result, yet none dared ask a question.

I ordered a general inspection of the slaves, yet when a *favorable* report was made, I did not rest content, and descended to examine each one personally. It was true; the child was *alone* infected!

For half an hour, I trod the deck to and fro restlessly, and caused the crew to subject themselves to inspection. But my sailors were as healthy as the slaves. There was no symptom that indicated approaching danger. I was disappointed again. A single case—a single sign of peril in any quarter, would have spared the poison!

That evening, in the stillness of night, a trembling hand stole forward to the afflicted boy with a potion that knows no waking. In a few hours, all was over. Life and the pestilence were crushed together, for a necessary murder had been committed, and the poor victim was beneath the blue water!

I am not superstitious, but a voyage attended with such calamities could not end happily. Incessant gales and head winds, unusual in this season and latitude, beset us so obstinately that it became doubtful whether our food and water would last till we reached Matanzas. To add to our risks and misfortunes, a British corvette espied our craft, and gave chase off Cape Maize. All day long she dogged us slowly, but, at night, I tacked off shore, with the expectation of eluding my pursuer. Day dawn, however, revealed her again on our track, though this time we had unfortunately fallen to leeward. Accordingly, I put *La Estrella* directly before the wind, and ran till dark with a fresh breeze, when I again dodged the cruiser, and made for the Cuban coast. But the Briton seemed to scent my track, for sunrise revealed him once more in chase.

The wind lulled that night to a light breeze, yet the red clouds and haze in the east betokened a gale from that quarter before meridian. A longer pursuit must have given considerable advantage to the enemy, so that my best reliance, I calculated, was in making the small harbor near St. Jago, now about twenty miles distant, where I had already landed two cargoes. The corvette was then full ten miles astern.

My resolution to save the cargo and lose the vessel was promptly made;—orders were issued to strike from the slaves the irons they had constantly worn since the mutiny; the boats were made ready; and every man prepared his bag for a rapid launch.

On dashed the cruiser, foaming at the bows, under the impetus of the rising gale, which struck him some time before it reached us. We were not more than seven miles apart when the first increased pressure on our sails was felt, and everything was set and braced to give it the earliest welcome. Then came the tug and race for the beach, three miles ahead. But, under such circumstances, it was hardly to be expected that St. George could carry the day. Still, every nerve was strained to effect the purpose. Regardless of the gale, reef after reef was let out while force pumps moistened his sails; yet nothing was gained. Three miles against seven were too much odds;—and, with a slight move of the helm, and "letting all fly," as we neared the line of surf, to break her headway, *La Estrella* was fairly and safely *beached*.

The sudden shock snapped her mainmast like a pipe-stem, but, as no one was injured, in a twinkling the boats were overboard, crammed with women and children, while a stage was rigged from the bows to the strand, so that the males, the crew, and the luggage were soon in charge of my old *haciendado*.

Prompt as we were, we were not sufficiently so for the cruiser. Half our cargo was ashore when she backed her top-sails off the mouth of the little bay, lowered her boats, filled them with boarders, and steered towards our craft. The delay of half a mile's row gave us time to cling still longer to the wreck, so that, when the boats and corvette began to fire, we wished them joy of their bargain over the remnant of our least valuable Negroes. The rescued blacks are now, in all likelihood, citizens of Jamaica, but, under the influence of the gale, *La Estrella* made a very picturesque bonfire, as we saw it that night from the *azotea* of our landlord's domicile.

FROM
Shipwreck of the Whaleship Essex

OWEN CHASE

On November 20, 1820, while hunting in the middle of the Pacific Ocean, the whaleship Essex *of Nantucket was stove in and sunk by a whale. Its crew of twenty escaped in three small boats. Salvaging some bread and water and a few navigational instruments from the wrecked ship, they set out on the long voyage to South America.*

Of the twenty crewmen, eight ultimately survived. Three were rescued from tiny Henderson Island, where they had elected to remain when the boats touched there in December 1820. Five others, in two separated boats, were picked up off the coast of Chile in February 1821. During three months at sea they had traveled 3700 miles. Six men who had died since leaving Henderson Island—and one who, after a desperate cast of lots, had been shot—were eaten by their starving companions.

First Mate Owen Chase begins his narrative of the terrible episode with this account of the wreck of the Essex.

Leviathan

I HAVE not been able to recur to the scenes which are now to become the subject of description, although a considerable time has elapsed, without feeling a mingled emotion of horror and astonishment at the almost incredible destiny that has preserved me and my surviving companions from a terrible death. Frequently, in my reflections on the subject, even after this lapse of time, I find myself shedding tears of gratitude for our deliverance, and blessing God, by whose divine aid and protection we were conducted through a series of unparalleled suffering and distress, and restored to the bosoms of our families and friends. There is no knowing what a stretch of pain and misery the human mind is capable of contemplating, when it is wrought upon by the anxieties of preservation; nor what pangs and weaknesses the body is able to endure, until they are visited upon it; and when at last deliverance comes, when the dream of hope is realized, unspeakable gratitude takes possession of the soul, and tears of joy choke the utterance. We require to be taught in the school of some signal suffering, privation, and despair the great lessons of constant dependence upon an almighty forbearance and mercy. In the midst of the wide ocean, at night, when the sight of the heavens was shut out, and the dark tempest came upon us, then it was that we felt ourselves ready to exclaim, "Heaven have mercy upon us, for nought but that can save us now." But I proceed to the recital.

On the 20th of November (cruising in latitude 0° 40′ S., longitude 119° 0′ W.), a shoal of whales was discovered off the lee bow. The weather at this time was extremely fine and clear, and it was about eight o'clock in the morning that the man at the masthead gave the usual cry of, "There she blows." The ship was immediately put away, and we ran down in the direction for them. When we had got within half a mile of the place where they were observed, all our boats were lowered down, manned, and we started in pursuit of them. The ship, in the meantime, was brought to the wind, and the main-topsail hove aback, to wait for us. I had the harpoon in the second boat; the captain preceded me in the first.

When I arrived at the spot where we calculated they were, nothing was at first to be seen. We lay on our oars in anxious expectation of discovering them come up somewhere near us. Presently one rose and spouted a short distance ahead of my boat; I made all speed toward it, came up with, and struck it; feeling the harpoon in him, he threw himself, in agony, over toward the boat (which at that time was up alongside of him), and, giving a severe blow with his tail, struck the boat near the edge of the water, amidships, and stove a hole in her. I immediately took up the boat hatchet, and cut the line, to disengage the boat from the whale, which by this time was running off with great velocity. I succeeded in getting clear of him, with the loss of the harpoon and line; and, finding the water to pour fast in the boat, I hastily stuffed three or four of our jackets in the hole, ordered one man to keep constantly bailing, and the rest to pull immediately for the ship; we succeeded in keeping the boat free, and shortly gained the ship.

The captain and the second mate, in the two other boats, kept up the pursuit, and soon struck another whale. They being at this time a considerable distance to leeward, I went forward, braced around the mainyard, and put the ship off in a direction for them; the boat which had been stove was immediately hoisted in, and after examining the hole, I found that I could, by nailing a piece of canvas over it, get her ready to join in a fresh pursuit, sooner than by lowering down the other remaining boat which belonged to the ship. I accordingly turned her over upon the quarter, and was in the act of nailing on the canvas, when I observed a very large spermaceti whale, as well as I could judge about eighty-five feet in length; he broke water about twenty rods off our weather-bow, and was lying quietly, with his head in a direction for the ship. He spouted two or three times, and then disappeared. In less than two or three seconds he came up again, about the length of the ship off, and made directly for us, at the rate of about three knots. The ship was then going with about the same velocity. His appearance and attitude gave us at first no alarm; but while I stood watching his movements, and observing him but a ship's length off, coming down for us with great celerity, I involuntarily ordered the boy at the helm to put it hard up; intending to sheer off and avoid him. The words were scarcely out of my mouth, before he came down upon us with full speed and struck the ship with his head, just forward of the fore chains; he gave us such an appalling and tremendous jar, as nearly threw us all on our faces. The ship brought up as suddenly and violently as if she had struck a rock, and trembled for a few seconds like a leaf. We looked at each other with perfect amazement, deprived almost of the power of speech. Many minutes elapsed before we were able to realize the dreadful accident; during which time he passed under the ship, grazing her keel as he went along, came up alongside of her to leeward, and lay on the top of the water (apparently stunned with the violence of the blow) for the space of a minute; he then suddenly started off, in a direction to leeward.

After a few moments' reflection, and recovering, in some measure, from the sudden consternation that had seized us, I of course concluded that he had stove a hole in the ship, and that it would be necessary to set the pumps going. Accordingly they were rigged, but had not been in operation more than one minute before I perceived the head of the ship to be gradually settling down in the water; I then ordered the signal to be set for the other boats, which, scarcely had I dispatched, before I again discovered the whale, apparently in convulsions, on top of the water, about one hundred rods to leeward. He was enveloped in the foam of the sea, that his continual and violent thrashing about in the water had created around him, and I could distinctly see him smite his jaws together, as if distracted with rage and fury. He remained a short time in this situation, and then started off with great velocity, across the bows of the ship, to windward. By this time the ship had settled down a considerable distance in the water, and I gave her up for lost. I, however, ordered the pumps to be kept constantly going, and endeavored to collect my thoughts for the occasion.

I turned to the boats, two of which we then had with the ship, with an intention of clearing them away, and getting all things ready to embark in them, if there should be no other resource left; and while my attention was thus engaged for a moment, I was aroused with the cry of a man at the hatchway, "Here he is—he is making for us again." I turned around and saw him about one hundred rods directly ahead of us, coming down apparently with twice his ordinary speed, and to me at that moment, it appeared with tenfold fury and vengeance in his aspect. The surf flew in all directions about him, and his course towards us was marked by a white foam of a rod in width, which he made with the continual violent thrashing of his tail; his head was about half out of water, and in that way he came upon, and again struck the ship. I was in hopes, when I descried him making for us, that by a dexterous movement of putting the ship away immediately, I should be able to cross the line of his approach, before he could get up to us, and thus avoid what I knew, if he should strike us again, would prove our inevitable destruction. I bawled out to the helmsman, "Hard up!" but she had not fallen off more than a point, before we took the second shock. I should judge the speed of the ship to have been at this time about three knots, and that of the whale about six. He struck her to windward, directly under the cathead, and completely stove in her bows. He passed under the ship again, went off to leeward, and we saw no more of him.

Our situation at this juncture can be more readily imagined than described. The shock to our feelings was such as I am sure none can have an adequate conception of that were not there: the misfortune befell us at a moment when we least dreamt of any accident; and from the pleasing anticipations we had formed, of realizing the certain profits of our labor, we were dejected by a sudden, most mysterious, and overwhelming calamity. Not a moment, however, was to be lost in endeavoring to provide for the extremity to which it was now certain we were reduced. We were more than a thousand miles from the nearest land, and with nothing but a light open boat as the resource of safety for myself and companions. I ordered the men to cease pumping, and every one to provide for himself; seizing a hatchet at the same time, I cut away the lashings of the spare boat, which lay bottom up across two spars directly over the quarter deck, and cried out to those near me to take her as she came down. They did so accordingly, and bore her on their shoulders as far as the waist of the ship. The steward had in the meantime gone down into the cabin twice, and saved two quadrants, two practical navigators, and the captain's trunk and mine; all which were hastily thrown into the boat, as she lay on the deck, with the two compasses which I snatched from the binnacle. He attempted to descend again, but the water by this time had rushed in, and he returned without being able to effect his purpose. By the time we had got the boat to the waist, the ship had filled with water and was going down on her beam ends: we shoved our boat as quickly as possible from the plank shear into the water, all hands jumping in her at the same time, and launched off clear of the ship. We were scarcely two boat lengths distant from her, when she fell over to windward, and settled down in the water.

Amazement and despair now wholly took possession of us.

We contemplated the frightful situation the ship lay in, and thought with horror upon the sudden and dreadful calamity that had overtaken us. We looked upon each other, as if to gather some consolatory sensation from an interchange of sentiments, but every countenance was marked with the paleness of despair. Not a word was spoken for several minutes by any of us; all appeared to be bound in a spell of stupid consternation; and from the time we were first attacked by the whale, to the period of the fall of the ship, and of our leaving her in the boat, more than ten minutes could not certainly have elapsed! God only knows in what way, or by what means, we were enabled to accomplish in that short time what we did; the cutting away and transporting the boat from where she was deposited would of itself, in ordinary circumstances, have consumed as much time as that, if the whole ship's crew had been employed in it. My companions had not saved a single article but what they had on their backs, but to me it was a source of infinite satisfaction, if any such could be gathered from the horrors of our gloomy situation, that we had been fortunate enough to have preserved our compasses, navigators, and quadrants. After the first shock of my feelings was over, I enthusiastically contemplated them as the probable instruments of our salvation; without them all would have been dark and hopeless.

Gracious God! what a picture of distress and suffering now presented itself to my imagination. The crew of the ship were saved, consisting of twenty human souls. All that remained to conduct these twenty beings through the stormy terrors of the ocean, perhaps many thousand miles, were three open light boats. The prospect of obtaining any provisions or water from the ship, to subsist upon during the time, was at least now doubtful. How many long and watchful nights, thought I, are to be passed? How many tedious days of partial starvation are to be endured, before the least relief or mitigation of our sufferings can be reasonably anticipated.

We lay at this time in our boat, about two ship lengths off from the wreck, in perfect silence, calmly contemplating her situation, and absorbed in our own melancholy reflections, when the other boats were discovered rowing up to us. They had but shortly before discovered that some accident had befallen us, but of the nature of which they were entirely ignorant. The sudden and mysterious disappearance of the ship was first discovered by the boat-steerer in the captain's boat, and with a horror-struck countenance and voice, he suddenly exclaimed, "Oh, my God! where is the ship?" Their operations upon this were instantly suspended, and a general cry of horror and despair burst from the lips of every man, as their looks were directed for her, in vain, over every part of the ocean. They immediately made all haste toward us. The captain's boat was the first that reached us. He stopped about a boat's length off but had no power to utter a single syllable: he was so completely overpowered with the spectacle before him that he sat down in his boat, pale and speechless. I could scarcely recognize his countenance, he appeared to be so much altered, awed, and overcome with the oppression of his feelings, and the dreadful reality that lay before him. He was in a short time, however, enabled to address the inquiry to me, "My God, Mr. Chase, what is the matter?" I answered, "We have been stove by a whale." I then briefly told him the story. After a few moment's reflection he observed that we must cut away her masts, and endeavor to get something out of her to eat.

Our thoughts were now all accordingly bent on endeavors to save from the wreck whatever we might possibly want, and for this purpose we rowed up and got on to her. Search was made for every means of gaining access to her hold; and for this purpose the lanyards were cut loose, and with our hatchets we commenced to cut away the masts, that she might right up again, and enable us to scuttle her decks. In doing which we were occupied about three quarters of an hour, owing to our having no axes, nor indeed any other instruments, but the small hatchets belonging to the boats. After her masts were gone, she came up about two-thirds of the way upon an even keel. While we were employed about the masts the captain took his quadrant, shoved off from the ship, and got an observation. We found ourselves in latitude 0° 40′ S., longitude 119° W. We now commenced to cut a hole through the planks, directly above two large casks of bread, which most fortunately were between decks, in the waist of the ship, and which being in the upper side, when she upset, we had strong hopes was not wet. It turned out according to our wishes, and from these casks we obtained six hundred pounds of hard bread. Other parts of the deck were then scuttled, and we got without difficulty as much fresh water as we dared to take in the boats, so that each was supplied with about sixty-five gallons; we got also from one of the lockers a musket, a small canister of powder, a couple of files, two rasps, about two pounds of boat nails, and a few turtles.

In the afternoon the wind came on to blow a strong breeze, and, having obtained everything that occurred to us could then be got out, we began to make arrangements for our safety during the night. A boat's line was made fast to the ship, and to the other end of it one of the boats was moored, at about fifty fathoms to leeward; another boat was then attached to the first one, about eight fathoms astern; and the third boat, the like distance astern of her. Night came on just as we had finished our operations; and such a night as it was to us! so full of feverish and distracting inquietude that we were deprived entirely of rest. The wreck was constantly before my eyes. I could not, by any effort, chase away the horrors of the preceding day from my mind: they haunted me the livelong night. My companions—some of them were like sick women; they had no idea of the extent of their deplorable situation. One or two slept unconcernedly, while others wasted the night in unavailing murmurs.

I now had full leisure to examine, with some degree of coolness, the dreadful circumstances of our disaster. The scenes of yesterday passed in such quick succession in my mind that it was not until after many hours of severe reflection that I was able to discard the idea of the catastrophe as a dream. Alas! it was one from which there was no awaking; it was too certainly true, that but yesterday we had existed as it were, and in one short moment had been cut off from all the hopes and prospects of the living! I have no language to paint out the horrors of our situation. To shed tears was indeed altogether unavailing, and withal unmanly; yet I was not able to deny myself the relief they served to afford me. After several hours of idle sorrow and repining I began to reflect upon the accident, and endeavored to realize by what unaccountable destiny or design (which I could not at first determine) this sudden and most deadly attack had been made upon us: by an animal, too, never before suspected of premeditated violence, and proverbial for its insensibility and inoffensiveness. Every fact seemed to warrant me in concluding that it was anything but chance which directed his operations; he made two several attacks upon the ship, at a short interval between them, both of which, according to their direction, were calculated to do us the most injury, by being made ahead, and thereby combining the speed of the two objects for the shock; to effect which, the exact maneuvers which he made were necessary. His aspect was most horrible, and such as indicated resentment and fury. He came directly from the shoal which we had just before entered, and in which we had struck three of his companions, as if fired with revenge for their sufferings. But to this it may be observed, that the mode of fighting which they always adopt is either with repeated strokes of their tails, or snapping of their jaws together; and that a case, precisely similar to this one, has never been heard of among the oldest and most experienced whalers. To this I would answer, that the structure and strength of the whale's head is admirably designed for this mode of attack; the most prominent part of which is almost as hard and as tough as iron; indeed, I can compare it to nothing else but the inside of a horse's hoof, upon which a lance or harpoon would not make the slightest impression. The eyes and ears are removed nearly one-third the length of the whole fish, from the front part of the head, and are not in the least degree endangered in this mode of attack. At all events, the whole circumstances taken together, all happening before my own eyes, and producing, at the time, impressions in my mind of decided, calculating mischief on the part of the whale (many of which impressions I cannot now recall) induce me to be satisfied that I am correct in my opinion. It is certainly, in all its bearings, a hitherto unheard of circumstance, and constitutes, perhaps, the most extraordinary one in the annals of the fishery.

FROM

Pacific War Diary: 1942–1945

JAMES J. FAHEY

For three years, Seaman First Class James J. Fahey was a member of the crew of a 40-mm. gun aboard the U.S. light cruiser Montpelier *in the South Pacific. On November 1, 1943, the* Montpelier*—flagship of Rear Admiral A. S. Merrill—led a force of light cruisers and destroyers in support of a troop landing at Empress Augusta Bay on the island of Bougainville. That night the American ships were hit by a superior Japanese force, and the next day by one hundred Japanese planes. Here, from Fahey's diary, is an ordinary sailor's account of the action.*

Battle Station

SUNDAY, *October 31, 1943:* It is the last day of the month and also the last day for mess cooking. These three months sure went fast. Now I shall go hungry again. The only good meal we get is at noon. I shall start standing gun watches again. On the regular watch on our 40-mm. machine gun mount we have about six men on watch. When you step into the mount, it is like going into a hot oven. You say to yourself, "How can anyone stand that terrific heat for four hours with the hot sun beating down on you and the heat from the blowers pouring it on, not to mention the hot steel of the mount that almost surrounds you." You could not stand on the steel deck without shoes on. The temperature is way over 100 degrees. The sweat just rolls off you and into your shoes and onto the steel deck. We have to keep wetting the canvas that covers the ammunition. The humidity just saps the strength from you and you do not get any breeze. You and another man stand one hour on the lookout and then you sit in the hot pointer's or trainer's seat for another hour, this is the toughest because you cannot move around. You just sit there in the hot steel seat and sweat. The glare from the sun and the water is very tough on the eyes. The 12 noon to 4 P.M. watch is always the hottest. It is also hard to stay awake when you are in the Japs' back yard at two or three in the morning when you are standing lookout in front of the gun mount. You have had very little sleep to start with and while you are on the lookout for Jap subs or torpedoes your feet just buckle under you. You are dead tired and actually fall asleep standing up. You force yourself to stay awake but it is a losing proposition. You continue to doze off for a split second, your head droops, feet buckle under you and then you are awake again to do the same thing all over again. While this is going on the mount captain is walking back and forth pushing the fellows and barking at them to stay awake. It is really the Agony in the Garden. This is what you call torture. If the guns are firing, we have no trouble staying awake. When we stand watch in port at night and one of the fellows should doze off in the pointer's or trainer's seat, he gets two buckets of water in the face. Everyone goes up to the fellow asleep and someone puts his hands in front of his eyes; if he does not move, we know he is asleep. The bucket brigade then goes into action. When he gets hit with the first bucket of water, it almost knocks him out of his seat, and when he opens his eyes, he gets the second bucket. It is better than a circus. The rest of the crew break their sides laughing. The payoff comes when he says that he was not sleeping, he was resting his eyes. It does not take very long to dry your clothes because the water is warm and the weather is very hot. This ceremony usually takes place on the midnight to four in the morning watch.

After all this talk about what we do while on watch, it looks like we are going to spend many days there, starting today. At 2:30 A.M., October 31, 1943, we left Tulagi in the Solomons. It's very dark as usual. Every time we hit the Japs it is pitch black. There is no moon. This way the Japs will not see us. We are going to travel about 500 or 600 miles up the Solomons to bombard the Japs on Buka and Bonis. This will take place after midnight. When we finish we will turn around and pull off our first daylight bombardment of the war, on the Shortlands. It is also heavily defended. Bonis is a strong base on the farthest tip of Bougainville. The Japs will have plenty of planes on the airfields here. Above Bonis is the Jap-held island of Buka. Buka is between Bougainville and the Jap fortress of New Britain and New Ireland. It looks like we will have our work cut out for us. All hands were told to get as much rest in the afternoon as we could. The sun is shining and it is hot as usual. The sea is calm. As I look out on the starboard side, I can see many transports, supply ships, invasion barges, etc. Large barrage balloons fly above many of the ships. They will come in handy against Jap planes. This is the first time I have seen these in a convoy. We must have about 70 or 80 ships with us.

Bougainville is about 200 miles long. It is also the largest island in the Solomons. The jungle there is about the thickest in the Solomons. It also has high mountains. Most of the waters around Bougainville are uncharted and we have to go by photos taken from the air or old charts that are not complete. You never know when the ship will get stuck on a reef and stay there. The Japs would love to see that happen right in their own back yard. Our five- and six-inch guns will fire thousands of shells during these bombardments.

November 1, 1943: At 12:30 A.M. this morning Admiral Merrill's task force of four light cruisers and eight destroyers started bombarding the Japs on Buka and Bonis. They are very close to each other. We kept up constant bombardment for almost one hour. The pilots in the Black Cats overhead kept us informed about what was happening to the Jap targets. We got close to shore and you could see many explosions on the beach. Our gunnery was good. We were destroying ammunition dumps, fuel dumps, troops and the Jap airfields with their planes parked there. The Japs sent planes into the air and dropped flares so that the shore guns could go to town on us. This also made it easy for the PT boats that came out of their hiding places. We made it too hot for the PT boats. One of them was blown to bits. We also had to be on the watch for Jap subs. The big Jap shore guns were also firing at us, their shells were exploding all around us. They came too close for comfort. A piece of shrapnel came through the bridge hitting Admiral Merrill's typewriter. The way things were exploding, it looked like a shooting gallery. We left the place a mass of flames and explosions. Hours later we could still see the big fires burning about 60 miles away. We are surrounded by Jap-held islands. We are the first warships to travel this far to the north. Still farther north is the powerful Jap-held base of Rabaul. We are about 600 miles from our base in Tulagi. When it gets light, the Jap Air Force will be out looking for us.

Later: After the bombardment of Buka and Bonis we headed south again. Our next target would be the Shortlands. They are south of Bougainville and are very formidable. On our way to bombard the Shortlands we spent our time carrying the empty powder cases, and fresh ammunition was carried up to be ready for our next bombardment and they were taken care of. One thing was sure we would not get any sleep. By bombarding Buka, the Japs would think that we were going to land there, and that would make our landing on Bougainville that much easier. While all this was going on, our troops were landing on Bougainville at Empress Augusta Bay. The crews on those transports and supply ships would work night and day getting them empty so they could be on their way south to the safety of their home base.

The hours passed as we sailed south in the direction of the Shortlands and about six in the morning we started bombarding the Japs on the Shortlands. This was something new for us, it was our first daylight bombardment. For the past year all our work was done in the dark. Now we will be able to see the enemy if he tries to sneak up on us. When we bombarded the Shortlands, one ship was behind the other, just like follow the leader. It consisted of four light cruisers and eight destroyers. Every ship gave the Japs on the island quite a broadside. It was not long before the Japs' big six-inch shore guns opened up on us. We held our breath as the shells straddled us. They were falling all around us. Big geysers of water could be seen shooting into the air as the shells exploded close by. Just a little closer and we would have had it. The Japs' marksmanship is very good. We are like a bunch of ducks in a shooting gallery as we pass in view of the Japs and their shore guns. One of our destroyers

was hit by a six-inch shell, but the casualties were light. Smoke could be seen rising from the destroyer. The Japs also had some torpedo boats nearby. Our ships were twisting and turning to keep from being hit as our guns blazed away at the Jap seaplane hangars, shore batteries, repair shops, airfields, troops, etc. Many fires were started as our guns hit their targets. Our bombardment lasted about three quarters of an hour. When we had finished, we continued on our way south with the Jap shore guns still firing at us.

We stayed at our battle stations for many hours and then we set the regular watch. The decks were covered with empty powder cases. We spent some time getting them out of the way. In the afternoon general quarters sounded. A big force of Jap planes including bombers was on its way down from Rabaul. They were going to hit the beachhead of Empress Augusta Bay, where our troops landed. Our task force was also an objective. Out of nowhere our planes came to the rescue. Both air forces were very large. It was a full-scale air battle. Our pilots were coming out on top. All the ships were getting low on fuel, especially the destroyers. We had been going at high speed for some time and covered many miles. We could expect more trouble. The Japs would not give up in a hurry without putting up a fight. They did not want to lose the big island of Bougainville because we would be able to knock out their big bases on New Britain, New Ireland and New Guinea with our planes and bombers.

Tuesday, November 2, 1943: We got two hours' sleep as we continued south, but 12:45 A.M. this morning general quarters sounded. Everyone was very tired as he ran to his battle stations in the early morning darkness, not knowing what we were in for. We did know that when we left our base at Tulagi, Sunday at 2:30 A.M., most of the time would be spent at battle stations without sleep. Our food during that time was mostly sandwiches. The reason for battle stations was that a task force of Jap warships was on its way down from Rabaul to sink our transports and supply ships that were unloading at Empress Augusta Bay, Bougainville. Its objective also included bombarding our Marines and Army troops on the shore. The Japs' force packed a bigger wallop than ours. They had two heavy cruisers with them. Our biggest ships were our four light cruisers. The Japs had eight-inch guns; our biggest were six-inch guns. The Japs had two heavy cruisers, two light cruisers and eight destroyers. We had the light cruisers *Columbia, Cleveland, Denver,* and *Montpelier,* and the destroyers *Ausburne, Dyson, Claxton, Stanley, Spence, Converse, Thatcher,* and *Foote.* The action took place off the shores of Empress Augusta Bay. Our troops on shore had a ringside seat. Our job was to prevent the Jap warships from sneaking into the bay during the darkness and inflicting damage on our ships and troops there. The Japs knew these waters better than we. We never knew when our ships would get stuck on one of those uncharted reefs. Our charts were about fifty years old and were not complete. During this action only the five- and six-inch guns were to fire. That would give the machine guns a chance to take in the fireworks. We would be ready if they needed us.

You sense a funny feeling as both task forces race towards each other. We know the Japs are coming but do the Japs know that they will run into us in their own waters? Time passes as we stand there on the forty-mm. gun mount. The twin five-inch mount is only a few feet away. The mount keeps moving around and you wonder if we will hit the Japs first or will they beat us to the punch. We keep getting reports on how close we are getting to the Japs. Finally . . . "Commence firing."

It is about 2:45 A.M. Tuesday, November 2, 1943, and all hell breaks loose. The battle is on. Our guns are pouring it on as they maneuver. It is very dark and heat lightning can be seen during the battle along with a drizzle. Our ship did not waste any time in that it hit a Jap heavy cruiser. Flames and explosions were everywhere. When it was all over, the ship was dead in the water. It finally sunk. Jap shells were falling all around us and some of our ships were also getting hit. Both sides were firing away at each other. The water was full of American and Japanese torpedoes as destroyers from both sides attacked. The big eight-inch salvos, throwing up great geysers of water, were hitting very close to us. The water sprayed the ship just in front of our mount. There are great explosions as some ships sink very fast. We received reports from the other ships that they had been hit. The cruiser *Denver* was hit and had another close call as a shell went through the smokestack. It would have been all over if it had gone down the stack. During all this action our ship was hit by two Jap torpedoes but they did not explode. There was also a near miss for one of our own destroyers as it came out of the darkness and came close to ramming our starboard side. It was going in the same direction in chase of a Jap warship. For a while we thought it would crash into our ship. Our force fired star shells in front of the Jap warships so that our destroyers could attack with torpedoes. It was like putting a bright light in front of your eyes in the dark. It is impossible to see. The noise from our guns was deafening. The guns on the port and starboard had plenty of firing as we kept cutting back and forth. They say the maneuvers Admiral Merrill pulled off in this sea battle would put German Admiral Sheer of World War I fame to shame. Sheer pulled his tactics in daylight off Jutland but Merrill had darkness to cope with and twice the speed. These maneuvers are very dangerous as collisions are the rule. It's a wonder the ships could work as a team in the darkness, each picking out his own target. During the action Jap float planes were overhead dropping flares. There are big explosions as some ships sink and others are dead in the water. The Jap warships lit the sea aglow with star shells. The destroyer *Foote* is now out of action, being hit by a Jap torpedo. The Jap admiral [Rear Admiral Sentaro Omori] was the best the Japs had and he tried every trick in the book. Admiral Merrill was better. When things looked bad and the sea was lit up by the Jap star shells, Admiral Merrill ordered a smoke screen. Thick black smoke engulfed the area. The Japs found it next to impossible to strike at us. We also were on the alert for Jap subs, and torpedo boats and to make sure none of the enemies' warships could sneak into the bay and fire on our transports and troops there. The battle raged hour after hour. No quarter was given by the Japs or us. It was a battle between two masters of naval warfare and the tide of battle could be turned at any time. During the battle one could see that the Jap star shells were brighter than ours. They really lit the place up. It's a funny sensation expecting to be hit by Jap or for that matter any shell or torpedo. I'll feel much better when it gets dark again. Sometimes we fired at Jap star shells and put them out. The sky was full of shells.

As the sea battle was coming to an end we passed a Jap ship under attack at close range. We did not fire on the Jap ship because we were very low on ammunition and our help was not needed. This action took place on our starboard side not too far away. It seemed like it was getting a little brighter as I watched the action. The Jap ship was dead in the water. I did not notice any other ships around but the three of us. The Jap ship was a mass of flames and red hot steel as the big guns covered it with exploding shells. It gave off a red glow that lit up the area around it. It must have been a nightmare in hell for the Japs as they were roasted and blown to bits. I don't see how anyone could escape. It was a horrible way to die, it was a slaughter. This type of warfare tops them all for horror. There is no safe place to hide and if you land in the water the huge sharks that are longer than a good-sized room are always close by. Our ships are now running low on ammunition and some of the destroyers have only star shells left, because of our earlier bombardments against the Japs. Our ship is also getting low on fuel. If this keeps up, we will only have machine guns and potatoes to fire at the Jap warships. After three hours of fighting, the Japs have had enough and head for their base at Rabaul. It's approximately 5:45 A.M. We started the engagement at 2:45 A.M. Losses for the Japs—at least One (1) heavy cruiser and Four (4) destroyers sunk and Two (2) cruisers and Two (2) destroyers were severely damaged. Our ship accounted for one destroyer and one cruiser, the rest of the task force took care of the rest. Every ship in the force was in on the kill. At daylight nothing could be seen on deck except empty shell cases. The men on the five- and six-inch mounts and turrets looked like a bunch of ghosts. They were all worn out from lack of sleep, heat, very little food and the bombardments. Oh yes, I forgot to mention the sea battle. The men had spent the past three hours in a hot steaming steel mount or turret passing shells or powder cases. The six-inch armor-piercing shells weigh 135 pounds and the heavy brass powder cases are approximately four feet long. They get very little air and the heat is unbearable. I imagine they believed that the firing would never stop. The steel decks were rivers of water from their perspiration. The weather from beginning to end was similar to a heat wave back home in August. Why they did not pass out from exhaustion was a miracle. They were all out on their feet. I would not want to be in their shoes for a million. When we go into action, the air blowers are shut off and the ones who are shut in really suffer. They actually gasp for fresh air. The ship keeps twisting and turning and they don't know what to expect from the enemy. The men who are many decks below in the handling rooms have a tough job sending the ammunition up. They are surrounded by tons of ammunition. If a torpedo ever happens to explode close by, they drown like a bunch of rats. It's a long way up to topside.

It's still Tuesday morning, November 2, the same day of the sea battle. It is a beautiful warm sunny day as we make our way south to our base at Tulagi. We have still to be on the alert for Jap planes for they will be out looking for us.

Later: Approximately 8:30 A.M. we were attacked by 70 Jap planes. Our four cruisers and seven destroyers had plenty of target practice. The destroyer *Foote,* our eighth destroyer, is dead in the water, as previously mentioned. All ships break loose as Jap planes come in on us from all directions. We fire every gun on the ship at the Japs, even our big six-inch guns. The first plane we hit was blown to bits by a six-inch shell. Jap planes can be seen falling all around us. The Japs are also doing some damage and one can see many bombs explode very close to our ships. At first you think they have scored a hit as the water shoots high into the air. Their machine guns are also cutting up the water. Our ship is also hit by a bomb that destroys one of our catapults that we use for shooting planes off. It's a good-size steel ramp. When the bomb exploded, the stern of the ship was covered with smoke. It looked very serious at first. If one of our planes had been on the ramp it would have been blown to bits. One of the machine-gun mounts was also knocked out by the bomb. No one was killed. About fifteen men were wounded. We also received a hit up forward and more casualties, all wounded. One of the fellows almost had his head taken off.

A few Japs parachuted when they were hit, but a few sailors

and Marines on the twenty mm. opened up on the ones in the chutes and when they hit the water they were nothing but pieces of meat cut to ribbons. The men were blasted out for doing this. They were told not to waste ammunition in such a way. They were also told that it was good shooting. The Japs were the first to do things like this. They asked for it and we returned the favor.

During the air battle, our air cover did a mop-up job on what was left of the Jap force. They were a little late getting here but we were very happy to see them. We secured from general quarters at noon and received some food for a change. We stayed in the waters near Bougainville all day. We are making sure nothing happens to our empty transports as they head for their base at Tulagi. If the Japs send down any more warships, we will have to use potatoes against them. We must have fired at least five thousand rounds of five- and six-inch ammunition during our sea battle. The concussion from the twin five-inch mount knocked out Fuller and ripped Babe's sweater off. It also knocked him to the steel deck twice during the air attack. Babe is a rugged Jewish boy from New York who weighs around 200 pounds. Sometimes when these twin five-inch mounts turn around, the men on the machine guns can look right into the barrels and almost touch them. The concussion from these, with all the steel around, is wicked on the eardrums. Many a man has had his eardrums broken with the guns. Our ship has close to a hundred guns on it: twenty-mm., forty-mm. machine guns and five-inch mounts, also six-inch turrets. The turrets have three guns each, five-inch mounts, two guns each. Admiral Merrill used the wisdom of Solomon when he let the men in his task force get some rest before going into action. At first we got very little sleep but after a while one can get along with what he can get. The little sleep we received went a long way. Old Bull Halsey knew what he was doing when he put Admiral Merrill in command of this task force. Old Bull knows how to pick them.

The new men we picked up before going to Australia were shaking like a leaf during the air battle, and we did not waste any time in kidding them about it.

We are still in the Solomons but expect to pull into port

sometime tomorrow. It will take some time for the destroyer *Foote* to reach port. A tug is now towing it back. We secured from general quarters at noon today Tuesday, November 3, 1943. During the sea battle the Japs must have had radar, their firing was good. They have the best star shells. They light the place up as if it were daytime. Their torpedo tossing is handled by experts but quite a few are duds. If all torpedoes had been alive, I wouldn't be here to tell about it. Every one that had hit us, and there were a few, was a dud. Their torpedoes pack an awful punch.

FROM

Authentic Narrative of the Death of Lord Nelson

WILLIAM BEATTY

At the Battle of Trafalgar, on October 21, 1805, the British Navy won its greatest victory and lost its greatest hero. The victory, over a combined French and Spanish fleet, destroyed Napoleon's naval power and ended the threat of an invasion of England. The British lost not a single ship. But among their casualties was their commander, Admiral Lord Nelson, the one-eyed, one-armed hero of St. Vincent, Aboukir, and Copenhagen.

Aboard Nelson's flagship, the Victory, *Surgeon William Beatty was busy tending the wounded and dying in the chaos below decks when he was called to the side of the mortally wounded admiral. Here is his eyewitness account of the death of Lord Nelson.*

Trafalgar

As the *Victory* drew near to the enemy, his Lordship, accompanied by Captain Hardy, and the captains of the four frigates (*Euryalus, Naiad, Sirius,* and *Phœbe*), who had been called on board by signal to receive instructions, visited the different decks of the ship. He addressed the crew at their several quarters, admonishing them against firing a single shot without being sure of their object; and expressed himself to the officers highly satisfied with the arrangements made at their respective stations.

It was now plainly perceived by all on board the *Victory* that, from the very compact line which the enemy had formed, they were determined to make one great effort to recover in some measure their long-lost naval reputation. They wore in succession about twenty minutes past seven o'clock; and stood on the larboard tack, with their heads toward Cadiz. They kept a good deal of sail set, steering about two points from the wind, with top sails shivering. Their van was particularly closed, having the *Santissima Trinidada* and the *Bucentaur* the ninth and tenth ships, the latter the flagship of Admiral Villeneuve; but as the admirals of the combined fleets declined showing their flags till the heat of the battle was over, the former of these ships was only distinguished from the rest by her having four decks, and Lord Nelson ordered the *Victory* to be steered for her bow.

Several officers of the ship now communicated to each other their sentiments of anxiety for his Lordship's personal safety, to which every other consideration seemed to give way. Indeed, all were confident of gaining a glorious victory, but the apprehensions for his Lordship were great and general; and I made known to Dr. Scott my fears that his Lordship would be made the object of the enemy's marksmen, and my desire that he might be entreated by somebody to cover the stars on his coat with a handkerchief.

Dr. Scott and Mr. Scott (Public Secretary) both observed, however, that such a request would have no effect; as they knew his Lordship's sentiments on the subject so well that they were sure he would be highly displeased with whoever should take the liberty of recommending any change in his dress on this account; and when I declared to Mr. Scott that I would avail myself of the opportunity of making my sick report for the day to submit my sentiments to the admiral, Mr. Scott replied, "Take care, Doctor, what you are about: I would not be the man to mention such a matter to him."

Notwithstanding, I persisted in my design, and remained on deck to find a proper opportunity for addressing his Lordship, but this never occurred, as his Lordship continued occupied with the captains of the frigates (to whom he was explaining his intentions respecting the services they were to perform during the battle) till a short time before the enemy opened their fire on the *Royal Sovereign*, when Lord Nelson ordered all persons not stationed on the quarter-deck or poop to repair to their proper quarters. Much concerned at this disappointment, I retired from the deck with several other officers.

The boats on the quarters of the ship, being found in the way of the guns, were now lowered down, and towed astern.

Captain Blackwood, of the *Euryalus,* remained on board the *Victory* till a few minutes before the enemy began to fire upon her. He represented to his Lordship that his flagship would be singled out and much pressed by the enemy, and suggested the propriety therefore of permitting one or two ships of his line to go ahead of the *Victory* and lead her into action, which might be the means of drawing in some measure the enemy's attention from her.

To this Lord Nelson assented, and at half-past nine o'clock he ordered the *Temeraire* and *Leviathan* by signal (the former of which ships, being close to the *Victory,* was hailed by his Lordship) to go ahead for that purpose, but from the light breeze that prevailed they were unable, notwithstanding their utmost efforts, to attain their intended stations. Captain Blackwood foresaw that this would be the case; and as the *Victory* still continued to carry all her sail, he wished Captain Hardy to acquaint his Lordship that, unless her sail was in some degree shortened, the two ships just mentioned could not succeed in getting ahead previously to the enemy's line being forced. This, however, Captain Hardy declined doing, as he conceived his Lordship's ardor to get into battle would on no account suffer such a measure.

About half an hour before the enemy opened their fire, the memorable telegraphic signal was made, that "ENGLAND EXPECTS EVERY MAN WILL DO HIS DUTY," which was spread and received throughout the fleet with enthusiasm. It is impossible adequately to describe by any language the lively emotions excited in the crew of the *Victory* when this propitious communication was made known to them: confidence and resolution were strongly portrayed in the countenance of all; and the sentiment generally expressed to each other was that they would prove to their country that day how well British seamen *could* "do their duty" when led to battle by their revered admiral.

The signal was afterward made to "prepare to anchor after the close of the day;" and Union Jacks were hoisted at the foretop mast and topgallant stays of each ship to serve as a distinction from the enemy's, in conformity with orders previously issued by the commander in chief. By his Lordship's directions also, the different divisions of the fleet hoisted the St. George's or White Ensign, being the colors of the commander in chief: this was done to prevent confusion from occurring during the battle, through a variety of national flags.

The *Royal Sovereign* now made the signal by telegraph that "the enemy's commander in chief was in a frigate." This mistake arose from one of their frigates making many signals.

Lord Nelson ordered his line to be steered about two points more to the northward than that of his second in command, for the purpose of cutting off the retreat of the enemy's van to the port of Cadiz; which was the reason of the three leading ships of Admiral Collingwood's line being engaged with the enemy previously to those of the commander in chief's line.

The enemy began to fire on the *Royal Sovereign* at thirty minutes past eleven o'clock; in ten minutes after which she got under the stern of the *St. Anna* and commenced a fire on her. Lieutenant Pasco, signal officer of the *Victory*, was heard to say while looking through his glass, "There is a topgallant yard gone." His Lordship eagerly asked, "Whose topgallant yard is that gone? Is it the *Royal Sovereign's?*" and on being answered by Lieutenant Pasco in the negative, and that it was the enemy's, he smiled, and said, "Collingwood is doing well."

At fifty minutes past eleven, the enemy opened their fire on the commander in chief. They showed great coolness in the commencement of the battle; for as the *Victory* approached their line, their ships lying immediately ahead of her and across her bows fired only one gun at a time, to ascertain whether she was yet within their range. This was frequently repeated by eight or nine of their ships, till at length a shot passed through the *Victory's* main topgallant sail; the hole in which being discovered by the enemy, they immediately opened their broadsides, supporting an awful and tremendous fire.

In a very short time afterwards, Mr. Scott, public secretary to the commander in chief, was killed by a cannon shot while in conversation with Captain Hardy. Lord Nelson being then near them, Captain Adair of the marines, with the assistance of a seaman, endeavored to remove the body from his Lordship's sight. But he had already observed the fall of his secretary, and now said with anxiety, "Is that poor Scott that is gone?" and on being answered in the affirmative by Captain Adair, he replied, "Poor fellow!"

Lord Nelson and Captain Hardy walked the quarter-deck in conversation for some time after this, while the enemy kept up an incessant raking fire.

A double-headed shot struck one of the parties of marines drawn up on the poop, and killed eight of them; when his Lordship, perceiving this, ordered Captain Adair to disperse his men around the ship, that they might not suffer so much from being together.

In a few minutes afterwards a shot struck the fore-brace bits on the quarter-deck, and passed between Lord Nelson and Captain Hardy, a splinter from the bits bruising Captain Hardy's foot and tearing the buckle from his shoe. They both instantly stopped, and were observed by the officers on deck to survey each other with inquiring looks, each supposing the other to be wounded. His Lordship then smiled and said, "This is too warm work, Hardy, to last long;" and declared that "through all the battles he had been in, he had never witnessed more cool courage than was displayed by the *Victory's* crew on this occasion."

The *Victory* by this time, having approached close to the enemy's van, had suffered very severely without firing a single gun: she had lost about twenty men killed, and had about thirty wounded. Her mizzen topmast and all her studding sails and their booms on both sides were shot away, the enemy's fire being chiefly directed at her rigging, with a view to disable her before she could close with them.

At four minutes past twelve o'clock, she opened her fire, from both sides of her decks, upon the enemy; when Captain Hardy represented to his Lordship that "it appeared impracticable to pass through the enemy's line without going on board some one of their ships."

Lord Nelson answered, "I cannot help it: it does not signify which we run on board of; go on board which you please; take your choice."

At twenty minutes past twelve, the tiller ropes being shot away, Mr. Atkinson, the master, was ordered below to get the helm put to port; which being done, the *Victory* was soon run on board the *Redoubtable* of seventy-four guns.

On coming alongside and nearly on board of her, that ship fired her broadside into the *Victory*, and immediately let down her lower deck ports; which, as has been since learned, was done to prevent her from being boarded through them by the *Victory's* crew. She never fired a great gun after this single broadside.

A few minutes after this, the *Temeraire* fell likewise on board of the *Redoubtable*, on the side opposite to the *Victory*; having also an enemy's ship, said to be *La Fougueux*, on board of *her* on her other side: so that the extraordinary and unprecedented circumstance occurred here of *four* ships of the line being *on board of each other* in the heat of battle, forming as compact a tier as if they had been moored together, their heads lying all the same way. The *Temeraire*, as was just before mentioned, was between the *Redoubtable* and *La Fougueux*.

The *Redoubtable* commenced a heavy fire of musketry from the tops, which was continued for a considerable time with destructive effect to the *Victory's* crew. Her great guns, however, being silent, it was supposed at different times that she had surrendered; and in consequence of this opinion, the *Victory* twice ceased firing upon her by orders transmitted from the quarter-deck.

At this period, scarcely a person in the *Victory* escaped unhurt who was exposed to the enemy's musketry; but there were frequent huzzas and cheers heard from between the decks, in token of the surrender of different of the enemy's ships. An incessant fire was kept up from both sides of the *Victory*: her larboard guns played upon the *Santissima Trinidada* and the *Bucentaur*; and the starboard guns of the middle and lower decks were depressed, and fired with a diminished charge of powder, and three shot each, into the *Redoubtable*. This mode of firing was adopted by Lieutenants Williams, King, Yule, and Brown, to obviate the danger of the *Temeraire's* suffering from the *Victory's* shot passing through the *Redoubtable*; which must have been the case if the usual quantity of powder, and the common elevation, had been given to the guns.

A circumstance occurred in this situation which showed in a

most striking manner the cool intrepidity of the officers and men stationed on the lower deck of the *Victory*. When the guns on this deck were run out, their muzzles came into contact with the *Redoubtable's* side; and consequently at every discharge there was reason to fear that the enemy would take fire, and both the *Victory* and the *Temeraire* be involved in her flames. Here then was seen the astonishing spectacle of the fireman of each gun standing ready with a bucket full of water, which as soon as his gun was discharged he dashed into the enemy through the holes made in her side by the shot.

It was from this ship (the *Redoubtable*) that Lord Nelson received his mortal wound. About fifteen minutes past one o'clock, which was in the heat of the engagement, he was walking the middle of the quarter-deck with Captain Hardy, and in the act of turning near the hatchway with his face toward the stern of the *Victory*, when the fatal ball was fired from the enemy's mizzen top; which, from the situation of the two ships (lying on board of each other), was brought just abaft, and rather below, the *Victory's* main yard, and of course not more than fifteen yards distant from that part of the deck where his Lordship stood. The ball struck the epaulette on his left shoulder and penetrated his chest. He fell with his face on the deck. Captain Hardy, who was on his right (the side farther from the enemy) and [had] advanced some steps before his Lordship, on turning round, saw the sergeant major (Secker) of marines with two seamen raising him from the deck; where he had fallen on the same spot on which, a little before, his secretary had breathed his last, with whose blood his Lordship's clothes were much soiled.

Captain Hardy expressed a hope that he was not severely wounded; to which the gallant chief replied: "They have done for me at last, Hardy."

"I hope not," answered Captain Hardy.

"Yes," replied his Lordship, "my backbone is shot through."

Captain Hardy ordered the seamen to carry the admiral to the cockpit; and now two incidents occurred strikingly characteristic of this great man, and strongly marking that energy and reflection which in his heroic mind rose superior even to the immediate consideration of his present awful condition. While

the men were carrying him down the ladder from the middle deck, his Lordship observed that the tiller ropes were not yet replaced, and desired one of the midshipmen stationed there to go upon the quarter-deck and remind Captain Hardy of that circumstance and request that new ones should be immediately rove. Having delivered this order, he took his handkerchief from his pocket and covered his face with it, that he might be conveyed to the cockpit at this crisis unnoticed by the crew.

Several wounded officers, and about forty men, were likewise carried to me for assistance just at this time; and some others had breathed their last during their conveyance below. Among the latter were Lieutenant William Andrew Ram and Mr. Whipple, captain's clerk. I had just examined these two officers, and found that they were dead, when my attention was arrested by several of the wounded calling to me, "Mr. Beatty, Lord Nelson is here: Mr. Beatty, the admiral is wounded."

Now, on looking round, I saw the handkerchief fall from his Lordship's face; when the stars on his coat, which also had been covered by it, appeared. Mr. Burke, the purser, and I, ran immediately to the assistance of his Lordship; and took him from the arms of the seamen who had carried him below. In conveying him to one of the midshipmen's berths, they stumbled, but recovered themselves without falling. Lord Nelson then inquired who were supporting him; and when I informed him, his Lordship replied, "Ah, Mr. Beatty! you can do nothing for me. I have but a short time to live: my back is shot through."

I said, "I hoped the wound was not so dangerous as his Lordship imagined, and that he might still survive long to enjoy his glorious victory."

The Rev. Dr. Scott, who had been absent in another part of the cockpit administering lemonade to the wounded, now came instantly to his Lordship; and in the anguish of grief wrung his hands, and said: "Alas, Beatty, how prophetic you were!" alluding to the apprehensions expressed by me for his Lordship's safety previous to the battle.

His Lordship was laid upon a bed, stripped of his clothes, and covered with a sheet. While this was effecting, he said to Dr. Scott, "Doctor, I told you so. Doctor, I am gone;" and after a short pause he added in a low voice, "I have to leave Lady

Hamilton, and my adopted daughter Horatia, as a legacy to my country."

I then examined the wound, assuring his Lordship that I would not put him to much pain in endeavoring to discover the course of the ball; which I soon found had penetrated deep into the chest and had probably lodged in the spine. This being explained to his Lordship, he replied he was "confident his back was shot through." The back was then examined externally, but without any injury being perceived; on which I requested his Lordship to make me acquainted with all his sensations. He replied that he felt a gush of blood every minute within his breast: that he had no feeling in the lower part of his body: and that his breathing was difficult, and attended with very severe pain about that part of the spine where he was confident that the ball had struck, "for," said he, "I felt it break my back."

These symptoms, but more particularly the gush of blood which his Lordship complained of, together with the state of his pulse, indicated to me the hopeless situation of the case; but till after the victory was ascertained and announced to his Lordship, the true nature of his wound was concealed by me from all on board except only Captain Hardy, Dr. Scott, Mr. Burke, and Messrs. Smith and Westemburg, the assistant surgeons.

The *Victory's* crew cheered whenever they observed an enemy's ship surrender. On one of these occasions, Lord Nelson anxiously inquired what was the cause of it; when Lieutenant Pasco, who lay wounded at some distance from his Lordship, raised himself up, and told him that another ship had struck, which appeared to give him much satisfaction.

He now felt an ardent thirst; and frequently called for drink, and to be fanned with paper, making use of these words: "Fan, fan!" and "Drink, drink!" This he continued to repeat, when he wished for drink or the refreshment of cool air, till a very few minutes before he expired. Lemonade, and wine and water, were given to him occasionally. He evinced great solicitude for the event of the battle, and fears for the safety of his friend Captain Hardy. Dr. Scott and Mr. Burke used every argument they could suggest to relieve his anxiety.

Mr. Burke told him, "The enemy were decisively defeated,

and that he hoped his Lordship would still live to be himself the bearer of the joyful tidings to his country."

He replied, "It is nonsense, Mr. Burke, to suppose I can live: my sufferings are great, but they will all be soon over."

Dr. Scott entreated his Lordship "not to despair of living," and said "he trusted that Divine Providence would restore him once more to his dear country and friends."

"Ah, Doctor!" replied his Lordship, "it is all over; it is all over!"

I sent many messages to Captain Hardy, requesting his attendance on his Lordship; who became impatient to see him, and often exclaimed, "Will no one bring Hardy to me? He must be killed: he is surely destroyed."

The captain's aide-de-camp, Mr. Bulkley, now came below and stated that "circumstances respecting the fleet required Captain Hardy's presence on deck, but that he would avail himself of the first favorable moment to visit his Lordship."

On hearing him deliver this message to me, his Lordship inquired who had brought it.

Mr. Burke answered, "It is Mr. Bulkley, my Lord."

"It is his voice," replied his Lordship. He then said to the young gentleman, "Remember me to your father."

An hour and ten minutes, however, elapsed from the time of his Lordship's being wounded before Captain Hardy's first subsequent interview with him, the particulars of which are nearly as follow.

They shook hands affectionately, and Lord Nelson said, "Well, Hardy, how goes the battle? How goes the day with us?"

"Very well, my Lord," replied Captain Hardy: "we have got twelve or fourteen of the enemy's ships in our possession; but five of their van have tacked, and show an intention of bearing down upon the *Victory*. I have therefore called two or three of our fresh ships around us, and have no doubt of giving them a drubbing."

"I hope," said his Lordship, "none of *our* ships have struck, Hardy."

"No, my Lord," replied Captain Hardy; "there is no fear of that."

Lord Nelson then said, "I am a dead man, Hardy. I am going fast: it will be all over with me soon. Come nearer to me. Pray let my dear Lady Hamilton have my hair, and all other things belonging to me." Mr. Burke was about to withdraw at the commencement of this conversation, but his Lordship, perceiving his intention, desired he would remain.

Captain Hardy observed that "he hoped Mr. Beatty could yet hold out some prospect of life."

"Oh! no," answered his Lordship; "it is impossible. My back is shot through. Beatty will tell you so."

Captain Hardy then returned on deck, and at parting shook hands again with his revered friend and commander.

His Lordship now requested me to return to the wounded and give my assistance to such of them as I could be useful to, "for," said he, "you can do nothing for me." I assured him that the assistant surgeons were doing everything that could be effected for those unfortunate men, but on his Lordship's several times repeating his injunctions to that purpose, I left him surrounded by Dr. Scott, Mr. Burke, and two of his Lordship's domestics.

After I had been absent a few minutes attending Lieutenants Peake and Reeves of the marines, who were wounded, I was called by Dr. Scott to his Lordship, who said: "Ah, Mr. Beatty!

I have sent for you to say, what I forgot to tell you before, that all power of motion and feeling below my breast are gone; and *you*," continued he, "very well *know* I can live but a short time." The emphatic manner in which he pronounced these last words, left no doubt in my mind that he adverted to the case of a man who had, some months before, received a mortal injury of the spine on board the *Victory*, and had labored under similar privations of sense and muscular motion. The case had made a great impression on Lord Nelson: he was anxious to know the cause of such symptoms, which was accordingly explained to him; and he now appeared to apply the situation and fate of this man to himself.

I answered, "My Lord, you told me so before," but I now examined the extremities, to ascertain the fact, when his Lordship said, "Ah, Beatty! I am too certain of it: Scott and Burke have tried it already. *You know* I am gone."

I replied, "My Lord, unhappily for our country, nothing can be done for you," and, having made this declaration, I was so much affected that I turned around and withdrew a few steps to conceal my emotions.

His Lordship said, "I know it. I feel something rising in my breast," putting his hand on his left side, "which tells me I am gone." Drink was recommended liberally, and Dr. Scott and Mr. Burke fanned him with paper.

He often exclaimed, "God be praised, I have done my duty," and upon my inquiring whether his pain was still very great, he declared it continued so very severe, that he wished he was dead. "Yet," said he in a lower voice, "one would like to live a little longer, too," and after a pause of a few minutes he added in the same tone, "What would become of poor Lady Hamilton, if she knew my situation?"

Finding it impossible to render his Lordship any further assistance, I left him to attend Lieutenant Bligh, Messrs. Smith and Westphall, midshipmen, and some seamen, recently wounded.

Captain Hardy now came to the cockpit to see his Lordship a second time, which was after an interval of about fifty minutes from the conclusion of his first visit. Before he quitted the deck, he sent Lieutenant Hills to acquaint Admiral Collingwood with the lamentable circumstance of Lord Nelson's being wounded.

Lord Nelson and Captain Hardy shook hands again, and while the captain retained his Lordship's hand, he congratulated him even in the arms of death on his brilliant victory, which, he said, was complete; though he did not know how many of the enemy were captured, as it was impossible to perceive every ship distinctly. He was certain, however, of fourteen or fifteen having surrendered.

His Lordship answered, "That is well, but I bargained for twenty," and then emphatically exclaimed, "*Anchor,* Hardy, *anchor!*"

To this the captain replied, "I suppose, my Lord, Admiral Collingwood will now take upon himself the direction of affairs."

"Not while I live, I hope, Hardy!" cried the dying chief, and at that moment endeavored ineffectually to raise himself from the bed.

"No," added he, "do *you* anchor, Hardy."

Captain Hardy then said, "Shall *we* make the signal, sir?"

"Yes," answered his Lordship, "for if I live, I'll anchor." The energetic manner in which he uttered these his last orders to Captain Hardy, accompanied with his efforts to raise himself, evinced his determination never to resign the command while he retained the exercise of his transcendant faculties, and that he expected Captain Hardy still to carry into effect the suggestions of his exalted mind, a sense of his duty overcoming the pains of death.

He then told Captain Hardy he felt that in a few minutes he should be no more, adding in a low tone, "Don't throw me overboard, Hardy."

The captain answered, "Oh! no, certainly not."

"Then," replied his Lordship, "you know what to do, and," continued he, "take care of my dear Lady Hamilton, Hardy; take care of poor Lady Hamilton. Kiss me, Hardy."

The captain now knelt down and kissed his cheek, when his Lordship said, "Now I am satisfied. Thank God, I have done my duty."

Captain Hardy stood for a minute or two in silent contemplation: he then knelt down again and kissed his Lordship's forehead.

His Lordship said, "Who is that?"

The captain answered, "It is Hardy," to which his Lordship replied, "God bless you, Hardy!"

After this affecting scene Captain Hardy withdrew and returned to the quarter-deck, having spent about eight minutes in this his last interview with his dying friend.

Lord Nelson now desired Mr. Chevalier, his steward, to turn him upon his right side; which being effected, his Lordship said, "I wish I had not left the deck, for I shall soon be gone." He afterward became very low, his breathing was oppressed, and his voice faint.

He said to Dr. Scott, "Doctor, I have *not* been a *great* sinner," and after a short pause, "*Remember*, that I leave Lady Hamilton and my daughter Horatia as a legacy to my country, and," added he, "Never forget Horatia."

His thirst now increased, and he called for "Drink, drink," "Fan, fan!" and "Rub, rub!" addressing himself in the last case to Dr. Scott, who had been rubbing his Lordship's breast with his hand, from which he found some relief. These words he spoke in a very rapid manner, which rendered his articulation difficult, but he every now and then, with evident increase of pain, made a greater effort with his vocal powers, and pronounced distinctly these last words, "Thank God, I have done long as he was able to give it utterance.

His Lordship became speechless in about fifteen minutes after Captain Hardy left him. Dr. Scott and Mr. Burke, who had all along sustained the bed under his shoulders (which raised him in nearly a semirecumbent posture, the only one that was supportable to him), forbore to disturb him by speaking to him; and when he had remained speechless about five minutes, his Lordship's steward came to me in another part of the cockpit and stated his apprehensions that his Lordship was dying.

I immediately repaired to him and found him on the verge of dissolution. I knelt down by his side and took up his hand, which was cold, and the pulse gone from the wrist.

On my feeling his forehead, which was likewise cold, his Lordship opened his eyes, looked up, and shut them again.

I again left him, and returned to the wounded who required my assistance, but was not absent five minutes before the steward announced to me that he believed his Lordship had expired. I returned and found that the report was but too well founded: his Lordship had breathed his last, at thirty minutes past four o'clock; at which period Dr. Scott was in the act of rubbing his Lordship's breast and Mr. Burke supporting the bed under his shoulders.

FROM

Around the World Submerged

EDWARD L. BEACH

Instead of a routine shakedown cruise in the Atlantic, the newly commissioned nuclear-powered submarine Triton *was assigned a dramatic secret mission: to circumnavigate the globe—submerged. The* Triton *left New London on February 10, 1960. It returned, its mission accomplished, on May 16. For eighty-three days, men and machines sustained a grueling test. Here its commander, Captain Edward L. Beach, describes the moment of crisis when his decision would determine the success or failure of the mission.*

Commander of the Triton

SUNDAY, *March* 6, was a day of rest, well deserved by all hands, and it was noteworthy for a special reason. Our growing concern over our fathometer had caused us to keep a closer-than-usual watch over it and over our regular search-sonar equipment, too. Searching out ahead, to our great pleasure, the latter at 1610 detected something that looked like a fifty-foot peak, or boulder, on the bottom. A moment later, as *Triton* herself passed over the spot, the fathometer registered the accuracy of the information. It was a comforting thought to know that our search sonar, designed to detect other ships and submarines, might be depended on to give us adequate warning of the approach of shoal water.

For two days, *Triton* roared toward Cape Horn, driving to make up lost time. On Monday, March 7, we reached the storied Land's End of the Western Hemisphere.

I had been giving some thought to how we should make proper observance of our passage from the Atlantic to the Pacific and finally hit upon a simple idea. In the *Triton Eagle*, I occasionally wrote a column called "The Skipper's Corner," to say things which it seemed might best be handled informally. On March 7, therefore, the following entry appeared in "The Skipper's Corner":

As for Cape Horn, *Triton* will make a photographic reconnaissance on it, and then Mr. Roberts will make a National Geographic reconnaissance. Following this, as we cruise by for the 3rd or 4th time, I intend to require every man on the ship to come to the conning tower for a look. It is not a usual thing for a sailor to round the Horn these days. Many spend a lifetime and never do. By far the majority of US Navy sailors have never done it. Quite obviously, if you ever brag about having been around the Horn, the next question will either be, "Did you see it?" or "What does it look like?"

We intend to take a picture and I think it will be possible to make enough copies for all hands. But more than this, I want every man aboard to be able to say he's seen it. Note: there will be no muster taken. If you don't want to see the Horn, no one will force you. But you'll wish you did later, because you'll probably never get the chance again.

And then, that morning, I let it be known that in the old days, when a sailor went around the Horn, he hoped not to see the fabled cape. If anyone aboard an old sailing ship, bucking wind and tide to double the cape, sighted the forbidding promontory looming through the haze, it was considered that bad luck would follow very soon in the form of shipwreck on one of the most inhospitable coasts in the world.

More modern traditions, I announced, were different. A sailor who gazed upon Cape Horn deliberately would experience good luck for the rest of his seafaring career. Not only that, but all sailors who rounded the Horn automatically attained certain privileges denied ordinary mortals (one I did not recommend was that we might all have a pig tattooed on the calf of the right leg). Tradition has it also that sailors who have rounded the Horn may with impunity throw trash and slops to windward, and because of their great victory over the forces of the wind, none of it will ever be blown back into their faces. They also have the traditional right to wear their hats on the side of their heads instead of square above the eyebrows, as is required by Navy regulations (no one may wear it on the *back* of his head).

We made no muster, but we did keep an unofficial count of the persons coming into the conning tower for a look, in some cases to photograph the famous landmark with their own cameras (which they had been permitted to bring provided all film was turned in for checking). Every man wanted a look, and it was necessary to go back and forth five times in front of the cape before all hands had had their view.

Triton's log for the passage may give some idea of the conditions the old-timers faced in the days of sail.

Our observations of the conditions make it quite clear why it was such a tremendously difficult thing for old-time seafarers to weather this famous Cape. In the first place, though we are safely submerged and comfortable, *Triton* is rolling rather heavily. There is an unusually rough sea topside. Lt. James C. Hay, recently reported aboard from West Milton, has already established himself as a most competent diving officer—but he is having difficulty in maintaining ordered depth today. Good practice for young officers, and planesmen, too. We estimate the waves as 10 to 12 feet high and the wind about 25 knots from the west.

There are occasional rain squalls and the cloud coverage is rather low to the water. It is also noticed, after a few navigational cuts, that we are being set backwards, to the east, by a current of some 3 knots. Under such conditions it is easy to see how an old windjammer, trying to beat her way around the Cape, might find it almost impossible. Heavy winds and a strong current were both dead against her. Even a steamer would have her troubles at a time like this.

Although the conditions we have observed could hardly be called a storm, there is no doubt that any ship riding around Cape Horn on the surface today would be having a rough and uncomfortable trip. By contrast we are comfortable and snug.

Joe Roberts had spent practically his entire life as a photographer, and was one of the *National Geographic's* best. He also happened to be endowed with a genial personality which generated real affection on the part of officers and crew alike. An illustration of this was an incident that occurred in the conning tower as we passed Cape Horn. After taking his *National Geographic* pictures with half a dozen expensive cameras which he had slung around his neck, Joe had been about to make room for others by going below, when a sailor with a box camera appeared in the conning tower. Photographing through the periscope is by no means a simple procedure and Joe put down his cameras and other paraphernalia and turned back to help.

Sailor after sailor—and some officers, too—came to the conning tower with cameras, and to each one Commander Roberts patiently showed the tricks of the game, helped calculate and adjust the periscope diopter setting for the particular camera, plus the camera settings for the type of film and the outside light. Money could not have purchased the instruction and assistance these men were getting for nothing, and I wished I had had the sense to bring my own camera.

We had hoped the passage to Easter Island would be uneventful, after the rather strenuous navigation around the Falkland Islands and Cape Horn. I looked forward to a twenty-five-hundred-mile run through deep water, few problems, and a chance to read Thor Heyerdahl's book, *Aku-Aku*, in which he describes his search for the origin of the Easter Islanders and his re-erection of one of the stone monoliths. It was, unfortunately, not to be so.

The tremendous capability of the nuclear power plant and the many changes in submarine operating procedures which it requires were brought firmly home the day after we passed Cape Horn, when we held a "loss of all main power" drill. All naval ships are required to carry out such exercises, for the obvious reasons that they develop the crew's ability to cope with the problem should it occur in battle or as a result of some mishap.

Triton had, however, traveled some two thousand miles at great speed since she had last "gotten a good trim," as submariners say. She had, moreover, changed from Atlantic waters off the River Plate to Pacific waters on the far side of Cape Horn, and was well on her way toward Easter Island. Our instruments, and those of Nick Mabry from the Hydrographic Office in Washington, gave us some idea of the change in salinity of the sea water—generally speaking, the Atlantic side of South America was saltier. We had taken aboard a good deal of water for various purposes, including running our evaporators and keeping our fresh water tanks full, and we had pumped varying amounts of water overboard to compensate for our computed decreased buoyancy.

Prior to the test, Tom Thamm sought me out.

"Captain," he said, "my calculations show us to be pretty heavy by the time you consider the reduced salinity and the changes which have taken place in our internal weights."

"Yes?" I said.

"According to these figures we ought to pump out about seventy thousand pounds before we have the drill . . ."

"Tom," I interrupted, "aren't your diving officers and diving chiefs keeping up with the trim as we go along?"

"Yes, sir, but I made a special computation because of this drill coming off, and that is what the figures show."

This would be an opportunity for a good lesson, I thought. "Permission not granted, Tom," I said. "The sort of casualty that we're simulating might happen at any time, and we would have to face it with the conditions existing at that time. Suppose we really were to lose all power right now, rather than an hour from now after you get all this water pumped out?"

I had Tom there and he knew it, though I could see that he did not fully approve. "Aye aye, sir," he said. "I'll stand by in the control room just in case."

I grinned at him. Tom was a perfectionist who didn't want to have anything go wrong in his department. If the ship were too badly out of trim, a short blast of high-pressure air in the main ballast tanks was the quickest way of expelling a lot of water and stopping her descent. Then, the air in the tanks would have to be vented off—partly, at least—as we came up. Otherwise, with reduced external pressure as the ship rose to shallower depths, the air in the tanks would expand even more, thus still further lightening her. Blowing precisely the right amount to balance exactly could not be guaranteed, and several blowings and ventings would undoubtedly be required before the trim pump could get rid of enough water. And later, Curt Shellman's carefully tended air compressors would have to perform considerable extra work to recharge the air banks.

In the unlikely event that Tom was wrong, that the ship was light instead of heavy, water would have to be taken in rapidly in order to keep her from broaching surface; but with the aid of sea pressure, this is always a much easier thing to do than to pump it out.

The particular problem that faced us had almost never been experienced in battery-driven submarines, for these normally operate at minimum speed while submerged in order to conserve their vitally important batteries, and any divergence from a perfect submerged trim is instantly evident. As a consequence, all old-fashioned submarines automatically stay in perfect trim, practically as a reflex action, whenever they operate submerged. Being even slightly out of trim causes difficulty in maintaining depth at slow speed. But at our sustained high speed, a few hundred tons of extra weight, or buoyancy, would be unnoticeable—until we slowed down.

Everyone in the ship was up and around during the drill period, late sleepers among the off-watch section having been jolted into consciousness by the daily test of the ship's various alarm systems, which had been programmed for fifteen minutes prior to the beginning of the exercise.

At the agreed-upon time, I too was in the control room, as

were Will Adams and Tom Thamm. At my signal, Will picked up the telephone and spoke briefly to Don Fears, who, naturally enough, just happened to be in number-one engine room.

Immediately, a strident voice bellowed on the ship's general announcing system. "Control, this is Maneuvering One. We've lost all power, both shafts."

I watched the engine-order telegraph indicators on the Diving Control Panel shift swiftly from "ahead full" to "stop."

For a moment, nothing else happened, though I knew our propellers were now only pinwheeling with the ship's motion through the water. Dick Harris, who had the Diving Officer's watch, stepped a few inches closer to his planesman; all three were intently scanning the instruments in front of them. Seated on the padded tool box in front of the fathometer, Tom Thamm was doing the same, while two feet farther aft, Chief Engineman E. C. Rauch had squared himself away in front of his Diving Panel and crushed out his half-smoked cigarette.

Elsewhere in the ship, wherever there was a critical station, I knew that the men on watch were standing by to take whatever action might be necessary, and because this was a scheduled drill, at every station there also stood, as observers, the off-watch personnel, the senior petty officer in charge, and the officer responsible.

We had been making just under twenty knots. As the ship slowed, I knew that both Dick and Tom were watching the depth gauges and the plane-angle indications for the first sign that we were, as everyone suspected, considerably heavier than the water we displaced. We waited a long minute, as *Triton* slowed and her bow and stern planes gradually lost effect. Suddenly, Harris reached his hand out behind him, motioned toward Rauch. "Pump auxiliaries to sea!" he snapped.

I had not seen yet any indications of the ship's being heavy. "How do you figure we're heavy, Dick?" I asked.

"Mostly intuition I guess, Captain," he replied. "There's really no sign here yet, but I know darned well she's heavy."

Another minute passed. We had slowed perceptibly and now it became evident that, to hold the ordered depth, the planesmen were required to maintain up angle on both bow and stern planes.

"We are heavy, all right," I said.

From Harris my response was a tight-lipped smile, but it was Third Class Quartermaster Roger A. Miller, standing watch on the bow planes, who put it into words with a deep-toned whisper which caromed off the deck and bulkheads and brought amused smiles to everyone within earshot.

"This old hog sure has lead in her tail!" said he as he lifted the bow planes another five degrees.

As speed dropped off rapidly, bow and stern planes soon were at the maximum angles of elevation and then, inexorably, *Triton* began to sink. In the meantime, Rauch, checking the rate-of-flow meter, was monotonously calling out the amount of water we pumped overboard: "5,000 out—7,000 out—10,000 out, sir—12,000 out—15,000 out."

Dick made no motion to stop him. *Triton's* speed through water had by now dropped to only three or four knots; she was still on an even keel, but the depth gauges were showing a gradually increasing speed of descent.

It was apparent soon that we should not be able to get enough water out of the ship before she had exceeded the maximum depth to which we were allowed to submerge her. Deliberately I waited as long as possible, then finally nodded to Dick, "I guess we won't be able to catch her, Dick. Blow tanks."

"Blow forward group! Blow after group!" Dick had the orders ready.

So did Rauch, whose fingers were already on the main ballast blow valve switches. With two quick motions, high-pressure air was roaring into *Triton's* main ballast tanks. Dick waited until he saw our downward motion perceptibly reduced, then gave the clenched fist signal to Rauch at the same time as the order, "Secure the air!"

The noise of air blowing stopped. We had lightened the ship by several hundred tons, and *Triton's* involuntary dive stopped well above the allowed limit. But this was not the end of the episode.

The depth gauges now started going in the other direction. *Triton* was rising to the surface, slowly at first and then with increasing speed. We had placed a large air bubble in our main ballast tanks which, like uncorked bottles inverted in the water, were open at the bottom and closed at the top. It was impossible to gauge the amount of air that had to be blown into the tanks so as to put the ship precisely and exactly in equilibrium at a given depth.

As we had put enough air into the tanks to stop the descent, it was apparent that the ship would now rise. As she rose, however, the size of the air bubble increased as the sea pressure reduced; and as the air bubble increased in size, it pushed even more water out through the bottom of the ballast tanks, thus making *Triton* still lighter. In this condition, we would continue to lighten and rise faster until we reached the surface.

Once, during the war, with the old *Trigger* leaking badly and surrounded by Japanese destroyers listening for us to start our pumps, we had survived just such a situation by putting an air bubble in one of our tanks and then either venting it slowly into the ship (we dared not use the main vents, which would have loosed a betraying bubble of air to the surface) or blowing it carefully. With the desperate skill of emergency, for fifteen hours Johnny Shepherd maintained precise control of our depth, as the accumulated leakage of water gradually made us heavier and heavier, until finally we outlasted the enemy. We had not dared to relieve Johnny.

The situation here was far less tense. There was no enemy; we could afford to let air bubbles come to the surface. Our only problem was to control the size of the bubble in our tanks to keep from broaching surface, on the one hand, or going too deep, on the other.

As *Triton* ballooned upward, I watched silently for signs of the required action. It is for situations like this that men are qualified in submarines. With approval, I saw Rauch keeping his eyes on Harris, his hand already resting lightly on the controls for the main vents. Thamm was watching too. *Triton* rose at an ever-increasing pace and finally Dick gave the order: "Open main vents."

I could hear the vent mechanism operating and all of us heard the rush of the entrapped air as it escaped from the tank. But Dick was still watching the depth gauges, "Shut main vents," he ordered. His objective was to catch some of the air still inside

the tanks in order to retain some of the resulting buoyancy. In the meantime, with approval, I noted that he had not ordered Rauch to stop the trim pump, that we were still pumping water from the midships auxiliary tanks to sea.

Triton's rise toward the surface ceased rather abruptly. By this time, we had no forward motion through the water at all. With the ship badly out of trim, she was controllable in depth only by the constant buoyancy of her great hull, plus the variable buoyancy of the expanding and contracting volume of air in the ballast tanks. Undersea ballooning was an apt simile.

But Dick had let out too much air, for *Triton* was now heavy and began to sink once more; as she sank, the air bubble remaining in the ballast tanks would be further and further compressed, with the result that the ship's buoyancy would continue to reduce and she would now progressively descend faster and faster—though slower than the first time. Dick was ready for this, however, and after we had sunk some little distance, he again ordered that tanks be blown, but for a considerably shorter time than before. Again, *Triton* halted her descent and began to rise; and, as she neared the surface, Dick opened the ballast tank vents and allowed most of the air to escape.

In the meantime, we had continued pumping water out of the ship. Gradually, our wild gyrations lessened as we got her correctly trimmed. With ballast tanks again full of water, no air trapped in them, *Triton* finally hovered, motionless, balanced precariously with her internal weight exactly equal to that of the water displaced.

It might be well to explain at this point a fact that submariners know well but that may not be so well known to others: it is impossible for a submerged body to be so delicately trimmed or balanced that it will remain indefinitely static, neither rising nor falling. Despite fanciful tales written by people who do not know their physics, things cannot just sink part way. A submerged submarine has no reserve buoyancy; that is to say, she gains no additional buoyancy by sinking a little deeper in the water (a surface ship, passing from more dense to less dense water, increases imperceptibly in draft). If an eight-thousand-ton submarine is one pound heavier than the water she displaces, she will slowly sink. The deeper she goes, the greater the pressure; even the strongest hull will be slightly compressed, thus reducing the volume of displaced water and increasing the disparity between her weight and that of the water displaced. She will go all the way down until she reaches the bottom. Conversely, a submerged submarine one ounce light will ultimately broach the surface. The only exception to this rule occurs when there is a layer, or stratum, of heavier water underlying a lighter layer. In this case, the submarine can "balance" on the boundary between the two, as long as the dissimilarity continues to exist. This is known as "riding a layer."

It is true that a submarine almost in perfect trim—as near to perfect trim as it can possibly get—might very very slowly sink in water of a certain density until it reaches a layer of water considerably cooler or more saline than the one for which trimmed, and there she will stay for a while. Ships have been known to ride thus, suspended between two layers of water of dissimilar densities, for many hours. There have even been stories about balancing a submarine so skillfully that the slight increase in displacement gained by raising a periscope would cause her slowly to drift toward the surface, and sink slowly when the periscope is withdrawn inside its bearings, but, practically speaking, such situations are rare and highly temporary.

The submarine riding on a layer will maintain depth so long as all the factors affecting her equilibrium remain exactly the same. But they never do. Considering the many changes constantly taking place in the weight of the submarine, due to leakage through propeller shaft glands, to name one unstoppable source, or water taken in by the evaporators, for instance, it is certain that within a short time the sub's trim will change. In all cases, the change is in the direction of becoming heavier and, without the intelligent hand of man, she will shortly resume her descent. Nothing, in other words, can float without control between the surface of the sea and the bottom.

Davy Jones might have been perturbed had he observed *Triton,* the world's greatest submarine, slither to a halt and commence a series of astonishing gyrations in depth, accompanied by a frenetic blowing and venting of air and grinding of pumps. He would indeed have been justified in suspecting something to have gone seriously wrong. Such was, however, far from the fact. We were well pleased with the results of our drill, which showed that we had more than adequate control of our huge ship, even under the hazardous conditions which result from a complete loss of power; and after a short time, the mock-casualty restored, *Triton's* great propellers began to turn purposefully once more and she settled down on her course to the northwest at a speed faster than any submarine had ever traversed these waters.

According to *Triton's* log, it was next day, at about ten-thirty at night, when a calamity of very real proportions confronted us. Intimation of the problem came when Don Fears called me on the ship's service telephone in my room. For a few days we had had a severe leak around the starboard propeller shaft, which had been growing steadily worse. Now, as Don put it, it was no longer incidental, but of some magnitude. Fears and Curt Shellman were both in the lower level of the engine room, and I got there as soon as possible.

Spotting the leak was easy. Great sheets of water were spurting out around the periphery of the flange and gland through which the propeller shaft passed into the sea, driving a solid white spray perpendicularly outward from the shaft itself around 360° of its circumference, soaking the overhead of the platform deck above, the curved side of the ship outboard of the shaft, and the tiny walk deck. A heavy canvas dropcloth had already been rigged to protect the machinery near the leak, while Curt Shellman and three of his engineers, all of them drenched, were struggling perilously close to the rapidly revolving propeller shaft in their effort to stem the flow of water.

The tremendous racket produced by the hydrantlike force of water striking deck plates and other structures in the engine room made it almost impossible to talk. I put my mouth next to Don Fears' ear and shouted, "Good Lord, Don, how long has it been this bad?"

Fears looked serious and shouted into my ear in turn. "This is why I called you, Captain. The leak we had before was getting slowly worse and I was thinking of calling you anyway, then suddenly she broke loose."

"What is the trouble?" I yelled.

Don shook his head. "Don't know for sure, sir. Curt and his people have been right on it, though. Maybe we'll have an answer pretty soon."

"You can't handle this with the drain pump, Don," I shouted, enunciating slowly and carefully above the din. "We can't let these bilges get too full!"

Don nodded understandingly. "We have the drain pump on the line already, Captain, but I think you're right. The pump won't be able to keep up with this flood!"

Quite apart from the ultimate safety of the ship herself, if this huge leak could not be stopped, there was a lot of electrical equipment and other delicate machinery in the engine room which would be damaged if the water level rose too high.

"Don," I said, "we'll have to stop the starboard shaft. That will help some. At least it will let Curt get closer to the problem. I don't like him working around the shaft like that while it's turning."

Don nodded, shouting in my ear. "Maybe we could come to a shallower depth, too, Captain. That would reduce the pressure and cut down the leak some."

I assented. It took but a second to dash up the ladder to the upper level, find a telephone, and call the Officer of the Deck. In a moment, the starboard propeller shaft began to slow down, and at the same time the ship angled gently upward. In deference to the amount of water already in the bilges, which would all be concentrated in the after end if too steep an angle were assumed, I had told the Officer of the Deck to bring her up handsomely—that is, slowly and steadily, with good control.

As the outside water pressure was reduced, the leak correspondingly decreased. Shellman cast me a grateful look. I beckoned to him. "Curt," I said, "we are locking the shaft so that it can't turn. This will let you get closer to it, at least."

Shellman was mopping his face with a rag. "Thanks, Captain. I was about to ask if we might do that. I'm afraid to put somebody outboard of the propeller shaft because there's not much clearance between it and the skin of the ship."

He did not need to say more. There was perhaps a foot-and-a-half clearance between the propeller shaft and the curve of *Triton's* pressure hull, or skin. As I watched the propeller shaft come to a complete stop, there came into view a great bolted coupling by which two sections of the shaft had been joined together. The huge coupling had been rotating previously in a sort of a blur, its machined edges a lethal hazard while the shaft was turning.

With the shaft at a complete halt, Curt and Chief Engineman Fred Rotgers climbed on top, braving the reduced spray of water, while "Rabbit" Hathaway, a compactly built engineman, squirmed under the shaft and into the confined space.

Several minutes later we had the answer. The spit of anger in Rotgers' voice as he reported the basic cause of the problem was not all due to the salt-water bath he had just experienced. "The —— nuts on the far side of the gland are so loose you can turn them by hand," he spluttered.

"How about the locking washers, Chief?" asked Shellman.

"I sure didn't see any. That's why they loosened up!" Rotgers glared as he spoke. It was evident that whoever had installed these bolts would have fared badly had the powerful Rotgers been able to get his hands on him at that moment.

"There are locking wires on the inboard side of the gland," reported Shellman, after a brief inspection.

Further investigation showed that loose bolts were not the end of the trouble. The propeller shaft water seal had been improperly installed, that is, not made tight, either because of the difficulty in reaching some of the bolts or through lack of locking devices. Under the vibration and stress of continual high speed, complication had followed upon complication. Looseness of the bolts on the outboard side had permitted the packing gland to become partially cocked on its seat, and now, tighten the bolts as we would, it remained jammed in a cocked position and could not be straightened. We heaved on the nuts with the biggest wrenches aboard, to the point where Curt feared further pressure might distort or damage the parts even more, but there was no stemming the leak.

Not sure, in fact, whether or not some improvement might have been made, we eased *Triton* down again into the depths, and the resulting effect, with the greater pressure outside, was striking, to say the least.

We had obviously not solved the problem. The next step was to put an emergency clamp around the leak, utilizing three damage-control clamps which had been designed for small patches, not for anything as massive as this. Down we went for a test again, but the pressure of the water was so strong that it simply pushed the clamps apart.

Midnight had long given way to morning as Curt Shellman, Fred Rotgers, Clarence Hathaway, and others struggled with the leak in the confined space. The watch had changed at midnight and again at four o'clock, but Shellman, Rotgers, and company stayed on the job. Two solutions were decided on: first, we would try to reinforce the three damage-control clamps which had failed; second, we would design an entirely new clamp, sacrificing for the purpose a section of molding from the wardroom passageway, which happened to be made of corrosion-resisting steel and was, by good fortune, of sufficient size for our use.

By breakfast time the first try was in place, damage-control clamps with backing plate for reinforcement. It had been a long, backbreaking job, performed in tight quarters under the most unfavorable conditions, with water squirting in under pressure the whole time the men worked. When we unlocked the propeller shaft for a full-fledged test, Curt Shellman's naturally haggard face assumed an even more worried expression, the deep circles under his eyes standing out almost as though the difficulty had caused him physical suffering. But all went well; the leak did not increase beyond manageable size, the drain pump was able to take care of the water leakage without difficulty, and Shellman permitted a half-smile to wrinkle the deep bags under his eyes. At noon, Fears reported that the modified clamp would hold, for the time at least, and that our newly manufactured one would be held in reserve.

Entry from the log dated March 12, 1960:

0020 Our fathometer is out of commission again. This is bad news. It has been giving us trouble off and on for the past several days. Each time, however, we have brought it back into operation. This time, as our electronics technicians and sonarmen check it over, they actually record the gradually decreasing installation resistance in the head. It appears to be flooded.

Ever since the initial difficulty with the fathometer, "Whitey" Rubb and Dick Harris had been giving me daily reports as to its condition, and I was well aware of their increasing fears as to its performance. All the instruction books we had on board for the fathometer had been pored over, and in anticipation, we had checked over the stock of electronic spares on board the ship, the back-up for all the complicated electronic-control equipment with which *Triton* was fitted. All spare parts which could conceivably be used in the fathometer—tubes, resistors, crystals, power amplifiers—all, no matter what type of equipment they were originally designed for, had been located, so that we could substitute as necessary.

As the careful watch over the fathometer continued, our worries increased. The receiver crystals had again burned out, and our new transformer had gone too. Both were abnormal casualties, and it appeared that the basic trouble was not in the electronic hookup of the fathometer, but in the installation of the fathometer head itself. This, unfortunately, was something with which we could not cope, even were the ship on the surface. We could, and did, take resistance and capacitance readings of various components through the electrical connections inside the ship to which we had access. But so far as inspecting the head, possibly eliminating a leak or replacing a bad component with a good one, we were completely helpless.

By 0200, complete loss of the fathometer was confirmed. Another set of crystals, just replaced in the receiver, had immediately burned out, and there was no question that the fathometer head itself was the cause. Chief Sonarman George McDaniel reported that while he was measuring the resistance to ground he recorded a rapidly reducing resistance to the point where the sonar head was completely grounded out.

All submarines are plagued with inability to maintain topside wiring free of water. A great number of cables must come through the pressure hull and therefore, over some percentage of their length, must be exposed to full sea pressure. Despite great care in installation, there are always some that flood, either through an unsuspected fault in the pressure sealing of the cable itself or because of improper installation. New ships, because of their miles of cabling, always have the greatest difficulty keeping their wiring dry.

Realizing that we would have to complete the rest of our cruise without a fathometer, a serious period of self-analysis faced me. Could we safely finish the trip without danger of running aground on some uncharted shoal or damaging the ship by striking bottom in one of the restricted passages we would later be required to navigate?

It was not as though this had suddenly become a consideration at four o'clock on the morning of the twelfth of March. I had been thinking it over ever since the first difficulty with the fathometer had arisen, and had generated some experiments with our search sonar and Mike Smalet's "monkey in a cage"—our name for his gravity-metering gadget.

Even before it finally broke down, I had become convinced that despite the loss of the fathometer we could still proceed along our way. Our search sonar reliably detected shallow water ahead and on either side, and particularly gave us immediate warning of sudden changes in the depth of the ocean bottom.

Smalet, who was as anxious as anyone that the trip proceed successfully, had advanced the theory that, although unexplained anomalies in the earth's crust had an effect on gravity, it was also true that gravity was fundamentally a function of mass and distance. A perceptible increase in gravity should therefore coincide with a reduction in the depth of the ocean, and vice versa. We had been trying out his theory whenever there was an opportunity, and to our delight found that there was indeed some such correlation.

However, a more subtle question had to be answered: should I report our trouble?

By this time, we had passed into the operational control of ComSubPac, whose headquarters were in Pearl Harbor. What would be his reaction upon receiving a message from the *Triton* stating that her fathometer was out of commission? What indeed would be the reaction in the Pentagon? It was in a sense my duty to report our problem, but would I not, in so doing, be passing on responsibility I should assume myself? How could any admiral in Pearl Harbor or Washington or New London evaluate the situation as well as I could? Unable to see the situation at first hand, might they not be obliged to adopt the cautious course?

In short, if I simply reported the loss of the fathometer without all the amplifying considerations we had so laboriously developed in the past week and a half, was there not a good chance that we should be ordered to cancel the remainder of our trip and proceed directly to Pearl Harbor for repairs?

This question, with all its nuances, was the big one. In the final analysis, I felt that continuation of our expedition depended as much upon my decision at this point as on anything we had done to date. Well I knew the Navy tradition; on the captain rests the responsibility for the right decision. And well I remembered what had happened to Father after the *Memphis* had gone aground in Santo Domingo harbor. The cause had been a tidal wave—unpredictable, therefore something against which one could not have been prepared. Pacing the deck of his ship on a warm, pleasant afternoon, at anchor with awnings rigged, gangways down, and liberty parties ashore, he had been the first to see danger. Within forty minutes, mast-high breakers swept in from the peaceful sea and *Memphis* was cast ashore on a coral reef, a total wreck. Father was exonerated of all blame for the catastrophe, except the impossible responsibility for not having anticipated a tidal wave. (Technically, "not having been ready to get underway immediately.")

This was, in fact, the major contention upon which his court-martial eventually turned. In the crux of the decision, which the court, true to Navy tradition, could but render against him, was the statement that nothing could divest the commanding officer of the ultimate responsibility for the safety of his ship. A comparable responsibility now burdened me.

Breakfast was served as I wrestled with the problem. This was not something that anyone else on board the *Triton* should be concerned with, but the more I thought of it the more certain I became that here, even more surely than off Montevideo, success or failure of our voyage lay in the balance.

Much has been written about the so-called "calculated risk," but one of the considerations or calculations which cannot be neglected is that, if failure is encountered, the penalty is no less severe than if the risk had been assumed without forethought.

All the training the Navy had given me, all the background of the Naval Academy and my years at sea, could lead to only one conclusion. As in Father's case and in every similar case, the final responsibility is on the commanding officer. I had to make the crucial decision, and it had better be the right one.

I resolved not to report our difficulty. Come what might, we would carry on and complete the voyage. Furthermore, I could not permit our situation to be fully appreciated by anyone else aboard. This load, like that of our special mission, could not be shared with anyone.